OXFORD WORLD'S CLASSICS

THE OXFORD SHAKESPEARE

General Editor · Stanley Wells

The Oxford Shakespeare offers new and authoritative editions of Shakespeare's plays in which the early printings have been scrupulously re-examined and interpreted. An introductory essay provides all relevant background information together with an appraisal of critical views and of the play's effects in performance. The detailed commentaries pay particular attention to language and staging. Reprints of sources, music for songs, genealogical tables, maps, etc. are included where necessary; many of the volumes are illustrated, and all contain an index.

ROGER WARREN, co-editor of *Twelfth Night* in the Oxford Shakespeare, is Senior Lecturer in English at the University of Leicester.

STANLEY WELLS is Chairman of the Shakespeare Birthplace Trust and Vice-Chairman of the Royal Shakespeare Theatre. He is Emeritus Professor of Shakespeare Studies at the University of Birmingham, General Editor of the Oxford Shakespeare, and co-editor of *Twelfth Night*.

THE OXFORD SHAKESPEARE

Currently available in paperback

The rest of the plays and poems are forthcoming

OXFORD WORLD'S CLASSICS

WILLIAM SHAKESPEARE

Twelfth Night, or What You Will

Edited by
ROGER WARREN
and
STANLEY WELLS

OXFORD
UNIVERSITY PRESS

OXFORD

UNIVERSITY PRESS

Great Clarendon Street, Oxford OX2 6DP
Oxford University Press is a department of the University of Oxford.
It furthers the University's objective of excellence in research, scholarship,
and education by publishing worldwide in

Oxford New York

Athens Auckland Bangkok Bogotá Buenos Aires Calcutta
Cape Town Chennai Dar es Salaam Delhi Florence Hong Kong Istanbul
Karachi Kuala Lumpur Madrid Melbourne Mexico City Mumbai
Nairobi Paris São Paulo Singapore Taipei Tokyo Toronto Warsaw

with associated companies in Berlin Ibadan

Oxford is a registered trade mark of Oxford University Press
in the UK and certain other countries

First published by the Clarendon Press 1994
First published as a World's Classics paperback 1995
Reissued as an Oxford World's Classics paperback 1998

British Library Cataloguing in Publication Data

Data available

Library of Congress Cataloging in Publication Data
Shakespeare, William, 1564–1616.
[Twelfth night]
Twelfth night, or, What you will / edited by Roger Warren and
Stanley Wells.
p. cm—(The World's classics)
I. Warren, Roger. II. Wells, Tanley W., 1930- . III. Title.
IV. title: Twelfth night. V. Ttitle: What you will. VI. Series.
PR2837.A2W28 1995
822.3'3—dc20 94-22803

ISBN 0-19-812366-3 (hbk.)
ISBN 0-19-283415-0 (pbk.)

5 7 9 10 8 6 4

Printed in Spain by Book Print S.L.

PREFACE

THIS is essentially a collaborative edition. The editors' contributions are roughly as follows: the text is based on that prepared by Stanley Wells for the Oxford *Complete Works*, with modifications by Roger Warren, chiefly concerned with lightening the punctuation in order to preserve the shape and rhythm of the verse lines as much as possible; the introduction was written by Warren and revised by Wells; and the commentary was written by Warren, incorporating much material prepared by Wells for a projected annotated Oxford *Complete Works*. Where we have disagreed about a reading (for example at 5.1.274), we have set out the conflicting arguments as clearly as possible, so as to emphasize that an edition is not a fixed thing, but offers opportunities for continual reassessment of the textual evidence.

The edition is collaborative in other ways too. We have been fortunate in having James Walker, a very experienced practical musician and composer for the theatre, to edit the music; and just before starting work on the edition, Warren participated in the preparation of Peter Hall's 1991 production at the Playhouse, London: the detailed discussion of each phrase that took place during the rehearsals was of great value in preparing the commentary. We have also learnt much from other productions, which we have tried to acknowledge in the introduction and commentary.

We should also like to thank all those who have helped with various suggestions, and especially to acknowledge the generous co-operation of the librarians at the Shakespeare Institute and the Shakespeare Centre, Stratford-upon-Avon.

ROGER WARREN
STANLEY WELLS

CONTENTS

LIST OF ILLUSTRATIONS

INTRODUCTION

Twelfth Night is one of the most popular of Shakespeare's plays in the modern theatre, and its success seems to have begun early; the sole surviving reference to it during Shakespeare's lifetime is to a performance. On 2 February 1602, John Manningham, then a law student of the Middle Temple in London, wrote in his diary:

At our feast we had a play called *Twelfth Night, or What You Will*, much like *The Comedy of Errors* or *Menaechmi* in Plautus, but most like and near to that in Italian called *Inganni*. A good practice in it to make the steward believe his lady widow was in love with him, by counterfeiting a letter as from his lady, in general terms telling him what she liked best in him, and prescribing his gesture in smiling, his apparel, etc., and then when he came to practise, making him believe they took him to be mad.[1]

This must have been an early performance. The play was probably written in 1601, either immediately before or straight after *Hamlet*.[2] Both plays were therefore written at the mid-point of Shakespeare's career, when he was at the height of his powers, so their theatrical success is not surprising.

The play has not, however, always been as popular in the theatre as it is today. Although it was among the earliest of Shakespeare's plays to be revived when the London theatres

---

[1] The document is reproduced in S. Schoenbaum, *William Shakespeare: A Documentary Life* (Oxford, 1975), p. 156. Presumably the actors were Shakespeare's company, the Lord Chamberlain's Men; they were unlikely to relinquish a new play to anyone else, and in any case the text was not generally available, since it was not published before the First Folio of 1623, and was only then entered in the Stationers' Register, on 8 November 1623. See Wells and Taylor, *Textual Companion*, p. 32.

[2] Other pointers to this date are: (i) references to 'the Sophy'—the Shah of Persia (2.5.170; 3.4.269)—probably postdate Sir Robert Shirley's return from Persia, in a ship named *The Sophy*, in 1599; (ii) an apparent allusion to the Arctic voyage of William Barentz in 1596–7 (3.2.24–6); an English account was entered in the Stationers' Register in 1598, the earliest surviving edition dated 1609; (iii) 'the new map with the augmentation of the Indies' (3.2.74) appears to be one published in Hakluyt's *Voyages* in 1599 and reissued in 1600; (iv) some of the snatches of song in 2.3 probably draw on Robert Jones's *First Book of Songs or Airs* (1600). See Wells and Taylor, *Textual Companion*, p. 123, for a more detailed discussion of the dating.

reopened after the restoration of the monarchy in 1660, only three performances in the later part of the seventeenth century are known, and Samuel Pepys attended each of them. On 11 September 1661 he entered the theatre simply because the King was going to be there. 'So I, against my own mind and resolution, could not forbear to go in, which did make the play seem a burden to me, and I took no pleasure at all in it.' Nevertheless he saw it again on Twelfth Night 1663, when he found it 'but a silly play, and not relating at all to the name or day', and yet again, though with no more enthusiasm, on 20 January 1669, 'as it is now revived' (which may imply adaptation, though no alteration survives from his period), this time calling it 'one of the weakest plays that ever I saw on the stage'.[1]

Pepys seems to have reflected the taste of his age: the play then left the repertory for over eighty years. William Burnaby drew on it for his *Love Betray'd* of 1703, a very free adaptation, mostly in prose, which retains fewer than sixty of Shakespeare's lines. Only two performances are known, one in February 1703 and the other in March 1705.[2] *Twelfth Night* shared in the general neglect of Shakespeare's comedies during the early part of the eighteenth century but returned to the English stage in January 1741, with Charles Macklin as Malvolio. After this, while not receiving as many performances as *The Merchant of Venice, As You Like It,* or *The Merry Wives of Windsor,* it remained in the repertory of either Covent Garden or Drury Lane for the rest of the century.[3] The acting version printed in Bell's edition in 1774 is substantially Shakespeare's text with a few cuts, including two of Feste's songs; J. P. Kemble's acting edition of 1811 also makes only comparatively minor changes, including the transposition of the

[1] *The Diary of Samuel Pepys*, ed. Robert Latham and William Matthews, 11 vols. (1970–83); 2.177, 4.6, 9.421.

[2] The play was reprinted by the Cornmarket Press in 1969. Charles Molloy's *The Half-Pay Officers*, of 1720, listed by e.g. Campbell and Quinn in *A Shakespeare Encyclopaedia* (1966) as an adaptation of *Twelfth Night*, bears scarcely any relation to Shakespeare's play. It is described by George C. D. Odell, *Shakespeare from Betterton to Irving*, 2 vols. (New York, 1920), 1.248, and was reprinted by the Cornmarket Press in 1969.

[3] Full information on performances from 1660 to 1800 is given in *The London Stage*, 11 vols. (Carbondale, Illinois, 1965–8).

first and second scenes, a practice which still occasionally happens at the present time.[1]

In 1820 Frederic Reynolds, along with the composer Henry Bishop, put on at Covent Garden a heavily adapted version introducing 'Songs, Glees, and Choruses, the Poetry selected *entirely* from the Plays, Poems, and Sonnets of Shakespeare' and adding also the masque from *The Tempest*. This adaptation, which was indulgently reviewed by Leigh Hunt,[2] continued in performance at intervals over several years; the text has not survived.

Shakespeare's play had been introduced to New York in 1804, and it was the American actresses Charlotte and Susan Cushman, appearing as Viola and Olivia, who brought it back to the London stage in 1846, at the Haymarket Theatre. Other notable nineteenth-century productions included those of Samuel Phelps at Sadler's Wells in 1848, Charles Kean at the Princess's Theatre in 1850, and one at the Olympic Theatre in 1865, in which the text was altered so that Kate Terry could play both Viola and Sebastian.[3] Henry Irving's production at the Lyceum Theatre in 1884, in which he played Malvolio with Ellen Terry as Viola, was not a great success, and Augustin Daly's took remarkable liberties with the text.[4]

These were all performances in the nineteenth-century pictorial tradition, but in 1895 William Poel's semi-professional Elizabethan Stage Society acted the play 'after the manner of the sixteenth century' (though not without abbreviation), impressing Bernard Shaw with 'the immense advantage of the platform stage to the actor'.[5] The winds of change were blowing, even though Beerbohm Tree's version at His Majesty's Theatre in 1901, in which he played Malvolio, reverted to traditional methods. It had what George Odell described as 'the most extraordinary single setting I have ever beheld. It

[1] Kemble's edition was reprinted by the Cornmarket Press in 1971 with a brief introduction by John Russell Brown. It is discussed by Odell, 2.52, 62–3.

[2] *Leigh Hunt's Dramatic Criticism 1808–1831*, ed. L. H. and C. W. Houtchens (1950), pp. 227–31.

[3] Jean Anouilh similarly adapted the play, in his own translation, for the French actress Susanne Flon, reviewed by Alan S. Downer, 'For Jesus' Sake Forbear', *SQ* 13 (1962), 219–30; pp. 226–8.

[4] Described and analysed by Odell, 2. 386, 406–7, and 441–2.

[5] *Our Theatres in the Nineties* (1932, reprinted 1948), 1.184–91; p. 189.

was the garden of Olivia, extending terrace by terrace to the extreme back of the stage, with very real grass, real fountains, paths and descending steps. I never saw anything approaching it for beauty and *vraisemblance*'—but the disadvantage was that it had to be used 'for many of the Shakespearian episodes for which it was absurdly inappropriate'.[1] This was the last major production of *Twelfth Night* in the high Victorian style. In 1912 Harley Granville Barker directed it at the Savoy Theatre, London, in a production which, influenced partly by Poel, laid the foundations for the many twentieth-century stagings of this play, some of whose insights have made an important contribution to the rest of this introduction.[2]

A 'Twelfth Night' Play?

It is interesting that the earliest recorded performance should have been at a celebratory feast: John Manningham saw it on 2 February, which was Candlemas, the festival of the blessing of candles to celebrate the Purification of the Blessed Virgin Mary, a Catholic feast which, like others, survived into post-Reformation England. Both the other early performances we know about were also given privately to celebrate festive occasions: by the King's Men at court on Easter Monday, 6 April 1618, and again at Candlemas, 2 February 1623, before Charles I at Whitehall. This inevitably prompts us to ask whether *Twelfth Night* was conceived and performed as a play especially suited to private performances on festive occasions. It seems unlikely that such a successful stage play would have been reserved for private performance; but on Twelfth Night 1601 Shakespeare's company performed an unspecified play before Queen Elizabeth I and her chief guest, Don Virginio Orsino, at Whitehall, and Leslie Hotson has argued in *The First Night of 'Twelfth Night'* (1954) that the play was rapidly put together for this occasion. Although his book sheds much valuable light on details of the text, from which the commentary in this edition has benefited, his main argument has not won general acceptance; it is likelier that the ducal visitor and the festive

[1] Odell, 2.455.
[2] Barker's production is described in detail by Dennis Kennedy, *Granville Barker and the Dream of Theatre* (Cambridge, 1985), pp. 136–47.

occasion suggested the name of Shakespeare's duke and the title of his play, which was probably written later that year.

Opinion varies about how far the title provides a clue for interpretation. In spite of Pepys's view that the play was irrelevant to the day, it was often performed on or around 6 January in the later eighteenth century. Like the feast of Candlemas, the elaborate festivities associated with Twelfth Night were a survival of medieval customs into post-Reformation England. L. G. Salingar conveniently summarizes those features of the play which relate to the period of licensed 'misrule', revelry, and topsy-turveydom traditionally associated with the Twelve Days of Christmas, of which Twelfth Night was the conclusion and the climax:

The sub-plot shows a prolonged season of misrule, or 'uncivil rule', in Olivia's household, with Sir Toby turning night into day; there are drinking, dancing, and singing, scenes of mock wooing, a mock sword fight, and the gulling of an unpopular member of the household, with Feste mumming it as a priest and attempting a mock exorcism in the manner of the Feast of Fools.[1]

Both the principal actions of the play present reversals of established norms such as the period of misrule encouraged: in the main plot, the Duke Orsino is educated out of his aberrant state of love-melancholy by his servant, who then becomes her 'master's mistress' (5.1.317); in the sub-plot, Olivia's steward aspires to become his mistress's master. And during the drinking scene, Sir Toby's quotation of an unidentified song, 'O' the twelfth day of December' (2.3.79), may be his drunken version of the carol 'The Twelve Days of Christmas', perhaps identifying the party as his own version of a Twelfth Night revel.[2]

Modern directors have taken diametrically opposed views of the usefulness of the associations of Twelfth Night to

---

[1] 'The Design of *Twelfth Night*', *SQ* 9 (1958), 117–39; p. 118. The topic is also discussed by François Laroque in *Shakespeare's Festive World* (Cambridge, 1991), pp. 227–8.

[2] In *Shakespeare's Festive Comedy* (Princeton, 1959), C. L. Barber argues that Shakespearian comedy draws on the forms and traditions of Elizabethan holidays (not just Twelfth Night) to create a pattern of festive release leading to psychological clarification: 'People are caught up by delusions or misapprehensions which take them out of themselves, bringing out what they would keep hidden or did not know was there' (p. 242).

performance, as Michael Billington's conversations with some of them in *Directors' Shakespeare* (1990), a valuable account of the theatrical issues, makes clear. For Terry Hands, '*Twelfth Night* meant just that—the sixth of January, the moment when you take down the decorations and Christmas is over. The festive moment has passed, and this is now the cruellest point of the year', and the drinking scene is an attempt 'to put their Christmas tree back up' (pp. 2, 8).[1] On the other hand, John Barton, who directed a long-running and almost universally admired production for the Royal Shakespeare Company (1969–71), finds the play less wintry than 'autumnal in mood' (p. 7). In this respect, Barton agrees with Peter Hall, who directed another much admired autumnal staging (Stratford-upon-Avon, 1958–60, and again at the Playhouse, London, in 1991); while for Bill Alexander, director of the RSC's 1987–8 production, 'the title was a kind of distraction' (p. 3).

That title, however, is not simply *Twelfth Night*. Both the earliest sources, John Manningham's diary and the First Folio of Shakespeare's plays (1623), the sole authority for the text of the play, call it *Twelfth Night, or What You Will*; perhaps the permissive *What You Will* is intended to qualify too rigorous an insistence upon Twelfth Night and its associations of misrule.[2] Such openness would be entirely characteristic of a play which establishes so subtle a balance between contrasting elements that it has often been characterized as 'elusive' in mood and overall effect. John Gielgud, who directed what seems to have been a rather unsuccessful production at Stratford-upon-Avon in 1955, comments: 'It is so difficult to combine the romance of the play with the cruelty of the jokes against Malvolio, jokes which are in any case archaic and difficult. The different elements in the play are hard to balance

---

[1] Hands's 1979 RSC production is discussed in Roger Warren, 'Shakespeare at Stratford and the National Theatre, 1979', *SS* 33 (Cambridge, 1980), 169–80; pp. 170–1.

[2] Barbara Everett argues that 'the "sub-title" is really no sub-title, but a generic, perhaps primary, and certainly important part of the title' ('Or What You Will', *EC* 35 (1985), 294–314; p. 304). She points out that 'Marston's *What You Will*, though not published till 1607, was almost certainly written and first performed not long before the first performance of Shakespeare's comedy', so this may have necessitated a change in Shakespeare's title (p. 313).

properly.'[1] For this reason, as Michael Billington points out in his introduction to *Directors' Shakespeare*, 'different characters become, at different times, the pivot of the play [but] the quartet of RSC directors suggests that Sir Toby is the motor that drives the plot and Feste the character who determines the mood' (p. ix).

It may be that one reason why John Barton's and Peter Hall's autumnal versions were so successful in achieving just that elusive balance between contrasting elements that Gielgud mentions, between sweet and sour, laughter and tears, was that autumn itself is a season of contrasts: serene, warm days edged by chilly nights, mist, and lengthening shadows. Keats catches precisely this quality in his ode 'To Autumn' where he defines the perfection of the autumn day by reminding the reader of those things that threaten it—the hint of transience in the 'soft-dying day' and in the 'gathering swallows', about to depart to escape the approach of winter. And he might be describing the quality of *Twelfth Night* itself when he writes in his 'Ode on Melancholy' that 'in the very temple of delight | Veil'd Melancholy has her sovran shrine'. This combination of happiness and sadness, to the point where an awareness of the one is essential to the full experience and appreciation of the other, is characteristic of the mood of *Twelfth Night*, epitomized in the lines in which Orsino and Viola discuss female perfection,

> ORSINO
> For women are as roses, whose fair flower
> Being once displayed, doth fall that very hour.
> VIOLA
> And so they are. Alas that they are so:
> To die even when they to perfection grow
>
> (2.4.37–40),

or in Viola's phrase about her imaginary sister 'Smiling at grief' (2.4.115), or in Feste's comparison of Orsino's mind to an opal, an iridescent jewel that changes its appearance in the varying light (2.4.74).

An autumnal mood also suits the revels of Sir Toby and Sir Andrew, which carry a sense of the best days being past, of

---

[1] *An Actor and his Time* (1979), p. 176.

having to make the most of every moment while it lasts. Feste perfectly catches this mood in the song he sings to them in the drinking scene: 'Present mirth hath present laughter. . . . | Youth's a stuff will not endure' (2.3.46, 50). Perhaps the need to indulge in 'present laughter' explains the rather desperate tone of the revelry in most performances, and more particularly how the joke against Malvolio comes to be pushed to the extreme of attempting to drive him mad. Making the most of passing moments is as much a part of Twelfth Night, the end of a period of mid-winter revels, as it is of autumn; and references to other seasons in the text—'More matter for a May morning' (3.4.137) and 'this is very midsummer madness' (3.4.53)—allude to other periods of Elizabethan revelry, May Day and Midsummer Eve, not necessarily to a particular season in which the action takes place—although Bill Alexander, the director who felt that 'the title was a kind of distraction', departed as far from mid-winter as possible and set his 1987 RSC version in the brightly-lit summer sunshine of a fishing village on the Illyrian coast. This leads naturally to the ways in which various stagings have presented Illyria, and to the more general question 'Where—or what—is Illyria?'

Illyria

Illyria was the ancient name of an area of the Adriatic coast roughly corresponding to what was for long known as Yugoslavia. In the classical world, Illyria had a reputation for piracy: the Illyrians' attacks on Adriatic shipping led to Roman intervention, and the area became the Roman province of Illyricum. Shakespeare was clearly aware of its reputation since his only other reference to it, in the phrase 'Bargulus, the strong Illyrian pirate' (*Contention* 4.1.108), is a translation of 'Bardulis Illyrius latro', from Cicero's *De Officiis* 2.11, a work used as a textbook in Elizabethan schools. This association of Illyria with piracy may have contributed to the vivid evocation of a ferocious sea-battle between Antonio and Orsino at 5.1.45–70, and to the ambiguous presentation of Antonio in general, discussed in a later section of this introduction.

In Shakespeare's day Illyria was a series of city-states controlled by the Venetian republic. Possibly Shakespeare conceives of Orsino and Olivia as neighbouring rulers of these city-states, for whom a marriage alliance might appear natural; yet Orsino and Olivia seem just as much to be neighbouring Elizabethan aristocrats; Olivia's household is presented in precise detail, complete with steward, waiting-gentlewoman, fool, and sponging elderly relative. The coexistence of the remote and the familiar in Shakespeare's Illyria—nicely characterized in a review by Hugh Leonard as 'a fairyland with back-streets' (*Plays and Players*, August 1966, p. 16)—suggests to some interpreters that it should be 'magical, romantic, *Illyrian* in that sense' (John Barton), or even a country of the mind: 'The place is defined by the characters and the journey they undertake . . . which is an emotional journey' (Terry Hands, in *Directors' Shakespeare*, pp. 8, 9). Each of these aspects of Illyria—the geographical or Mediterranean, the specifically English, the magical, and the sense of a country of the mind—can be illustrated by the prominence each has been given in notable stagings, though of course to emphasize one aspect need not exclude the others, and in the most balanced productions does not do so.

For Shakespeare's company, working on an unlocalized stage and wearing what was for them modern dress, the question of design choices presumably did not arise; and the staging of the play is exceptionally undemanding of theatrical resources.[1] Later actors and directors, since at least the middle of the nineteenth century, have sought to provide a visual equivalent for the play's poetic and dramatic qualities. In the nineteenth century there was a fashion for elaborately realistic and sometimes would-be 'historical' settings. Since Illyria in Shakespeare's time 'was under the rule of the Venetian republic', a note in H. H. Furness's 1901 New Variorum edition explains, 'the custom has long prevailed of treating the piece as a romantic and poetic picture of Venetian manners in the seventeenth century. Some stage managers have used Greek dresses. For the purposes of the stage, there must be a "local habitation" ' (p. 4). In a New York production of 1904, for instance, a kind of 'Illyrian' national dress was evolved, using elements of Greek, Balkan, even Turkish costumes. The twins

[1] Peter Thomson considers '*Twelfth Night* and Playhouse Practice' in his *Shakespeare's Theatre*, 2nd edn. (1992), pp. 91–113.

each wore a skirted robe with a sleeveless jacket trimmed with braid, a fez, and a sash around the waist with a scimitar.[1] Harley Granville Barker's Savoy production in 1912 reacted against such 'realistic' designs by setting a stylized garden with brightly coloured, cone-shaped formal trees against a yellow and black abstract drop-cloth for Orsino's court; but even he made a concession to prevailing 'Illyrian' styles by dressing Orsino in oriental robes, complete with turban.[2]

Although Bill Alexander at Stratford-upon-Avon in 1987 attempted to evoke the actual Illyria of Shakespeare's time, his aim was not the historical but the timeless. 'Those white-washed buildings were the same, arguably, in the sixteenth century as they are in the twentieth century.' The costuming was 'Elizabethan Illyrian', that is, 'Greek–Yugoslav dress of that period'—and in fact it was not far removed from the nineteenth century's attempts to create an 'Illyrian' style. But Alexander also addressed the important question why, since so much of the society in the play seems so English, Shakespeare bothered to set it in Illyria at all: 'I think he does it for its compression value: . . . when people are displaced, their characteristics become heightened' so that there is 'an intensification of human behaviour' (*Directors' Shakespeare*, pp. 12, 32). His evocation of the historical Illyria, then, was ultimately directed at sharpening the audience's sense of the psychology of the play.

And so, in a completely contrasting style, was Peter Hall's very English view at Stratford-upon-Avon in 1958. Derek Granger in his review pointed out that the play 'marvellously lends itself to a close pictorial re-working' and that Lila de Nobili's designs were 'permissibly explicit; we are in fact in a Caroline park on a sunny late afternoon at the very end of September; the light is gold and gauzy, the shadows are umber, the sunflowers glow against the garden wall and there is just the hint of a nip in the air' (*Financial Times*, 23 April 1958). The use of painted gauzes allowed the perspectives of a seventeenth-century long gallery for Orsino's court (see fig. 1)

---

[1] There is a photograph of the twins in *SS* 32 (Cambridge, 1979), facing p. 88.

[2] There are several photographs in Dennis Kennedy, *Granville Barker and the Dream of Theatre* (Cambridge, 1985), pp. 136–47.

1. Orsino (Derek Godfrey, seated centre) and Viola (Dorothy Tutin, standing behind him) listen to Feste (Max Adrian) singing 'Come away death' in a seventeenth-century long gallery. Peter Hall's production, Stratford-upon-Avon, 1960.

to blend swiftly into Olivia's walled garden. The advantage of these designs, as A. Alvarez put it when the production was revived in 1960, was that they provided 'a kind of visual parallel for the play's complexities' (*New Statesman*, 28 May 1960), and in particular reflected its changing moods; as one vista melted into another, the production precisely caught that shifting, 'elusive' quality often mentioned in connection with the play, its balancing of happiness and melancholy. That balance was further enchanced by Hall's decision to set the play some thirty years after its probable date of composition, in a Caroline world of lace collars, silks, and plumed hats which recalled Van Dyck's images of Charles I's court, in which autumnal colours often temper court splendour with a hint that the golden moment cannot last. Roy Walker summarized some advantages of presenting Illyria like this: the 'choice of Cavalier costume gave the maximum thematic contrast with Malvolio's Puritan habit, served the opposition of amours and austerity, and . . . eased the problem of the identical twins with a hair-style equally suitable to boy and girl'.[1]

The Illyria of John Barton's RSC production (1969–71) was in some respects a visual distillation of Hall's. Christopher Morley's design was a receding, slatted gauze box which proved very flexible. Set with candelabra and dimly lit, it resembled Hall's in suggesting Orsino's enclosed ducal hall; but when the gauze box was back-lit, it evoked a mysterious world beyond. This was crucial to Barton's view of the 'magical, romantic' nature of Illyria, and it was especially effective at the first appearance of Viola: the doors at the back of the gauze box flew open and she suddenly materialized amid swirling spray, rising like Venus from the sea; her long flowing hair also carried a suggestion of Alice in Wonderland. But the magical was balanced with the wittily human as Viola gradually recovered her bearings and resolved on positive action, especially once she assumed her page's disguise. Barton back-lit the gauze not only to suggest 'magic and the sea and the world outside that they'd come from' (*Directors' Shakespeare*, p. 10), but also to intensify moments that were

[1] 'The Whirligig of Time', *SS 12* (Cambridge, 1959), 122–30; pp. 128–9.

2. The reunion of the twins (Gordon Reid as Sebastian and Judi Dench as Viola), watched by Feste (Emrys James, centre). John Barton's 1969–71 RSC production.

at once mysterious and intensely human, above all for the reunion of the twins (see fig. 2), and he underscored such moments with the recurrent sound of the sea, a device adopted by several directors since. Barton's production was first given in a season that concentrated on Shakespeare's late romances; and one consequence was to make the audience especially aware of the ways in which *Twelfth Night* anticipates those plays: in the use of the sea as both destroyer and renewer; in the sense of characters undertaking emotional journeys; and in the final renewal of a family relationship which is as important as (or more important than) the coming together of lovers upon which comedy usually concentrates.[1]

An Illyria very far removed from all these was Peter Gill's at Stratford-upon-Avon in 1974. Here, more than in any other production, Illyria was a country of the mind. The key

[1] This production is discussed in Stanley Wells, *Royal Shakespeare* (Manchester, 1977), pp. 43–63, and in Lois Potter, *'Twelfth Night': Text and Performance* (1985).

to this interpretation was a huge, dominating mural of Narcissus gazing infatuatedly at his reflection in the water, suggesting the extent to which the characters are prisoners of their own obsessions. As Irving Wardle put it, Orsino, Olivia, and Malvolio, 'in his own way the greatest narcissist of the lot (and the only one who finally resists cure)', are all 'intoxicated with their own reflections, and the function of Viola and Sebastian is to put them through an Ovidian obstacle course from which they learn to turn away from the mirror and form real attachments' (*The Times*, 24 August 1974). But the production was concerned with body as well as with mind: Peter Ansorge focused something essential about the play as well as the staging when he defined this Illyria as 'a highly refined, erotic trap . . . in which the characters must learn to read the subtext of their desires' (*Plays and Players*, October 1974, p. 31). So as well as presenting various visual images of Illyria, these stagings used design to focus important aspects of the play to which subsequent sections of this introduction must return.

'Most like . . . that in Italian called "Inganni" '

In the diary entry describing the *Twelfth Night* performance he saw in 1602, John Manningham called the play 'much like *The Comedy of Errors* or *Menaechmi* in Plautus' (the principal source of *The Comedy of Errors*), but added that it was 'most like and near to that in Italian called *Inganni*'. He shrewdly identified the main influences on both the twins story and the love story. There were at least two Italian comedies called *Gl'Inganni* ('The Mistakes'), one by Nicolò Secchi (performed in 1547, first published in Florence in 1562 and frequently reprinted) and one by Curzio Gonzaga (published in Venice in 1592). Both appear to derive from an anonymous play, *Gl'Ingannati* ('The Deceived'), first performed at Siena in 1531 by a literary society called the 'Intronati' ('Thunderstruck by Love') and published in Venice in 1537. All these dramatize the central situation of *Twelfth Night*: a girl disguised as a page woos another lady on behalf of the master whom she loves; the lady then falls in love with the 'page', but subsequently marries 'his' twin brother. The story recurs in two English prose narratives: Barnaby Riche reworks it in *Riche his Farewell to Military Profession* (1581); and there is a variant in an episode in Emanuel Forde's romance *The Famous History of Parismus* (1598).[1] It was, in other words, a story that was 'in the air' at the time; and it is worth considering some points of comparison (and contrast) between these works and *Twelfth Night*, not to 'prove' debts which are unprovable, but to indicate the *kind* of story that Shakespeare is using, and modifying, for his main plot.

After a prologue and two introductory scenes which contain two references to Twelfth Night (*la notte di beffana*—the Epiphany), the disguised heroine of *Gl'Ingannati* makes her first appearance and instantly establishes the tone of the play:

It is indeed very rash of me, when I think of it, to come out in the streets so early, considering the wild practices of these licentious youths of Modena. Oh, how awful it would be if one . . . seized me by force, and, dragging me into a house, wanted to make sure whether I am a man or a woman! (Bullough's translation, cited throughout, p. 292)

Here there is a titillating, salacious flirting with the sexual ambiguities of the disguised heroine. To some extent, this is inherent in the situation, however and by whoever it is dramatized; but this bald statement announces the main source of interest in *Gl'Ingannati*; and a similarly blunt statement occurs later when the heroine describes her master whom she loves: 'He looked me up and down from head to foot so closely that I feared he would recognize me' (p. 296). Unlike Viola, this disguised heroine has followed and is now serving a man who deserted her, so there is a double risk of recognition, both of sex and of identity; but even allowing for this, *Gl'Ingannati* expresses the potential of the situation in a blunter way than Orsino does:

> Diana's lip
> Is not more smooth and rubious; thy small pipe

[1] Several of these texts are conveniently gathered together in Geoffrey Bullough, *Narrative and Dramatic Sources of Shakespeare*, vol. 2 (1958), pp. 286–372. They are discussed in Bullough, in Robert C. Melzi, 'From Lelia to Viola', *Renaissance Drama*, 9 (1966), 67–81, and in Salingar (see p. 5 n. 1 above).

> Is as the maiden's organ, shrill and sound,
> And all is semblative a woman's part.
>
> (1.4.31–4)

All these Italian versions have the heroine hint at her love for her master, as Viola does in her allegory of a sister who died of love (2.4.88–115), but once more this is inherent in the situation: a disguised heroine needs some statement of her feelings, however reticent. The heroine's assumed name in *Gl'Ingannati*, Fabio, may have suggested Fabian's name to Shakespeare, though another possibility is suggested in the Commentary to 2.5.1. In Curzio Gonzaga's *Gl'Inganni*, the heroine assumes the name 'Cesare': this looks like the origin of Viola's choice of 'Cesario' for her male disguise. It is interesting that Viola, like the Italian heroines, does not use her brother's name, whereas the heroine in Barnaby Riche's version does, thus making the confusion of the twins much more complete, more 'plausible', and, for the brother, even more bewildering.

Shakespeare may have read these Italian plays, or possibly come across the stories through performances by the *commedia dell'arte*, which often drew upon published Italian plays and which was especially fond of plots involving twins (was that where John Manningham too came across *Gl'Inganni*?);[1] but the immediate stimulus was almost certainly provided by Barnaby Riche's story of Apollonius and Silla in *Riche his Farewell to Military Profession*, perhaps by way of Matteo Bandello's version of the story in his *Novelle* (1554) or François de Belleforest's French translation of it (1570).

Riche's narrative sets out to show how lovers drink from 'the cup of error':

> for to love them that hate us, to follow them that fly from us, to fawn on them that frown on us, to curry favour with them that disdain us, ... who will not confess this to be an erroneous love, neither grounded upon wit nor reason? (Bullough, p. 345)

This sentence might even have been the spark that set off Shakespeare's choice of main plot; he echoes its phrasing at Olivia's declaration of her love for 'Cesario': 'Nor wit nor

[1] For *commedia* performances in England, see K. M. Lea, *Italian Popular Comedy*, 2 vols. (Oxford, 1934), 2.339–455.

reason can my passion hide' (3.1.150). When Riche's Duke Apollonius courts Lady Julina 'according to the manner of wooers: besides fair words, sorrowful sighs, and piteous countenances, there must be sending of loving letters [to] become a scholar in love's school' (p. 351), he anticipates not only Orsino's formal wooing of Olivia, but still more the lesson in courtship given by Proteus in *The Two Gentlemen of Verona*:

> Say that upon the altar of her beauty
> You sacrifice your tears, your sighs, your heart.
> Write till your ink be dry, and with your tears
> Moist it again . . .
>
> (3.2.72–5)

And when Duke Apollonius (Orsino) sends Silla (Viola) to woo Lady Julina (Olivia), and Julina falls 'into as great a liking with the man as the master was with herself' (pp. 351–2), the phrasing is close to Olivia's 'Unless the master were the man' (1.5.284) and to Viola's soliloquy on the complicated situation (2.2.33–9). Closer still is the similarity between Julina's 'it is enough that you have said for your master; from henceforth, either speak for yourself or say nothing at all' (p. 352) and Olivia's

> I bade you never speak again of him;
> But would you undertake another suit,
> I had rather hear you to solicit that
> Than music from the spheres.
>
> (3.1.105–8)

Riche's handling of the crisis of the story is closer than the Italian plays to *Twelfth Night*. Julina protests to Duke Apollonius that she is married to Silvio/Silla, 'whose personage I regard more than mine own life' (p. 356), a phrase that Shakespeare transfers to Viola/Cesario, who protests that she loves Orsino 'more than my life' (5.1.131); Julia urges Silla 'Fear not then . . . to keep your faith and promise which you have made unto me' (p. 358), as Olivia urges Viola: 'Hold little faith, though thou hast too much fear' (5.1.167). But Shakespeare's revelation of the heroine's sex is necessarily very different from Riche's, since he was using a boy actor. Riche says: 'And here withal loosing his garments down to his stomach', the 'page' 'shewed Julina his breasts and pretty teats, surmounting far the whiteness of snow itself' (p. 361). Riche's handling of this revelation, with its somewhat titillating lingering over the heroine's breasts, is a measure of the important difference between Riche's tone and Shakespeare's, despite the similarities of plot and the verbal echoes;[1] and still more is Riche's suggestive address to the 'gentlewomen' readers to avoid Julina's example: 'For God's love take heed, and let this be an example to you, when you be with child, how you swear who is the father' (p. 359). Although in some ways Riche is more romantic than the Italians, his tone here is much closer to theirs than to Shakespeare's—as it is also in the treatment of the relationship between the equivalents of Sebastian and Olivia: whereas Olivia's predecessors take the heroine's twin to bed, and in Secchi's and Riche's versions become pregnant and so precipitate the crisis of the story, Olivia marries Sebastian.

In some respects, Shakespeare's tone is closer to the other work that may have provided him with his immediate stimulus, Emanuel Forde's *Parismus* of 1598. This narrative seems to have given him the names of his two heroines. Prince Parismus, about to be married to the daughter of Queen Olivia, sleeps with Violetta, who under cover of darkness mistakes him for 'her accustomed friend'; she subsequently follows Parismus disguised as the page Adonius and, while staying at a hermit's cell, has to share a bed with Parismus and his friend Pollipus:

Poor Adonius with blushing cheeks put off his apparel, and seemed to be abashed when he was in his shirt, and tenderly leapt into the bed . . . , where the poor soul lay close at Parismus' back, the very sweet touch of whose body seemed to ravish her with joy: and on the other side not acquainted with such bedfellows, she seemed as it were metamorphosed with a kind of delightful fear. (Bullough, p. 367)

Forde's alternation between 'he' and 'she' when describing Violetta/Adonius underlines the ambiguity of the disguised

---

[1] Other interesting verbal similarities are the use of 'leasing' (rather than 'lying') by Riche (Bullough, pp. 357, 360) and by Feste (1.5.92); and of 'denay', rather than 'deny' by Riche (pp. 357, 359) and by Orsino (2.4.124). Silla's passions are said to be 'contagious' (p. 347), like Feste's singing (2.3.52); Julina's bitterly ironical remark that she has 'so charily preserved mine honour' (p. 360) recalls Olivia's that she has 'laid mine honour too unchary out' (3.4.195).

heroine. Her 'delightful fear' is again something that is inherent in the relationship of the heroine and the master she loves, as most performances of the Viola/Orsino scenes bring out. For example, Hilary Spurling, reviewing the RSC's 1966 production, noted how 'an aura of desire, narrowly and deliciously averted, hangs over all the scenes between Orsino and his "dear lad", Viola/Cesario. At one point, as his page, she undresses him, draws off his gloves, half-caressing, half-shrinking from the touch' (*Spectator*, 24 June 1966).

But then *Parismus* takes a surprising turn. Parismus himself is reunited with the daughter of Queen Olivia, and Violetta sympathetically looks after Pollipus, who is in love with her but does not recognize her in her page's disguise, and she gradually comes to love him:

Often time he would spend many hours in secret complaints and protestations of his loyal love. . . . [She] beheld the . . . constancy of his resolution, for that he determined to spend his life in her service, and also the pleasure she took in his company, being never from him in the day time, and his bedfellow in the night, that she was privy to all his actions, using many kindnesses, which he full little thought proceeded from such affection. (Bullough, pp. 368–9)

While the situation is not exactly the same as in *Twelfth Night*, since Pollipus' constant resolution is to Violetta herself rather than to another woman, and Violetta, unlike Viola, only gradually falls in love, the image of a disguised heroine attending and ultimately curing her beloved's love-sickness, while their relationship matures without the man being aware of it, is very likely to have had its effect on the genesis of *Twelfth Night*. And both Forde and Shakespeare share a quality notably absent from Riche and the Italian plays: tenderness.

A Central Comedy

If Forde, Riche, and the Italians provided Shakespeare with different elements of his main plot, those features were modified through the experience of writing his own earlier plays. In *The Two Gentlemen of Verona*, for instance, Julia follows her lover Proteus in boy's disguise, only to find that he has transferred his attentions to Silvia, and she becomes an agent in his wooing. There is a bittersweet exchange between Proteus and Julia which anticipates both Viola's expressing her love obliquely and her 'ring' soliloquy (2.2.17–41). Disguised as the page Sebastian, Julia refers to herself as a woman:

> She dreams on him that has forgot her love;
> You dote on her that cares not for your love.
> 'Tis pity love should be so contrary.
>
> (4.4.79–81)

But in this version, as Harold Jenkins points out, 'the lady fails to fall in love with the page at all, which is really a little surprising of her, since she had done so in Shakespeare's source [Montemayor's *Diana*]. It is almost as though Shakespeare were reserving this crowning situation, in which the mistress loves the woman-page, for treatment in some later play'.[1]

John Manningham recognized that *Twelfth Night* was also 'much like *The Comedy of Errors* or *Menaechmi* in Plautus'. Although Shakespeare derived the central scenes of confusion over the twins from Plautus' *Menaechmi* (and from another Plautus play, *Amphitruo*), he also placed these within a framework story of a family separated by shipwreck and ultimately reunited after much wandering, which was drawn chiefly from the story of Apollonius of Tyre that he used again much later in his career for the main plot of *Pericles*. He introduced other material into *The Comedy of Errors* which is relevant to *Twelfth Night*. He moved the setting from Epidamnus in Plautus to Ephesus, partly because, as the centre of the cult of Diana, Ephesus had a reputation for witchcraft and the occult in the ancient world (and in the Bible), and would therefore provide an apt context for scenes of apparent madness and exorcism; this is much developed in *Twelfth Night* both in the way in which Orsino, Olivia, and Malvolio seem to be suffering from various kinds of madness, and in the mock-exorcism of Malvolio by Feste as Sir Topaz. By setting the action of the two plays in Ephesus and Illyria, Shakespeare located them,

---

[1] 'Shakespeare's *Twelfth Night*', Rice Institute Pamphlet 45 (1959), reprinted in *Shakespeare: the Comedies*, ed. Kenneth Muir, Twentieth Century Views (Englewood Cliffs, New Jersey, 1965), 72–87, and in *'Twelfth Night'*: *Critical Essays*, ed. Stanley Wells (New York and London, 1986), 171–89, from which page references are taken; p. 180.

however approximately, on Mediterranean sea-coasts. *The Comedy of Errors* opens under the shadow of bloody inter-city trade war, and this reappears in *Twelfth Night* to sharpen the acrimonious confrontation between Antonio and Orsino at the start of the final scene.

But of course the most important connection between *The Comedy of Errors* and *Twelfth Night* is in the handling of the twins. In Plautus, as in *Errors*, they are the same sex. The Italian plays, and *commedia dell'arte* scenarios based on them, established a new tradition by making them a boy and a girl, and Shakespeare may have been attracted to this variant for personal reasons: he was the father of boy and girl twins, Hamnet and Judith.[1] However that may be, the twins introduce a vein of particularly intense emotion into *Twelfth Night*. Shakespeare's son Hamnet died in 1596 at the age of eleven, and Shakespeare may have known what modern research into bereaved twins has demonstrated: that the death of a twin seems to cause a sense of desolation different in kind from other bereavements, and the surviving twin often tries to 'compensate' for the loss by attempting to assume the other's identity.[2] Shakespeare had already touched on a twin's sense of lost identity when separated from a brother in *The Comedy of Errors*:

> I to the world am like a drop of water
> That in the ocean seeks another drop ...
> So I, to find a mother and a brother,
> In quest of them, unhappy, lose myself.
> (1.2.35–40)

Such perceptions may have helped to sharpen the poignancy of Viola's initial reaction to her brother's loss—

> And what should I do in Illyria?
> My brother he is in Elysium (1.2.2–3)—

and to her decision to assume her brother's *persona* for her disguise:

---

[1] This means, of course, that they cannot be physically *identical*, an advantage when casting them.

[2] This evidence is usefully summarized by Joan Woodward, 'A Twin's View of *The Comedy of Errors*', in the RSC programme for that play, 1990–1, preserved in the archives of the Shakespeare Centre, Stratford-upon-Avon.

> Even such and so
> In favour was my brother, and he went
> Still in this fashion, colour, ornament,
> For him I imitate.
>
> (3.4.371–4)

This speech has another, more down-to-earth function: Shakespeare takes care to make the twins' identical clothing seem plausible here, while in *Errors* two pairs of twins separated since infancy wear identical clothes on one particular day.

In fact, the treatment of the twins is one measure of the difference between the two plays. *The Comedy of Errors* is basically a comedy of situation with psychological touches, *Twelfth Night* a comedy of character built upon a comedy of situation. In *The Comedy of Errors*, despite the fact that Antipholus of Syracuse has come to Ephesus specifically *looking* for his brother, he still fails to make the obvious deduction when everybody appears to recognize him and calls him by his name—although it is true that Shakespeare has to some extent prepared for this by making Antipholus aware of Ephesus' evil reputation as a centre of

> nimble jugglers that deceive the eye,
> Dark-working sorcerers that change the mind,
> Soul-killing witches that deform the body (1.2.98–100),

so that he half-expects strange things to happen to him. By contrast, when Antonio mistakes Viola for Sebastian, she immediately deduces the facts: 'He named Sebastian. I my brother know | Yet living in my glass' (3.4.370–1). Yet she conceals this information from others, pretending at the start of the final scene that Antonio's words to her seem merely 'distraction' (5.1.62), until the truth is confirmed by Sebastian's appearance. This holding-back greatly intensifies both the pathos and the ecstasy of their climactic reunion.

There are also important resemblances, not so much in story-line as in mood and technique, between *Twelfth Night* and another of Shakespeare's earlier comedies, *Love's Labour's Lost*. Like Orsino and Olivia, the young lords in this play are idealists, swearing to renounce the world (and specifically the company of women) for three years' secluded study. The play is about their growing up. The ladies of the French court lure them from their idealism to an acceptance of a more down-to-earth reality, as Viola lures Orsino and Olivia from theirs. Although this involves the lords in breaking their oaths to study, and Olivia breaks her promise to retire for seven years in mourning for her brother, at least these forswearings are on the side of life. The lords, like Orsino and Olivia, begin an emotional journey to maturity, but this is not necessarily a solemn thing: in *Love's Labour's Lost*, its first stage culminates in the brilliant *tour de force* of a multiple eavesdropping scene, in which the lords overhear one another admit their love for the ladies—a scene which in its technical bravura anticipates Malvolio's letter scene in *Twelfth Night*.

The climax of the lords' journey to maturity in *Love's Labour's Lost* is much more sombre, as a black-clad messenger interrupts the festivities at the end of the play with news of the death of the Princess's father. Faced with such a harsh intrusion of reality, and with parting from the ladies, the lords are compelled to drop the conventional forms of wooing they have used so far and say just what they feel. But the shadow of death has been cast across the brilliant surface of the play on several earlier occasions, from the King's urge in his opening speech to evade mortality by seeking an immortality guaranteed through the achievements of learning, to Catherine's poignantly simple statement about her sister who died of love: Cupid 'made her melancholy, sad, and heavy, | And so she died' (5.2.14–15); this anticipates Viola's expression of her own love through an allegory of a sister who died of love:

> She pined in thought,
> And with a green and yellow melancholy
> She sat like patience on a monument,
> Smiling at grief.
>
> (2.4.112–15)

In some respects the treatment of death in *Love's Labour's Lost* is tougher than in *Twelfth Night*: Catherine's sister actually died, whereas Viola leaves the issue of death ambiguous, for obvious metaphorical reasons. But *Love's Labour's Lost* anticipates in important ways the persistent vein of melancholy and awareness of mortality that shadows the revels in *Twelfth*

Night and deepens the happiness achieved. It is as if Shakespeare feels that the resolutions of comedy must be put to the test of being set against harsher experience if they are to be convincing.

In its emphasis upon the emotional journeys of the characters; in making the reunion of the members of a family as important as the love story; in the use of storm and of sexual disguise; and in setting ultimate happiness against harsher experiences, *Twelfth Night* looks forward to the late romances as well as back to the earlier comedies. At the climax of *Pericles*, Shakespeare even reworks Viola's image of her sister sitting 'like patience on a monument' in order to express the way in which Marina lures Pericles from the 'extremity' of his violent despair by her smiling patience:

> thou dost look
> Like patience gazing on kings' graves, and smiling
> Extremity out of act.
>
> (Scene 21. 126–8)

In *Cymbeline*, Shakespeare creates a heroine, Innogen, who closely resembles Viola in her candid integrity but who is put through much harsher, more extreme experiences, and who expresses her sense of utter desolation at the apparent death of her husband with a spare simplicity which is a further paring-down of Viola's direct style: 'I am nothing; or if not, | Nothing to be were better' (4.2.369–70). And when at the end of *Twelfth Night* Orsino shows to Viola 'a savage jealousy | That sometime savours nobly' (5.1.115–16), he anticipates the far more explosive sexual violence of Posthumus in *Cymbeline* and Leontes in *The Winter's Tale*. Leontes in particular goes on an emotional journey from a jealousy which borders on sadism to a spiritual 're-creation' performed in a 'wide gap of time' (5.3.155), that time in which Viola also puts her trust (2.2.40–1). The sea which separates but also reunites the twins in *The Comedy of Errors* and *Twelfth Night* is an instrument both of destruction and restoration in *The Tempest* too: 'Though the seas threaten, they are merciful. | I have cursed them without cause' (5.1.181–2). *Twelfth Night* is a central comedy in more than just its chronological position half-way through Shakespeare's working life.

Kinds of Love

In reviewing Peter Hall's 1991 production of *Twelfth Night*, John Gross began by glancing briefly at academic criticism of the play:

Twelfth Night is about deception, about the difference between true love and its egocentric counterfeits. Orsino is in love with love, Olivia is in love with grief, Malvolio is in love with himself. So say the textbooks, and up to a point they are obviously right.

But when you put it that way, half the magic evaporates. The play's moods are much too various to be summed up in a formula, its colours much too delicate; the lessons it teaches are less important than the world it creates, and its language races ahead—magnificently—of anything that the plot requires. (*Sunday Telegraph*, 3 March 1991)

The tension which Gross focuses here between what the 'textbooks' say and the rich experience that the play offers in performance may be demonstrated by considering Orsino's opening scene.

Gareth Lloyd Evans conveniently reflects a common critical view of Orsino. His 'first speech has all the languid self-indulgence of a man [who lives] in an illusion of love'.[1] But when Alan Howard actually played the part like that at Stratford-upon-Avon in 1966, Lloyd Evans complained, because Howard gave the impression 'of high-class petulance, inbred stupidity and self-indulgence'.[2] It is interesting, however, that even a performance of Orsino which, reflecting critical fashion, verged on caricature, nevertheless suggested more than caricature, at least to Hilary Spurling in her review: this Orsino stands

listening in an attitude of conscious ecstasy, a rose in one outstretched hand, [and his] delivery of the famous first speech . . . shows a Renaissance delight in luxury and artifice. Also more than a hint, in his glistening eyes and sensuous lips, of Renaissance barbarity—'my desires, like fell and cruel hounds, | E'er since pursue me.' (*Spectator*, 24 June 1966)

What she focuses here is the sheer range of Orsino's language. In speaking of its 'Renaissance delight in luxury and artifice',

---

[1] *Shakespeare III, 1599–1604* (Edinburgh, 1971), p. 40.
[2] 'Shakespeare, the Twentieth Century and "Behaviourism" ', *SS 20* (Cambridge, 1967), 133–42; p. 134.

she points out that Orsino's opening speech starts off from an artificial Renaissance code of behaviour like that followed by Riche's Duke Apollonius or recommended by Shakespeare's Proteus in the passages quoted on p. 17 above: to that extent, he exemplifies the traditional melancholy lover; but as John Gross puts it, the language 'races ahead' of this basic situation, and complicates it:

> If music be the food of love, play on,
> Give me excess of it, that surfeiting,
> The appetite may sicken and so die.
>   (1.1.1–3)

Orsino's desire to be fed by the music to the point where he becomes sick of it can be interpreted as an expression merely of self-indulgence; but the additional implication that the music acts as a stimulus for, as much as a satiation of, the appetite is clarified by an illuminating parallel usage in Sonnet 56, where Shakespeare uses the same metaphor of feeding, not to express delusion, but to suggest that love needs to be constantly stimulated in order to avoid killing 'The spirit of love with a perpetual dullness' (7–8):

> Sweet love, renew thy force. Be it not said
> Thy edge should blunter be than appetite,
> Which but today by feeding is allayed,
> Tomorrow sharpened in his former might.
>   (1–4)

It is this stimulus that Orsino seeks in his opening speech; and if his lines suggest excess, they also suggest an emotional responsiveness, a potential for feeling, which is developed in the sensuous beauty of the following lines about the music:

> O, it came o'er my ear like the sweet sound
> That breathes upon a bank of violets,
> Stealing and giving odour.
>   (1.1.5–7)

It is true that he quickly tires of the music—'Enough, no more, | 'Tis not so sweet now as it was before'—but at least his changeableness ensures that he will not 'kill | The spirit of love with a perpetual dullness', as the Sonnet puts it. His language does not only indicate limitation or absurdity.

3. Actaeon transformed into a stag, and torn to pieces by his own hounds, for watching Diana bathing, from an edition of Ovid's *Metamorphoses* published at Leipzig in 1582.

Nor is his ensuing comparison of the 'spirit of love' to the sea simply extravagant. As Harold Jenkins says, 'if the spirit of love is . . . as unstable as the sea, it is also as living and capacious':[1]

> O spirit of love, how quick and fresh art thou,
> That notwithstanding thy capacity
> Receiveth as the sea, naught enters there,
> Of what validity and pitch so e'er,
> But falls into abatement and low price
> Even in a minute!
>
> (I.I.9–14)

The image has a vigorous life as well as extravagance. So, to an even greater extent, has Orsino's subsequent comparison of himself to the huntsman Actaeon, torn in pieces by his own hounds (see fig. 3), to which Hilary Spurling alludes in her account of Alan Howard's performance:

[1] 'Shakespeare's *Twelfth Night*' (see p. 20, n. 1), p. 178.

O, when mine eyes did see Olivia first
Methought she purged the air of pestilence;
That instant was I turned into a hart,
And my desires, like fell and cruel hounds,
E'er since pursue me.

(1.1.18–22)

This speech, even more than Orsino's first one, demonstrates the double effect of the language. On the one hand, Orsino's image of Olivia as a purifying goddess and his comparison of himself to a classical huntsman might be thought simply examples of what Hilary Spurling calls 'Renaissance artifice'; but the use to which they are put is not artificial at all. The 'pestilence', plague, was an everpresent threat to the audience listening to Orsino; and the ferocity of the 'fell and cruel hounds' makes real and immediate the pangs of frustrated desire—and this ferocity lurking beneath the artifice pre- pares, incidentally, for Orsino's homicidal outburst when he thinks himself betrayed in the final scene. So from the start of the play, the language is two-edged: if it is artificial and even satirical in that it draws upon fashion and conven- tion, that fashion is tempered by an immediacy and vigour which suggest that Orsino is at least capable of powerful feeling and, most important, of development under Viola's influence.

A further dimension is given to the scene by the music. It is almost as if the printed text is a blueprint for the total experience of words and music together—which of course is how Shakespeare has conceived it, 'hearing' the musical phrases, played and repeated, blending with the spoken text.[1] The music can take many forms. In the first performances it may have been a single instrument or a consort, but the plangent sound of the lute blends particularly well with the language, especially in expressing the 'dying fall' of line 4. In any case, the combination of musical beauty and sensuous language is a crucial part of an audience's experience of the

[1] Peter Thomson goes so far as to say that the 'highly wrought language of his first speech is designed to be a verbal accompaniment to the melody' rather than the other way round (*Shakespeare's Theatre*, 2nd edn., 1992, p. 92).

scene, and further complicates any view that Orsino is being satirized or caricatured.

There is, however, a further suggestion of artifice and the following of convention in Valentine's account of Olivia's mourning for her dead brother:

> The element itself till seven years' heat
> Shall not behold her face at ample view,
> But like a cloistress she will veilèd walk
> And water once a day her chamber round
> With eye-offending brine—all this to season
> A brother's dead love . . .
>
> (1.1.25–30)

The word 'element' seems to have been a fashionable affectation; it is used by Malvolio to express superiority (3.4.119) and mocked by Feste as 'over-worn' (3.1.58): whether the affectation here is Olivia's own or Valentine's veiled criticism of her is not clear, but such subsequent phrases as 'like a cloistress', 'water . . . her chamber', 'eye-offending brine', and 'season' also suggest affectation. It is good to mourn the dead, but not to carry mourning to extremes; and there could be no greater contrast than with Viola's style as she arrives on stage a mere ten lines later, shipwrecked and mourning the brother *she* has lost:

> And what should I do in Illyria?
> My brother he is in Elysium.
>
> (1.2.2–3)

Elysium is the heaven of classical mythology, but there is nothing artificial or 'literary' about the lines: Viola expresses her sense of bereavement with a direct simplicity which is characteristic of much of her language, except when she is being consciously 'poetical' (discussed in the next section), and which differs sharply both from Orsino's elaborate style and from the language used by Valentine to describe Olivia. That contrast swiftly and economically sets up the main line of the romantic plot: as Orsino and Olivia come into contact with Viola, her unaffected directness draws them from their affectations, and reveals the positive qualities that those mannerisms partly conceal.

The process has begun in Viola's very next scene, now in her disguise as the page Cesario. Orsino's first words to her are:

Thou know'st no less but all: I have unclasped
To thee the book even of my secret soul.

(1.4.13–14)

In noticeable contrast to the language he used to describe his love for Olivia, he now comes quickly to the point. He has met somebody whom he trusts, and has simply opened his heart to his page without fuss. Their relationship, and the foundation of their ultimate marriage, based not on wooing from afar but on getting to know one another, is established in a mere two lines.

Shakespeare also does a great deal of work in a short space of time in the scene where Olivia first appears (1.5). Here he introduces no fewer than three major characters—Olivia herself, Malvolio, and Feste—so that the audience can compare Olivia's and Malvolio's reactions to Feste. When Feste proves Olivia a fool 'to mourn for [her] brother's soul being in heaven' (1.5.65–6), she is able to accept the 'proof' and to laugh at herself. Shakespeare specifically invites the audience to compare Olivia's reaction with Malvolio's by having her ask Malvolio for his opinion, and he is not amused: 'I marvel your ladyship takes delight in such a barren rascal' (1.5.78–9)—words that Feste does not forget, and turns back upon Malvolio in the final scene. Olivia shrewdly characterizes Malvolio: 'O, you are sick of self-love, Malvolio . . . There is no slander in an allowed fool, though he do nothing but rail; nor no railing in a known discreet man, though he do nothing but reprove' (1.5.85–91). By equating Malvolio's faults with Feste's, Olivia delicately but firmly puts Malvolio in his place; and by allying herself with the wise fool rather than with the repressive steward, she emerges as a much more complex and interesting character than the first scene has led us to expect. Far from being either the purifying goddess described by Orsino, or the cloistered idealist shutting herself away for seven years described by Valentine, she is a great lady in charge of her household whom grief has not deprived either of a sense of humour or of a capacity to size up other people. Both stand her in good stead in her first encounter with Viola.

'Make me a willow cabin': Viola and Olivia

The Viola/Olivia scene opens with an exchange about the most appropriate expression for a declaration of love, and so recalls the complexities of Orsino's language in the first scene, appropriately enough since Viola is his ambassador. Unable to recognize Olivia, or pretending not to recognize her, Viola launches into Orsino's prepared speech, 'Most radiant, exquisite, and unmatchable beauty', only to break off and ask anticlimactically 'if this be the lady of the house, for I never saw her' (1.5.162–4), thus drawing attention to the risk of inappropriateness in conventional compliments. Far from being in any way thrown by Viola's irony, Olivia is quick to catch her tone and to match her in distrusting cliché:

VIOLA . . . I will on with my speech in your praise, and then show
    you the heart of my message.
OLIVIA Come to what is important in't, I forgive you the praise.
VIOLA Alas, I took great pains to study it, and 'tis poetical.
OLIVIA It is the more like to be feigned, I pray you keep it in.

(1.5.181–9)

Viola and Olivia are equals in poise and wit, and as so often Shakespeare uses wit to suggest relationship, or potential relationship. The two characters strike up an immediate rapport, which during the course of the scene develops on Olivia's side into interest and finally love; as with the Viola/Orsino relationship, Olivia's love has its origins in their compatible personalities.

Once Olivia has got rid of her attendants, what she calls a 'skipping . . . dialogue' (l. 193) begins to intensify. First, when she unveils at Viola's request and asks 'Is't not well done?', Viola's witty quip 'Excellently done, if God did all' is countered by Olivia's unperturbed, equally quick-witted reply: ' 'Tis in grain sir, 'twill endure wind and weather' (224–7). And when Viola goes on to suggest that Olivia must not die without leaving a 'copy' of her beauty, a child, Olivia wittily plays upon the word 'copy', taking the scene back into prose as she does so. Now it is she, not Viola, who deflates poetic compliments, mockingly reducing the various aspects of her beauty to a list of items on a 'schedule' or inventory, 'as, *item*, two lips, indifferent red; *item*, two grey eyes, with lids to them; *item*, one neck, one chin, and so forth' (ll. 235–7). The two of them are more clearly matched than ever in witty presence of mind.

The major transition in the scene comes when Viola, ironically in view of what is to happen, raises the idea of herself, as Cesario, loving Olivia, and demonstrates how she would go about her wooing in her famous 'willow cabin' speech (ll. 257–65). This is the perfect example of a passage which starts off from a basis of fashion and convention but goes far beyond the merely extravagant. As Harold Jenkins points out, 'the willow is the emblem of forsaken love and those songs that issue from it in the dead of night . . . are easily recognizable as the traditional love-laments'. But as he also says, the parody 'is of the kind that does not belittle but transfigures its original' and Olivia 'starts to listen'.[1] The situation is again two-edged. Part of the reason that Olivia starts to listen is that she is susceptible to this kind of language when delivered with this power, and an atmosphere of erotic ambiguity is established which dominates the Viola/Olivia scenes as it does the Viola/Orsino ones. The dramatist Simon Gray writes illuminatingly about this ambiguity: the speech 'is not a classic of romantic persuasiveness for nothing. If it is ironic in its exaggerations, it is also insidiously enticing in its rhythms . . . and consequently the comedy in [Viola's] relationship with Olivia is both intensely erotic and dangerous' (*New Statesman*, 28 August 1969).

Olivia registers the power of the willow cabin speech with the simple phrase 'You might do much.' She then takes the scene on to its next stage by asking 'What is your parentage?', the significance of which is that she is attempting to find out if 'Cesario' is of the rank that would qualify 'him' as a potential husband. Her defences are down, her interest clear. In the soliloquy at the end of the scene, Shakespeare has given her a valuable sense of self-mockery: she herself is surprised

[1] 'Shakespeare's *Twelfth Night*' (see p. 20 n. 1), p. 177.

at the speed and suddenness with which she has fallen in love: 'How now? | Even so quickly may one catch the plague?' (ll. 284–5). At the same time the comparison of love to the ever-threatening plague, echoing the first scene, gives a touch of sombre reality to her situation, and this duality is further developed in her second scene with Viola. There is certainly comedy of situation in Olivia's declaration of love to the 'page', but it is balanced by the lyrical freshness and beauty of her imagery, and then by her increasing desperation:

> Cesario, by the roses of the spring,
> By maidhood, honour, truth, and everything,
> I love thee so that maugre all thy pride,
> Nor wit nor reason can my passion hide.
> (3.1.147–50)

As so often in Shakespearian comedy, an event is seen from more than one perspective: what may appear humorously incongruous to an onlooker is no joke to the person experiencing it. The language takes the character well beyond mere confusion of situation. Olivia's emotions have been roused and fired, and moreover she is aware both of the pain and the irony of her situation as an oncoming wooer.

But the moment needs careful handling, and the age of the character (and of the actress) is an important consideration. In an account which emphasizes the openness of the text to a variety of interpretations, particularly in the matter of the characters' ages, John Russell Brown points out that Olivia can be of 'mature years', a gracious lady of the manor, or 'a very young girl' who forgets 'her "discreet" bearing in breathless eagerness' as she falls in love with Cesario.[1] But the limitations of this openness have often been rather sharply demonstrated in performance. At the 1980 Canadian Shakespeare

---

[1] *Shakespeare's Plays in Performance* (1966), p. 209. In an earlier book, Brown emphasizes the youth of the characters. He calculates that since Sebastian is the same age as Viola and 'still beardless enough to be imitated', they cannot be more than about nineteen; Orsino is of 'fresh and stainless youth' and believes that the man should be older than the woman, so must be older than Olivia; 'by the same token Olivia should be younger than Sebastian and hence younger than Viola'. This may, as he says, 'be pushing consistency too far'; but it is worth remembering at a time when Shakespeare's heroines are usually played by actresses rather than boy actors (*Shakespeare and his Comedies* (1957), pp. 176–7).

Festival in Stratford, Ontario, for instance, a mature Olivia threw herself at a young Viola only to be greeted by a strident comment from a woman in the audience, 'That's really quite embarrassing'—perhaps because Olivia appeared to be cradle-snatching, perhaps because one woman was making love to another. Olivia, of course, falls in love with the 'boy'; but it is part of the sexually ambiguous potential of the scene, as Trevor Nunn privately suggests, that Olivia unconsciously senses and responds to the feminine qualities of the 'boy'. Nunn argues particularly from the impression given by the matching youth, compatible personalities, and sympathy beneath the wit-combats, of Dorothy Tutin and Geraldine Mc-Ewan at Stratford-upon-Avon in 1958; but extreme youth can also bring its problems, as Robert Speaight explains: 'Olivia must, at least, be the competent mistress of a great household; a serious young woman capable of sudden silliness, or—if you prefer—a silly young woman capable of sudden seriousness. To make her incapable of any seriousness whatsoever blunt[s] the impact of Viola on her fantasy.'[1] A careful balance needs to be struck between youth and maturity, between innocence and experience.

'She never told her love': Viola and Orsino

The long scene between Viola, Orsino, and Feste (2.4) is the emotional heart of the play. It is also the scene which best exemplifies the play's 'elusive' quality, its shifting, bittersweet mood; and as in the first scene the music makes a powerful contribution. The scene falls into three clearly defined sections: Feste sings 'Come away death' in the middle of the scene, with intimate conversations between Viola and Orsino on either side. But the song permeates the first section of the scene as well, since Orsino asks the musician or musicians to play the tune before Feste arrives, and the characters' reactions to it focus the changing moods of the scene—by turns melancholy, heartfelt, humorous, ironic—and especially the steadily developing relationship of Orsino and Viola. For example, Viola's 'masterly' description of the music—'It gives

---

[1] *Shakespeare on the Stage* (Boston and Toronto, 1973), p. 281.

a very echo to the seat | Where love is throned' (2.4.20–1)—
leads Orsino to ask questions about Viola herself and with
whom she is in love. Her oblique replies, and witty puns like
'by your favour', implying both 'by your leave' and 'someone
who resembles you', establish the only way in which her
disguise allows her to speak of her love—through hints and
half-truths; and Orsino's reactions, like 'She is not worth thee
then' and 'Too old, by heaven', show a valuable capacity to
laugh at himself, a significant development from his first scene
(ll. 22–8).

The second phase of the scene begins with Feste's arrival
and the discussion of the song. There is a slight problem here.
Orsino calls it 'old and plain', a folk-song such as people sing
when sitting at work in the sun, about 'the innocence of love'.
But the text is actually quite elaborate. The point is probably
that the *sentiment* of the song, concerning a lover who is
about to die of unrequited love and who asks to be buried
uncommemorated and forgotten, is about primal emotions. It
is certainly perfectly suited to its hearers, as Feste's songs
always are: it fuels Orsino's love-melancholy, but it is also
very relevant to Viola, who no doubt thinks that she may
well go to her grave without being able to declare her love.
So for all its elaboration, the song celebrates unspoken emotion and is thus absolutely relevant to the content of the
scene. It is easy when reading to forget the reactions of
characters who are not speaking, which of course staging
brings out: Ronald Bryden, for instance, wrote of the 'glimpses
of unspoken tenderness' in John Barton's production, such as
Judi Dench's Viola 'biting her lip as she watches the effect of
Feste's hymn to death on Orsino' (*Observer*, 24 August 1969).
But the song is relevant to Feste too: since he is almost
certainly of an older generation—'a fool that the lady Olivia's
father took much delight in' (2.4.11–12)—a song that is 'old
and plain' suits this singer as it does his audience, for different
reasons, and its melancholy fits the wry manner he displays
elsewhere.

The impression that the song is suited to the singer also
derives from the enjoyment Feste gets out of it—'I take pleasure
in singing, sir'—and it is his involvement in his art which
motivates his barbed reaction when Orsino offers to pay him:

'pleasure will be paid, one time or another'. Feste is not slow to accept—or to ask for—money elsewhere (2.3.25, 30–4; 3.1.42–53; 4.1.20–2; 5.1.22–43), but here he seems to bridle at Orsino's assumption that art is simply something to be used and that it can be switched off and on to order. And when Orsino dismisses him, Feste delivers one of the most remarkable speeches in the play:

Now the melancholy god protect thee, and the tailor make thy doublet of changeable taffeta, for thy mind is a very opal. I would have men of such constancy put to sea, that their business might be everything, and their intent everywhere, for that's it that always makes a good voyage of nothing.   (ll. 72–7)

Here Feste openly criticizes Orsino's moody changeableness: 'changeable taffeta' was a standard Elizabethan term for shot silk, which keeps changing colour with the light, as the opal also does (see the notes to 2.4.73–4). He then accuses Orsino of lacking constancy—something that Orsino specifically prided himself upon at l. 18. Not surprisingly, Orsino is stung by this and dismisses everyone except Viola. While Feste's 'opal' and 'changeable taffeta' are apt descriptions for at least a part of Orsino's personality, they might also serve as apt images for the shifting moods of both the scene and the play as a whole.

Partly, no doubt, because he is smarting at Feste's criticism of his inconstancy, Orsino is at his most self-centred when he proclaims that no woman's love is like his (ll. 92–102). Such male chauvinism is too much for Viola, the living denial of it, and she bursts out 'Ay, but I know—'. This was a particularly memorable moment in Dorothy Tutin's performance in Peter Hall's 1958–60 production, well caught by Michael Billington as 'a soaring cry from the heart halted just in time and brought down in the vocal scale to a more moderate "Too well what love women to men may owe" ' (*Directors' Shakespeare*, p. xviii).[1] This impassioned broken line is very characteristic of Viola. In her candour, she cannot bear to hear Orsino going on about what is not true, and has to stop him

---

[1] Dorothy Tutin's performance is preserved in a sound recording (Argo ZPR 186–8 (1961)), as are those of two other members of Hall's cast, Patrick Wymark (Sir Toby, 1958–60) and Derek Godfrey (Orsino, 1960).

even at the risk of almost revealing her identity. And the half-line emphasizes that in her page's disguise she is frustrated from making the declaration of love she longs to make. But her impassioned outburst also reawakens Orsino's interest in Viola herself and her feelings expressed at the start of the scene, and this leads to the emotional climax, Viola's oblique statement of her love in the allegory of an imaginary sister.

Once more, as in her 'willow cabin' speech, Viola starts off from convention but transforms it: the traditional Elizabethan comparison of ladies' skin to damask roses, and the proverb, which Shakespeare also uses in Sonnet 35, that the 'canker' (worm) 'lives in sweetest bud' (l. 4), perfectly express the hidden grief eating away at her heart:

> She never told her love,
> But let concealment, like a worm i'th' bud,
> Feed on her damask cheek.   (ll. 110–12)

Viola then proceeds to transform the traditional image of the pining, melancholy lover into something more complex:

> She pined in thought,
> And with a green and yellow melancholy
> She sat like patience on a monument,
> Smiling at grief.   (ll. 112–15)

That final phrase, with smiles and tears inseparable, is very characteristic both of the play and of Viola herself: she can see the humorous as well as the sad side of situations. In her earlier soliloquy when Malvolio gave her Olivia's ring, for instance, she was able to combine sympathy for Olivia with a witty appreciation of the irony of her situation:

> Poor lady, she were better love a dream!
> . . . As I am man,
> My state is desperate for my master's love.
> As I am woman, now alas the day,
> What thriftless sighs shall poor Olivia breathe!
>   (2.2.26–39)

Viola's speech draws Orsino from his self-absorption to an interest in her and her story: 'But died thy sister of her love, my boy?' Her reply is packed with a variety of emotional implications:

> I am all the daughters of my father's house,
> And all the brothers too; and yet I know not.
> (ll. 119-21)

G. K. Hunter brings out some of these implications:

the doubleness of expression involves more than a pattern of wit; it evokes Viola's complex relationship of frustration and fulfilment, which is what the page role allows to her, at the same time as it reminds us of her brother, and her aloneness in the world. . . . Viola says, 'a woman may die of love', 'I may die of love for you', 'I am alone in the world—but I am not even sure of that', . . . and no doubt other things as well.[1]

Performers naturally seize upon this potential. Judi Dench, for instance, has a vocal characteristic, a little break or catch in the voice, which she can exploit to great expressive effect; she used it here on 'brothers', with a slight hesitation before the word: she was clearly thinking of Sebastian.

But Viola does not simply sit and pine: in the scene's final change of mood, she snaps out of her sorrow and has to remind Orsino, who is now absorbed in her and her story, of Olivia: 'Sir, shall I to this lady?' This moment, with Orsino more interested in Viola than Olivia, makes it clear that the basis of their relationship and ultimate marriage is fully established. One reason why Orsino has no more scenes until the finale is that no more are needed: Shakespeare's economical craftsmanship has done the work. As Gareth Lloyd Evans wrote of Orsino in John Barton's production, he 'has mewled about ideal love and compromises with a sweet actuality which, unknown to him, is as near to the ideal as he will ever achieve'.[2] He and Viola are friends first, lovers subsequently; at the end of the play, he marries someone he has come to know.

The final moments of this scene are usually highly charged in performance, as Orsino becomes more engrossed in Viola, and this interest is often expressed in physical ways which arise naturally out of the intensity of the scene. At Salzburg in 1972, for instance, Klaus Maria Brandauer actually kissed

---

[1] *John Lyly: The Humanist as Courtier* (1962), p. 366.
[2] 'Interpretation or Experience? Shakespeare at Stratford', *SS 23* (Cambridge, 1970), 131-5; p. 135.

'Cesario'; and in Peter Gill's 1974 RSC production, John Price's Orsino clasped Jane Lapotaire's androgynous Viola sympathetically to his bare chest, thus making the moment even more difficult for her; behind them, on the walls of William Dudley's set, was scrawled a line from Sonnet 23: 'O learn to read what silent love hath writ' (l. 13). This Viola was the perfect image of 'silent love'. Since she was also very convincing in her boy's disguise, and since Orsino responded so physically to 'Cesario', this staging focused attention on the sexually ambiguous potential of the relationships in this play, not only those between Orsino and Viola, and Viola and Olivia, but more particularly that between Antonio and Sebastian, which was also very physically expressed, with passionate embraces between them at parting and at reunion.

Antonio and Sebastian

The relationship between Antonio and Sebastian is another of the differing 'kinds of love' depicted in the play; but Shakespeare has dramatized it in a way that makes it hard to focus precisely. The difficulties begin in their first scene (2.1). It is surprising that this is in prose; even if the scene is regarded as a simple narrative link, the usual medium for that in a Shakespeare play is blank verse, as in the next scene for these two characters (3.3). Moreover, it is very unlike the vigorous, energetic prose so far spoken, being formal, even mannered, with its abstractions and balanced cadences, as in Sebastian's 'The malignancy of my fate might perhaps distemper yours' (ll. 4–5). It is possible that this style is meant to suggest a sense of strain in the relationship, Antonio loving Sebastian but being uncertain how best to express it, Sebastian half-aware of this, perhaps partly reciprocating it, while also preoccupied with his grieving for Viola. The verse lines embedded in the prose, for instance 'though it was said she much resembled me' (ll. 22–3), may suggest intense emotion reined in by the controlled, contained style, and Sebastian is close to tears at ll. 37–8. Strong feeling beneath the formal surface is also implied in Antonio's phrase 'If you will not murder me for my love, let me be your servant' (ll. 31–2), which employs the Petrarchan conceit of the cruel mistress murdering her loving servant; and once Sebastian has left, the constraint of prose gives way to the liberation of verse as Antonio expresses his love directly: 'I do adore thee so | That danger shall seem sport, and I will go' (ll. 42–3).

Some of the tensions beneath the prose in this scene may linger beneath the verse of their next conversation. In Sebastian's

> My kind Antonio,
> I can no other answer make but thanks,
> And thanks; and ever oft good turns ... (3.3.13–15),

the third line is two syllables short, which may suggest an embarrassed pause after 'And thanks', Sebastian appreciating Antonio's generosity but implying that he is trying to find the right way of telling Antonio that he cannot fully reciprocate his love—before the conversation turns to the less emotionally fraught topic of seeing the sights of the town. Antonio's generosity emerges again when he gives Sebastian his purse; and this motivates his outraged sense of betrayal when 'Cesario' subsequently denies him the purse in the scene of his arrest. This moment is typical of the technique of the play: the comedy of situation created by the mock duel draws from Antonio an outburst of intense suffering, and a public declaration of his love for Sebastian, whom he relieved with 'sanctity of love' and to whose 'venerable' 'image' he offered 'devotion'. His passion is summed up in the intense phrase 'O, how vile an idol proves this god!' (3.4.352–6). Here Antonio uses not so much the language of Petrarchan conceit as the expression of intense love in terms of religious devotion such as Shakespeare uses in some of his most powerful Sonnets:

> How many a holy and obsequious tear
> Hath dear religious love stol'n from mine eye (31.5–6)

or

> Let not my love be called idolatry,
> Nor my belovèd as an idol show ...
> (105.1–2)

And although Viola has caused his statement of anguished disappointment through her apparent ingratitude, it is a nice irony that in fact she agrees with Antonio in being generous and hating ingratitude (3.4.344–7). This obliquely makes the point that, like Viola, Antonio provides a kind of emotional ground bass for the declarations of love in the play—often wrung from him by the twists of the plot, both here and in the final scene, which will be considered later.

At the same time, the play does not sentimentalize Antonio. The suspicion of piracy, for instance, which hangs about him is never conclusively dispelled. The evidence centres on two accounts of the sea-battle between Antonio and Orsino at 3.3.26–37 and 5.1.45–70. While not denying that he is Orsino's enemy, Antonio does deny that he is 'thief or pirate' (5.1.68–70); yet earlier he admits to Sebastian that the quarrel

> might have since been answered in repaying
> What we took from them, which for traffic's sake
> Most of our city did. Only myself stood out . . .
> (3.3.33–5)

This is presumably intended to communicate Antonio's stubborn integrity; but if he alone did not return the spoils, was he not technically guilty of piracy? Moreover, there is a noticeable discrepancy between Antonio's claim that his participation in the sea-fight was not of 'a bloody nature' (3.3.30), and the Officer's accusation that in the battle Orsino's 'young nephew Titus lost his leg' (5.1.57), implying that this was Antonio's fault. The truth probably lies somewhere in between, Antonio attempting to play down his ferocity and perhaps piracy to Sebastian, his enemies exaggerating both. Even so, the discrepancy suggests that Antonio is not being wholly candid with Sebastian, though his basic integrity is not in doubt.

There is a discrepancy of a different kind, a double time scheme, involving Sebastian's and Viola's rescue and arrival in Orsino's city. At 1.4.3, it is stated that 'three days' have elapsed since Viola arrived at court, but in the final scene both Antonio and Orsino refer to 'three months' elapsing since the shipwreck (5.1.89, 94). This seems to be Shakespearian sleight of hand, in order to underline the maturing affection of Orsino for Viola and Antonio for Sebastian, but Joseph Pequigney uses this ambiguity as part of his attempt to '*secure* the homoerotic character of the friendship':

for months [Sebastian] has continuously remained with an adoring older man who is frankly desirous of him, who showered him with 'kindnesses' [3.4.341] and who, moreover, saved him from death at sea and nursed him back to health. It is the classic homoerotic relationship, wherein the mature lover serves as guide and mentor to the young beloved.[1]

He further suggests that Sebastian's use of the alias Roderigo (2.1.15) is 'unexplained' but that it can be 'seen as a means to hide his identity, his true name and family connections, during a drawn-out sexual liaison with a stranger in strange lands'. The alias can equally be explained as Sebastian's circumspection while unsure how far he could trust Antonio (perhaps because of the suspicion of piracy), or simply as a common motif in myth or folk-tale that to reveal your identity places you in other people's power. This is, for example, one of the reasons why Marina is so reluctant to reveal her identity in *Pericles* (Scene 21, 90–130, 175–7). But even if the arguments put forward by Pequigney and others[2] do not 'secure' the Antonio/Sebastian relationship as homoerotic, it is certainly true that the text permits, even if it does not demand, a homoerotic interpretation.[3]

The Gulling of Malvolio

Yet another aspect of love and lovers' behaviour is dramatized in the Malvolio story. By presenting Malvolio as an extravagant wooer of Olivia, the play provides a perspective on the Orsino/Olivia/Viola story and binds the main plot and the sub-plot tightly together, with Olivia at the centre of both, wooed by Orsino, Viola/Cesario, Sir Andrew, and Malvolio.

[1] 'The Two Antonios and Same-Sex Love in *Twelfth Night* and *The Merchant of Venice*', ELR 22 (1992), 201–21; pp. 202, 204–5.

[2] Stephen Orgel, for example, calls Antonio and Sebastian an 'overtly homosexual couple' ('Nobody's Perfect: Or Why Did the English Stage take Boys for Women?', *South Atlantic Quarterly*, 88 (1989), 7–29; p. 27).

[3] In an account of sexual ambiguity and hermaphroditism in the Renaissance, Stephen Greenblatt suggests that the blurring of accustomed sexual distinctions in the play, especially as represented by an all-male cast, is such that Sebastian and Viola become 'indistinguishable' figures. Perhaps this pushes the play's sexually ambiguous potential rather far; but his discussion focuses 'the sexual energies that [are] transfigured in the comedies and the melancholy darkness that lies just beyond the transfiguration' (*Shakespearean Negotiations* (Berkeley, 1988), pp. 91, 184).

Malvolio has made a big impact from the beginning. In his account of the earliest recorded performance, John Manningham thought it 'a good practice'—a good practical joke— 'to make the steward believe his lady widow was in love with him' (Olivia's mourning black must have misled Manningham into forgetting that she was mourning a brother, not a husband).[1] He also seems to have found the later stages of the gulling—'making him believe they took him to be mad'—all part of the fun: Shakespeare's contemporaries were notoriously cruel in their attitude to madmen. Manningham's account does not necessarily imply that Malvolio was played exclusively for broadly humorous effect; but when, in a commendatory poem to Shakespeare's *Poems* written before 1636 and published in 1640, Leonard Digges says that

> The Cockpit galleries, boxes, all are full
> To hear Malvolio, that cross-gartered gull (ll. 59–60),

the word 'gull' (fool) does not suggest that much sympathy was wasted on Malvolio. But after the only major gap in the play's post-Restoration performing history, Charles Macklin revived the play in 1741 and played Malvolio himself; he was also a famous Shylock, but none of the reviews suggests that he emphasized the strong vein of humour in Shylock's part, so it is possible that the tendency of leading actors (and commentators) to look for pathos, sympathy, or quasi-tragedy in Malvolio began with Macklin.

The first firm evidence for such an interpretation, however, comes in Charles Lamb's description of Robert Bensley as Malvolio in his essay 'On Some of the Old Actors'. Lamb argues that 'Malvolio is not essentially ludicrous' but the 'master of the household to a great Princess' and that the humour derives from the incongruity between his puritanical rectitude and the context in which he finds himself: 'his morality and his manners are misplaced in Illyria.' When Robert Bensley's Malvolio was lost in his fantasies of greatness, Lamb 'rather admired than pitied the lunacy', and he

---

[1] Stephen Greenblatt (see previous note) argues that this slip is the 'normalization' of the 'major male wish-fulfillment fantasy' of marrying a wealthy widow (pp. 69, 176).

'never saw the catastrophe of this character, while Bensley played it, without a kind of tragic interest'.[1]

Lamb's essay was published in 1823, but Bensley's last performances as Malvolio were in 1792, when Lamb was only seventeen, so it is possible that the 'tragic interest' was Lamb's rather than Bensley's, especially since Sylvan Barnet provides evidence that Bensley's performance contained grotesque elements too;[2] but it represents a reading of the character that has been attempted by many actors since. Henry Irving, for instance, seems to have drawn upon Lamb's essay for his quasi-tragic Malvolio in 1884, a performance widely regarded as a failure.[3] Even so, while most actors have seized upon the opportunities for broadly comic effect in the part, they have also striven for something 'human' and complex.

A notable example of this approach was Laurence Olivier's Malvolio at Stratford-upon-Avon in 1955. In a lecture given in Stratford at the time, Olivier said that since the part must be funny and yet 'tragic, too', he had chosen to play Malvolio as a social 'upstart' so that the notion of Olivia being in love with him would be absurd yet also pathetic (quoted in *The Times*, 27 August 1955). Ivor Brown described the result: 'a diligent, self-made domestic official, over-eager to keep order, a common, uneasy [social] climber with a tortured lisp. . . . The actor, not so much over-weening as under-weening, provided a plausible and untheatrical Malvolio, brilliant in many details.'[4] Some of those details, however, seemed to offer moments of farce that were at odds with the search for a plausibly human characterization, as when Olivier fell backwards off a bench in his ecstasies during the letter scene, or when his trousers fell down from under his nightshirt in the drinking scene. The relative disappointment with which this performance was received may have derived from the uneasy

---

[1] *Essays of Elia* (1823), much reprinted, and quoted here from *'Twelfth Night': Critical Essays*, ed. Stanley Wells (New York and London, 1986), 49–60; pp. 52–4.

[2] 'Charles Lamb and the Tragic Malvolio', *PQ* 33 (1954), 178–88.

[3] Alan Hughes discusses Irving's production and performance in *Henry Irving, Shakespearean* (Cambridge, 1981), remarking that from 4.2 onwards 'Malvolio became too human' (p. 201). He lightened his interpretation in later performances.

[4] *Shakespeare Memorial Theatre* 1954–56 (1956), pp. 6–7.

alternation between farcical gags and a striving for sympathy. It is worth trying to assess how far the text itself strikes a balance between these two extremes.

The first point to make is that Malvolio's name is against him. 'Malvolio' means 'ill-will', formed from Italian *mal* (bad) and *voglia* (desire) on analogy with, and in contrast to, 'Benvolio' in *Romeo and Juliet* who is Romeo's good friend and a would-be peacemaker. The name Shakespeare has created for him carries a suggestion of adverse criticism and even of caricature. Leonard Digges's allusion to 'Malvolio, that cross-gartered gull' quoted above is given in the modernized spelling of the Oxford *Complete Works* of Shakespeare. But the original spells the name 'Malvoglio', so if this is the author's spelling rather than the compositor's, Digges had clearly grasped the significance of the name; this *may* imply that the part was performed as a caricature in the first half of the seventeenth century, and support John Manningham's relish of the 'practice' against Malvolio. However that may be, Shakespeare reinforces the negative implications of the name when he introduces Olivia and Malvolio together and contrasts her generous reaction to Feste with Malvolio's dismissive one (1.5.68–93). Yet it is interesting that what were by general consent the two outstanding Malvolios of recent years, Donald Sinden (in John Barton's production) and Eric Porter (in Peter Hall's), both got a big laugh on their very first word in answer to Olivia's 'What think you of this fool, Malvolio? Doth he not mend?', which is 'Yes' (1.5.68–70).[1] This is not something which anyone is likely to pick up from reading alone; it marks the distance between text and performance. Nor did either actor impose anything upon the line; each simply packed into that monosyllable the censorious sourness of the whole sentence—'Yes, and shall do, till the pangs of death shake him'—and of Malvolio's attitudes in general. Charles Lamb was right to say that Malvolio is 'cold, austere, repelling'—but he is also very funny. In this part, as often elsewhere, Shakespeare makes his points through laughter.

Lamb was also, however, right to stress that Shakespeare establishes Malvolio as a reliable, even essential, steward in

[1] Sinden details his approach in *Players of Shakespeare 1*, ed. Philip Brockbank (Cambridge, 1985), pp. 41–66.

a great household: his repressiveness and lack of generosity
need not interfere with his efficient discharge of his duties,
and may even help them. He is obviously useful, for instance,
in dealing with unwelcome embassies from Orsino, as Olivia's
casual instructions imply: 'Go you, Malvolio. If it be a suit
from the Count, I am sick, or not at home—what you will to
dismiss it' (1.5.103–4). Malvolio will cope. If he fails to do so
in this case, that is because he comes up against someone
more able than himself, whose positiveness and efficiency
make her a more valuable servant for *her* master than Malvolio is for his. Malvolio is contrasted with Viola as well as
Olivia, especially in his encounter with her over the ring (2.2).
With the ring, Olivia has sent an invitation: 'If that the youth
will come this way tomorrow, | I'll give him reasons for't'
(1.5.295–6). But Malvolio's version of this characteristically
turns a positive suggestion into a negative one, 'that you be
never so hardy to come again in his affairs, unless it be to
report your lord's taking of this' (2.2.9–11). For all his
efficiency, or officiousness, on Olivia's behalf, he actually does
her a disservice here because he is not sensitive to what Olivia
means, as Viola is: quickly sizing up the situation, with
characteristic generosity she conceals Olivia's rash indiscre-
tion from her steward: 'She took the ring of me, I'll none of
it' (2.2.12). This tiny exchange points the difference between
an ungenerous nature and a generous one with brilliant
economy.

When Malvolio breaks up the drinking party (2.3), he is
again legitimately exercising his stewardship. Maria makes the
point just before his entry: 'If my lady have not called up her
steward Malvolio and bid him turn you out of doors, never
trust me' (2.3.68–70); and sure enough Malvolio says 'My
lady bade me tell you . . .' when he does appear (ll. 89–90).
But other evidence suggests that his representing Olivia will
not be among the audience's main impressions of the scene.
First, there is the nature of Malvolio's entry. The Folio text's
direction is merely a terse '*Enter Malvolio*', but that gives no
idea of the size and impact of the theatrical moment. The
drunken singing has been escalating; Maria's attempt to check
it only intensifies it; and then Malvolio appears, the man who
runs the household dragged out of bed in the middle of the

night. In Granville Barker's 1912 production, Malvolio appeared in his normal severe garb with its white puritan collar (see fig. 4), but most productions dress him in a nightshirt, usually with his steward's chain over it, and sometimes with a dressing-gown and a nightcap, or his steward's hat, as well; at Stratford-upon-Avon in 1966, Ian Holm had his hair in curlers beneath the nightcap (see figs. 5–7). The audience's chief impression is of an incongruity, more or less riotous depending on the staging, between Malvolio and the others, in which they are unlikely to think of him primarily as Olivia's representative.

What is more, Malvolio does not mention Olivia at first. He accuses the others of madness and calls them 'tinkers', an extremely abusive term. He only mentions Olivia in order to threaten Toby with dismissal: 'she is very willing to bid you farewell' (2.3.94). This is the cue for Sir Toby and Feste to adapt a lover's song of farewell in order to raise the question of Malvolio himself, rather than Sir Toby, being dismissed (ll. 95–105). Then the scene turns ugly as Sir Toby rises to Malvolio's challenge—spurred into doing so, it is interesting to note, by Feste's jibe 'you dare not'—and pulls rank on Malvolio: 'Art any more than a steward?' (ll. 106–7). The crucial point about Malvolio's stewardship here is that it is used to emphasize the personal conflict between Malvolio and Toby, which leads directly into the next major development of this area of the play—the plot against him. As she conceives this, Maria makes the point that he is only 'a *kind* of puritan', implying that his puritanism is a façade: 'The dev'l a puritan that he is, or anything constantly but a time-pleaser, an affectioned ass . . .' (ll. 130, 136–7). What lies behind the efficient steward and repressive puritan emerges in Malvolio's most extended scene, his discovery of the letter.

Before Malvolio enters, Maria tells the others that he 'has been yonder i'the sun practising behaviour to his own shadow' (2.5.14–15), and it is important that Malvolio should be entertaining fantasies of greatness, and specifically about being married to Olivia, before he even reads the letter: he is thus the more susceptible to its contents. Fantasizing about being 'Count Malvolio', he cites an instance where the barriers of class were crossed—'the Lady of the Strachey married

4–7. Malvolio rebukes the revellers: four stagings.

4. Harley Granville Barker's production, Savoy Theatre, 1912: Malvolio (Henry Ainley), Sir Toby (Arthur Whitby), Maria (Leah Bateman Hunter), Feste (Hayden Coffin), Sir Andrew (Leon Quartermaine).

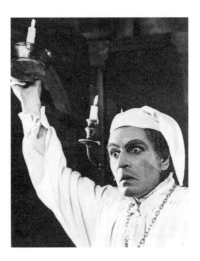

5. John Gielgud's production, Stratford-upon-Avon, 1955: Laurence Olivier as Malvolio.

6. Clifford Williams's production, Stratford-upon-Avon, 1966: Sir Toby (Brewster Mason), Feste, between his legs (Norman Rodway), Maria (Patsy Byrne), Malvolio (Ian Holm), Sir Andrew (David Warner).

7. John Barton's production, Stratford-upon-Avon, 1969: Maria (Brenda Bruce), Feste (Emrys James), Sir Andrew (Barrie Ingham), Malvolio (Donald Sinden).

the yeoman of the wardrobe' (ll. 32–7)—in the process revealing his interest in salacious gossip beneath his puritan exterior. The letter itself begins with a short poem and an 'alphabetical position' which draws upon the Elizabethan love of verbal games and acrostics:

> 'I may command where I adore,
>   But silence like a Lucrece knife
> With bloodless stroke my heart doth gore.
> M.O.A.I. doth sway my life.'
>
>   (ll. 100–3)

The quatrain is a parody of those Elizabethan love poems which are more intent on displaying ingenuity than on expressing feeling. Both the yellow stockings and the cross-gartering are also associated with traditional lovers' behaviour (see the Commentary to 2.5.144–5), and in his enthusiasm to wear them 'even with the swiftness of putting on' (l. 162), Malvolio allows his hitherto concealed fantasies of being a courtly lover to take over from the severe fronts of steward and puritan that have so far concealed them. The crowning touch in this transformation comes with his sudden address to Jove (ll. 162–8), and his assumption that the ruler of the classical gods, famed for his amorous exploits, is the perfect patron deity for him in his moment of triumph. That it should be a 'kind of puritan' who talks like this only emphasizes the incongruity between Malvolio the puritan steward and Malvolio the courtly lover.

This incongruity is much developed when he amazes Olivia by appearing before her wearing the yellow stockings and cross-garters, and quoting phrases that mean nothing to her (3.4.14–61); in the process, his place in the total scheme of the play becomes clear. As Irving Wardle wrote of Eric Porter's performance, Malvolio becomes the play's 'supreme victim of erotic delusion' (*Independent on Sunday*, 3 March 1991); so his love-delusions, as Harold Jenkins points out, 'fall into perspective as a parody of the more delicate aberrations of his mistress and her suitor. Like them Malvolio aspires towards an illusory ideal of love, but his mistake is a grosser one than theirs, his posturings more extravagant and grotesque'.[1] Oli-

---

[1] 'Shakespeare's *Twelfth Night*' (see p. 20 n. 1), p. 185.

8. Malvolio (Eric Porter) reads the letter. Behind the box-tree are
Fabian (Dinsdale Landen), Sir Toby (Patrick Wymark), and Sir Andrew
(Ian Richardson). Peter Hall's production, Stratford-upon-Avon, 1960.

via herself makes the point just as he appears: 'I am as mad
as he, | If sad and merry madness equal be' (3.4.14–15). The
strong element of sheer fantasy he expresses in the letter scene
and repeats in his soliloquy after Olivia has left in this one,
when he once more attributes his success to Jove (3.4.72–80),
makes the crucial point that as a lover he is so much more
extreme in his behaviour than Olivia and Orsino that by
comparison with him their 'delicate aberrations' seem modest

and susceptible of cure. We have already seen the start of Orsino's cure in his involvement with 'Cesario'; Malvolio's seems much less likely in view of the element of sheer fantasy involved in his love delusions. In this soliloquy, these fantasies are expressed with stewardly logic, working out how everything fits: 'Why, everything adheres together that no dram of a scruple, no scruple of a scruple, no obstacle, no incredulous or unsafe circumstance—what can be said?—nothing that can be can come between me and the full prospect of my hopes' (3.4.75–9). This is where the real importance of Malvolio's stewardship emerges: the more the actor makes Malvolio a steward of genuine capacity and substance in the early scenes, as Eric Porter for instance did, the greater the incongruity here; the more seriously Malvolio takes himself, the funnier he is—a basic principle of Shakespearian comedy, or any comedy.

There is no hint so far of potential heartbreak or quasi-tragedy in the presentation of Malvolio. But just after his exit in 3.4, the gulling plot takes another and more sinister turn. Maria's 'device' has completely succeeded, but when she proposes to pursue it still further, Fabian says 'Why, we shall make him mad indeed', and Sir Toby seizes upon the idea: 'Come, we'll have him in a dark room and bound' (3.4.126–30). Before we see that (4.2), however, the attention shifts to the other major intrigue of this section of the play, the mock duel between Viola and Sir Andrew; and these scenes of intrigue raise some problems which have not affected the course of the play so far.

Problems of the Intrigue Actions

The first two acts of the play, together with 3.1 and 3.4 up to Malvolio's exit, display structural mastery and economy, but it is a common theatrical experience that around the middle of the play, the rhythm seems to falter, especially in the very long 3.4. This scene consists of five main sections: Malvolio's appearance in yellow stockings (ll. 1–136), Sir Andrew's challenge (137–93), the third and final interview between Viola and Olivia (194–210), the mock duel (211–300), and Antonio's intervention and arrest (301–86). Performances that have moved well often seem to lose their way here, and the scene to fall into its discrete parts; it proves hard to discover the rhythm of individual sections or the overall shape of the scene.

The difficulties in fact begin earlier, with the abrupt, unexplained introduction of Fabian into the letter scene as a substitute for Feste. The crudeness of this contrasts strikingly with the theatrical expertise of the play so far. Shakespeare seems originally to have intended that Feste should 'make a third' in the plot against Malvolio (2.3.162), but then changed his mind. Perhaps he wanted to maintain Feste's detachment as an ironic commentator, or perhaps he decided not to involve him in the earlier stages of the plot so that his eventual participation, in the Sir Topaz scene, will have maximum impact, both because it is unexpected, and because Feste can be the centre of attention in that scene, whereas if he is involved in the box-tree scene he will have to share the focus with several other characters.

By comparison with the casual ease with which the plot against Malvolio is introduced into the drinking scene (2.3.125–64), the next intrigue action, the preparation in 3.2 for the mock duel in 3.4, is laboriously done. Fabian not only plays a major part in spurring Sir Andrew on to challenge Viola, he does so at length and in a very elaborate, even laboured, style, with formally balanced phrases and contrived comparisons:

She did show favour to the youth in your sight only to exasperate you, to awake your dormouse valour, to put fire in your heart and brimstone in your liver. . . . you are now sailed into the north of my lady's opinion, where you will hang like an icicle on a Dutchman's beard unless you do redeem it by some laudable attempt either of valour or policy. (3.2.16–27)

This sounds, not like the utterance of a dramatic character, but like a set speech, which is precisely what it is. Shakespeare is cranking the duel plot into action, and the effort shows. Moreover, Fabian's style introduces a vein of garrulity into a hitherto economically written play. And it is infectious. Sir Toby immediately catches his tone:

Taunt him with the licence of ink. If thou 'thou'st' him some thrice, it shall not be amiss, and as many lies as will lie in thy sheet of paper, although the sheet were big enough for the bed of Ware in England, set 'em down, go about it. (3.2.41–5)

Then, when he seems to have finished, he adds: 'Let there be gall enough in thy ink; though thou write with a goose-pen, no matter. About it' (3.2.45–7). It is true that, earlier in the play, Sir Toby has hardly been verbally reticent; but this speech provides the model for a whole series of extended speeches throughout the duel scene (3.4.178–89, 213–43, 264–98). They create a major theatrical problem.

The sense of elaborate contrivance in Fabian's speech just quoted lies partly in its use of topical reference. The laboured comparison of Sir Andrew hanging in 'the north' of Olivia's favour 'like an icicle on a Dutchman's beard' is probably an allusion to William Barentz, who led an expedition to the Arctic in 1596–7. Of course topical allusions occur earlier in the play as well, and throughout Shakespeare's works, but they seem to proliferate hereabouts: Sir Toby's reference to the Bed of Ware, Sir Andrew's 'I had as lief be a Brownist as a politician' (3.2.29), and so on. Such references are presumably what John Gielgud means when he says that one of the difficulties of the play lies in jokes which are 'archaic and difficult' (see p. 6 above). Another director, John Caird, corroborates Gielgud's view: what Gielgud calls 'archaic' jokes, Caird calls 'dead' ones—archaic or dead, that is, for modern audiences: 'it's very interesting that most of the dead jokes are in a particular part of the play . . . where we nearly always find there's a rhythmic problem' (*Directors' Shakespeare*, p. 21). Caird goes on to relate the specific problem to a larger one which seems to arise regularly in rehearsals and performances: 'Mainly, *Twelfth Night* is a play of almost perfect rhythm: if you just play the rhythms in the text and the rhythm from one scene to another, . . . it's miraculous . . . the way it motors itself along.' But Caird adds that in Act 3, Scenes 2 and 4 'you have major problems', notably because Sir Toby becomes 'incredibly prolix'—and prolix, moreover, on matters such as the rules of duelling, with which a modern audience is least familiar. A Toby who is too drunken, or too sluggish, or who enjoys his jokes too much, can bring the play to a standstill.

One way in which modern performances attempt to overcome this difficulty is to emphasize the darker side of Sir Toby's jollity, his constant exploitation of other people, and especially the cruelty latent in his relationship with Sir Andrew. A part of this process has been a tendency to sentimentalize Sir Andrew, whose reply to Sir Toby's remark that Maria adores him, 'I was adored once too' (2.3.169), often played for pathos, is frequently cited as an example of the way that Shakespeare rounds out his characters; but it is equally possible that the remark is not pathetic at all, but rather Sir Andrew's resentful attempt to keep up with Sir Toby, as he does elsewhere (2.5.172, 175, 178, 181, 197), implying 'You're not the only one to be loved'. Maria does after all characterize him as 'a great quarreller' (1.3.27), a man always suspecting slights and offences but without the wit to work out precisely what those might be. This certainly helps to launch the whole business of his challenge to Viola; and it may imply a young, or youngish, aggressive Sir Andrew, a prodigal squandering his inheritance, and so an especially easy victim for Sir Toby to exploit (see Commentary to 1.3.103).

In several modern productions, however, Sir Andrew has been much older, particularly in John Barton's version where, in Simon Gray's words, 'Sir Toby Belch and Sir Andrew Aguecheek sit collapsed, their eyes rheumy with retrospection, while Feste, as he sings "What is love? 'Tis not hereafter", watches them with tender irony' (*New Statesman*, 28 August 1969). These two knights, with their balding heads and straggling wisps of hair, were both of an age to recall, with a nostalgia fuelled by drink, that 'Youth's a stuff will not endure'. This closeness in age did not prevent Sir Toby rejecting Sir Andrew in the last act with the utmost brutality; and whether Sir Andrew is played young or old, a tougher relationship with Sir Toby helps to counterbalance the problem of slackening tension in the middle of the play.

Feste—and Sir Topaz

The replacement of Feste by Fabian in much of Act 3 is a double disadvantage, for Feste's interesting presence is as much missed as Fabian's is an unwelcome intrusion. It has often been argued that Shakespeare's creation of Feste was inspired by the arrival in his company, the Lord Chamberlain's Men, of Robert Armin, a singer and subtle comic actor, as a replacement for Will Kemp, who seems to have left the company during 1599, and who specialized in more broadly humorous roles like Dogberry in *Much Ado About Nothing*. It should be emphasized that there is no proof that Armin played Feste (whereas there is evidence from speech-headings in the 1600 quarto of *Much Ado* that Dogberry was written for Kemp), but it is likely; and if he did, then his presence may have influenced more than Feste's role alone, since Feste's qualities are also those of the play as a whole. In his own sharply witty, musical personality, tinged with melancholy, Feste, as Alan Pryce-Jones wrote of Max Adrian's performance in Peter Hall's 1960 version, embodies 'the interplay of light and shadow which makes [the play] memorable' (*Observer*, 22 May 1960). And in moving, like Viola, between the two worlds of Orsino's court and Olivia's great house, he helps to give the play its unity, and to hold its component parts together.

Half-way through the play, Shakespeare brings together these two characters who are at its centre in a dialogue which contributes virtually nothing to the story-line but a great deal to tone and mood, and which focuses Feste in particular. Much of their conversation is about the misleading-ness of conventional language. Feste's remark that he is not Olivia's fool but her 'corrupter of words' (3.1.34–5) is a perfect piece of self-definition: he plays with and perhaps distorts language, uses wit, to reveal truths, as when he analyses aspects of Olivia, Orsino, and Malvolio; now he turns his analytic eye on Viola too. Several productions have suggested that the wise fool achieves what others fail to do, and penetrates her disguise: 'Now Jove in his next commodity of hair send thee a beard' (3.1.43–4). She, equally, understands him, and after he has gone provides a perceptive analysis of him:

> This fellow is wise enough to play the fool,
> And to do that well craves a kind of wit.
> He must observe their mood on whom he jests,
> The quality of persons, and the time . . .
>
> (3.1.59–62)

And the last couplet of the speech perfectly captures Feste's paradoxical nature:

> For folly that he wisely shows is fit,
> But wise men, folly-fall'n, quite taint their wit.
>
> (3.1.66-7)

An audience might well take that final line as an apt comment on the behaviour of Malvolio in the previous scene, in contrast to that of the wise fool.

His wisdom seems to derive in part from age and experience. In the acting edition of his 1912 production, Granville Barker argued that Feste 'is not a young man': 'There runs through all he says and does that vein of irony by which we may so often mark one of life's self-acknowledged failures',[1] and he cast in the role an elderly musical comedy performer, Hayden Coffin, who, Michael Billington suggests, 'presumably brought with him just that touch of frayed melancholia you often find in veterans of the popular stage past their prime' (*Directors' Shakespeare*, p. xiv). The impression of age comes from his being of a generation with 'the lady Olivia's *father*' (2.4.11–12), and still more from the sense that he gives of having experienced a great deal of life beyond Olivia's garden wall.[2]

An important aspect of the role is Feste's use of theological terminology to prove Olivia a 'fool' at 1.5.52–67, where he 'catechizes' his 'madonna', puts her through the question-and-answer form of a catechism, which tests the orthodoxy of religious belief. The climax of this mock clericalism comes in the extraordinary episode in which Feste plays the priest Sir Topaz and 'exorcizes' the apparently mad Malvolio. Behind this scene, almost certainly, lies the Twelfth Night festivity of the Feast of Fools, and particularly the figure of the Bishop of Fools or Abbot of Unreason, who guyed and parodied the ceremonies of the Church as the Lord of Misrule reversed secular norms.[3]

---

[1] *Shakespeare's Comedy of 'Twelfth Night'* with a Producer's Preface by Granville Barker (1912), p. viii. The Preface is conveniently reprinted in *Granville Barker's Prefaces to Shakespeare: 'A Midsummer Night's Dream', 'The Winter's Tale', 'Twelfth Night'*, with a Foreword by Richard Eyre (1993), p. 96.

[2] Karen Greif describes the increasing prominence of Feste in twentieth-century productions in 'A Star is Born: Feste on the Modern Stage', *SQ* 39 (1988), 61–78.

[3] See Enid Welsford's classic study *The Fool* (1935), pp. 197–217.

But how, precisely, does Shakespeare set up the Sir Topaz scene? An important clue is provided by the Folio stage direction '*Malvolio within*'. This makes it clear that Malvolio is heard but not seen. In the Elizabethan theatre, he must have been offstage or more likely under the stage. This would have been a particularly appropriate place for a man apparently possessed by devils, since the area under the stage was known as 'the hell'; and it is usually where he is placed in most modern productions too, with only his hands visible, reaching out through a grille in the floor.[1] This has the important consequence of placing the physical focus of the scene firmly on Feste rather than Malvolio. The whole scene is mediated through Feste and his theatrical interpretations. It is not even the dialogue it seems to be on the page, since the speakers are so unequally balanced.

Opinion varies over what this focus implies about Feste himself. Gareth Lloyd Evans argues that the association with the traditional Twelfth Night entertainment of the Feast of Fools means that Feste is 'not stepping out of his posture as relatively uncommitted observer of the human scene'.[2] For Simon Gray, however, Feste in this scene forgoes his detachment and enters the fray: 'Feste *enjoys* tormenting Malvolio' (*New Statesman*, 28 August 1969). Gray points out that although Feste agrees to fetch Malvolio the materials to write his letter to Olivia, he 'subsequently and callously fails to deliver the letter itself' until Olivia's investigation compels him to do so (5.1.279–82). And there is a third possibility that combines Evans's and Gray's interpretations, which is that Feste's very detachment from Malvolio's plight as he concentrates on his impersonations may actually intensify the cruelty. It is, at any rate, in this scene that audiences often begin to feel uneasy about the treatment of Malvolio.

By focusing upon the tormentor rather than the tormented, and by keeping Malvolio out of sight, Shakespeare has not necessarily mitigated the cruelty of the scene; what he has

---

[1] While also suggesting that F's *within* may indicate use of the stage trap, John H. Astington traces the placing of Malvolio below the stage back to Jacques Copeau's production of 1914 ('Malvolio and the Dark House', *SS 41* (Cambridge, 1989), 55–62).

[2] *Shakespeare III, 1599–1604* (Edinburgh, 1971), p. 53.

done, presumably deliberately, is to make it much harder for an actor of Malvolio to play for gratuitous sympathy—provided, that is, that the Folio direction '*Malvolio within*' is observed. It would not do for Irving's tragic Malvolio. Edward Aveling in his review explained that the stage was divided in two, so that Malvolio was as visible as his tormentors. 'The mental and physical horror of darkness and the longing yearning for deliverance from a prison cell were never so realized, I think, before', wrote Aveling: 'there is the sense of the grievous wrong done to him, and the utter hopelessness of redress. My readers may be inclined to smile at me, but I declare in all seriousness the effect ... on me was that of intense tragedy.'[1] Aveling's suspicion that his readers may be inclined to smile at him is perhaps a tacit admission of the distance between this tragic Malvolio and anything that is suggested by the way in which Shakespeare has written the scene.

Even so, Bill Alexander's 1987–8 RSC staging went further still. Perhaps taking his cue from the reference to bear-baiting at 2.5.7,[2] Alexander not only made Antony Sher's Malvolio visible, but had him chained to a stake, his wild eyes suggesting someone whose hold on sanity was very tenuous, and during the scene Feste pushed him over the edge. In the final scene he was quite insane, lashing out at his tormentors, and singing snatches of Feste's song from the end of the prison scene. So much for Orsino's comment that Malvolio's letter 'savours not much of distraction' (5.1.305), and for the contained, pained dignity of his appeal to Olivia in organized verse, unlike the prose he has spoken up to this point (5.1.321–35). Clearly both Irving and Alexander/Sher went beyond interpreting the scene to rewriting it; but in the process they served to emphasize how the scene itself is written, and what it does not say—amongst other things, that Malvolio is mad. Nor is he mad in the final scene, even in a quasi-tragic reading; if Malvolio has a tragedy, it is that he remains irremediably sane. But the questions of madness, and

---

[1] Quoted in the Signet edition of the play, ed. Herschel Baker (revised edn., New York, 1987), p. 219.

[2] And perhaps from Ralph Berry's article '*Twelfth Night*: The Experience of the Audience' (*SS* 34 (Cambridge, 1981), 111–19: 'The audience becomes spectators, Malvolio the bear' (p. 118)).

of tragedy or otherwise, need to be addressed by considering Malvolio's last appearance in its context in the final scene, where it is one among many other considerations.

The Finale

In the long final scene, Shakespeare brings all the elements of the play together in a brilliantly theatrical *tour de force* which manipulates events so as to throw maximum emphasis on the emotional realities of the characters, often presented in extreme terms, a technique that he was to develop further in his final plays, especially in *Cymbeline*.[1]

In an opening episode, however, he establishes a more abstract framework for an intellectual dialectic that underpins the play. With self-conscious paradox Feste answers Orsino's question 'How dost thou, my good fellow?' with 'Truly sir, the better for my foes and the worse for my friends.' Orsino tries to reduce him to commonplaces, but Feste insists that his friends 'praise me, and make an ass of me', whereas his foes 'tell me plainly I am an ass, so that by my foes, sir, I profit in the knowledge of myself, and by my friends I am abused' (5.1.9–21). From this paradoxical point of view, Feste has been acting as a friend even to his foe Malvolio throughout the play. An actor can use this facet of Feste's behaviour to create a sense of an ultimate benignity behind his satire, and wisdom under his folly. Max Adrian in Peter Hall's 1960 production, for instance, shed tears at the end for his failure to teach Malvolio knowledge of himself, and the issues raised in this opening episode return when Feste and Malvolio face each other later in the scene.[2]

The tense situation that follows the arrival of Antonio draws from him, from Orsino, and from Viola declarations of love that have been wholly or partly concealed so far. The ferocity of the exchange between the old adversaries Antonio and

[1] The dramaturgy of this scene is studied in Jörg Hasler, *Shakespeare's Theatrical Notation: the Comedies* (Berne, 1974), pp. 160–78, reprinted in '*Twelfth Night': Critical Essays*, ed. Stanley Wells (New York and London, 1986), 279–302.

[2] Compare R. Chris Hassel, Jr.: 'he is persistently trying to correct unacknowledged follies in the play, trying to transform them into humility' (*Faith and Folly in Shakespeare's Romantic Comedies* (Athens, Georgia, 1980), p. 170).

Orsino serves to bring out the intensity of their other emotions as well. Viola's description of what Antonio said to her when he rescued her from the mock duel as 'distraction' (5.1.62) picks up the topic of madness from the Sir Topaz scene and from Sebastian's sensation in the previous scene that either he must be mad or Olivia must be (4.3.11–16); it is also the first of various references during the scene to madness (ll. 93, 275–6, 281, 285, 305, 364) or to witchcraft (ll. 70, 221–2, 229–30) which emphasize the highly charged, emotional state of many of the characters. Antonio is the first to mention 'witchcraft' (l. 70) in his impassioned attempt to find words to express his indignation at what he takes to be his betrayal by Sebastian, and this leads him publicly to declare that love:

> His life I gave him, and did thereto add
> My love without retention or restraint,
> All his in dedication. For his sake
> Did I expose myself, pure for his love,
> Into the danger of this adverse town . . .
> (ll. 74–8)

This speech, like Antonio's outrage at 3.4.350–61, is a good example of the way in which theatrical devices like disguise or mistaken identity are used in Shakespearian comedy to focus emotional realities.

What applies to Antonio applies still more to Orsino. When he evokes the bloody sea-battle in which he and Antonio previously faced one another, he brings into the play an experience much tougher than we have associated with him so far. It allows a glimpse of what Orsino can be like when not overwhelmed by love-melancholy, a ruler and military commander, just as Sebastian's tribute to Olivia in the previous scene (4.3.16–20) testifies to what *she* is like when not proposing to retire from the world or rashly falling in love: a great lady in command of her household. These aspects of the two characters emerge more fully under the pressure of events. When Orsino, like Antonio, thinks himself betrayed by Cesario, the savagery of the sea-battle, as it were, suddenly flares up again in his personal responses (reminding us that his name means 'little bear'), as he threatens to 'Kill what I love—a savage jealousy | That sometime savours nobly' (5.1.115–16).

The rest of the speech makes it clear that it is Viola, not Olivia, whom he proposes to kill:

> I'll sacrifice the lamb that I do love
> To spite a raven's heart within a dove.
>
> (ll. 126–7)

The repeated threat to kill what he loves is a subtle psychological point: the emotional tension spurs Orsino to admit in public, and perhaps also to himself, where his real feelings lie—with Viola/Cesario, not with Olivia. This is the natural and inevitable development of their relationship so far, their growing together in 1.4 and especially in 2.4.

The extreme situation draws from Viola a more consciously public statement of her love for Orsino; it also contains relief, no doubt, at being able to speak about it at last:

> OLIVIA
> Where goes Cesario?
> VIOLA   After him I love
> More than I love these eyes, more than my life,
> More by all mores than e'er I shall love wife.
> If I do feign, you witnesses above,
> Punish my life for tainting of my love.
>
> (ll. 130–4)

But of course this speech, which is so positive a declaration of her love for Orsino, must seem exceptionally cruel to Olivia—and even from Viola's point of view she is not (for once) considering the feelings of others or letting Olivia down lightly. It is one of the characteristics of comedy that something which seems of intense importance to one person may look quite different to others, hurtful to Olivia, perhaps even funny to the audience. Olivia's 'Ay me detested, how am I beguiled!', her 'Cesario, husband, stay', and Orsino's reactions 'Husband?' and 'Her husband, sirrah?' (ll. 135–41) can all draw laughter in performance without in any way endangering the truth of what the characters are feeling, in the process reminding us that their passionate declarations are being released through the mechanics of an intrigue action.

The violence that is latent in the exchanges between Antonio, Orsino, Viola, and Olivia finally breaks out as Sir Andrew and Sir Toby appear with broken heads—and to say this is not to deny the laughter which normally greets their appearance; but it does not last long. Sir Toby receives Sir Andrew's offer of help with the devastating reply: 'Will *you* help—an ass-head, and a coxcomb, and a knave; a thin-faced knave, a gull?' (5.1.199–200). In a scene where concealed or hitherto suppressed feeling keeps rising to the surface, this is one of the most striking examples. It is the climax of the Toby/Andrew relationship and a revelation that throws a retrospective light on all that has gone before. In view of this, it is not surprising that modern productions have concentrated on the cruelty latent in the relationship. Irving Wardle, reviewing John Barton's production, said that this moment 'almost suggests Falstaff rejecting Hal' (*The Times*, 23 August 1969). So far as the text is concerned, this is the last we see of Sir Toby and Sir Andrew. Anne Barton, emphasizing the division in the play's closing moments between the worlds of romance and a tougher reality, remarks that 'Sir Toby and Sir Andrew are not present to witness the revelations and accords of the closing moments. . . . Only by the special dispensation of art can some people, Viola and Orsino, Olivia and Sebastian, be left in Illyria.'[1] It is part of the sadness of *Twelfth Night* that it does not work towards an all-inclusive harmony.

It is also characteristic of the shifting tone of the play that the brutality with which Sir Andrew is dismissed should be followed by the moment of greatest wonder as the twins finally come face to face. This is at once a moment of magical simplicity and of great complexity, and although it belongs primarily to Viola and Sebastian, other characters participate in it, too. Orsino and Antonio, both released from the agonizing sense of betrayal by Sebastian's entry, comment on the similarity of the twins, but the simplest yet most potentially complex reaction comes from Olivia: 'Most wonderful!' (l. 219). This line can evoke many responses, often simultaneously, both on stage and in the audience. In part, Olivia is admitting the factual situation that she has married Sebastian rather than Cesario, and Geraldine McEwan at Stratford-upon-Avon in 1958, who had emphasized the humorous potential

---

[1] 'As You Like It and Twelfth Night: Shakespeare's Sense of an Ending', in *Shakespearian Comedy*, ed. Malcolm Bradbury and David Palmer, Stratford-upon-Avon Studies, 14 (1972), 160–80; pp. 177–8.

of the role throughout, was here able to turn the line with a witty, self-aware irony that drew much laughter. This was a reminder that the moment grows out of the similar one in *The Comedy of Errors* as the Antipholus twins at last come face to face and Adriana comments 'I see *two* husbands' (5.1.333). But there is at least as much wonder as humour in Olivia's line; and Maria Ricossa at Stratford, Ontario in 1985 delivered it in smiling wonder mixed with an amazed fascination and, above all, a generous sympathy with the twins: she was caught up in the magic of their reunion and shared in their happiness, which helped, of course, to lend conviction to the happy ending for herself and Sebastian.

But it is the reunion of the twins themselves which forms the emotional climax. In their first lines, the spectre of mystery or even witchcraft reappears from earlier in the scene. Sebastian, who until this moment has had no hint that Viola might be alive, expresses his shock at seeing his mirror image by making the point that only a god (or by implication a devil—see Commentary to l. 221–2) can be in more than one place at once:

> Do I stand there? I never had a brother,
> Nor can there be that deity in my nature
> Of here and everywhere.   (ll. 220–2)

Viola sustains the tension in answering his questions about her parentage and where she is from:

> Of Messaline. Sebastian was my father.
> Such a Sebastian was my brother too.
>   (ll. 226–7)

Something of the tense, emotionally charged atmosphere, and the timing, perhaps dictated by the short sentences, may be gauged from J. C. Trewin's account of how Peggy Ashcroft handled these lines at the Old Vic, London, in 1950: 'There is a long pause now before Viola, in almost a whisper (but one of infinite rapture and astonishment) answers: "Of Messaline." Practically for the first time in my experience a Viola has forced me to believe in her past.'[1] Viola goes on

---

[1] Quoted in John Russell Brown, *Shakespeare's Plays in Performance* (1966), p. 210.

to raise the suggestion of witchcraft again by saying 'If spirits can assume both form and suit | You come to fright us' (ll. 229–30).

'Spirit' could mean 'devil' in Elizabethan English, but with Sebastian's reply

> A spirit I am indeed,
> But am in that dimension grossly clad
> Which from the womb I did participate (ll. 230–2),

the scene securely banishes any hint of the supernatural or diabolical by celebrating the human and natural, especially when the name 'Viola' is used for the first time in the play; Shakespeare has reserved it for the moment when it will have greatest impact:

> Were you a woman, as the rest goes even,
> I should my tears let fall upon your cheek
> And say 'Thrice welcome, drownèd Viola.'
>
> (ll. 233–5)

Actors handle the next section of their reunion, the corroborating detail—'My father had a mole upon his brow' etc.—in very different ways. Some take it rapidly, tentatively, testingly, still hardly able to believe their good fortune; others use it as a means of releasing the emotional intensity of the preceding lines, allowing these prosaic matters of identification to draw entirely legitimate laughter, perhaps even laughing a little themselves. This exchange has sometimes been cut, presumably to avoid laughter at its obvious artificiality as a theatrical contrivance; but the mingling of laughter and tears is of the essence in this play, and artifice is deliberately manipulated to focus emotional realities in this scene as a whole. It is also characteristic of Shakespeare to draw attention to the conventions associated with the fiction he is representing, especially towards the end of a play. While the lines may seem merely prosaic, they may also expand the stage situation into an image of a timelessly recurrent, or archetypal, situation. In this respect, the episode anticipates the technique of the endings of Shakespeare's final plays, where lines like 'Guiderius had | Upon his neck a mole, a sanguine star' (*Cymbeline* 5.6.364–5) or

> That she is living,
> Were it but told you, should be hooted at
> Like an old tale. But it appears she lives . . .
> (*The Winter's Tale* 5.3.116–18)

serve to intensify rather than to detract from the tenderness
of a family reunion in each play, just as the *Twelfth Night*
passage intensifies the joy of a smaller family reunion.

In placing the reunion of brother and sister at the heart of
this scene, the technique of *Twelfth Night* not only looks
forward to the endings of the late plays but back to that of
The Comedy of Errors, another multiple family reunion:
throughout his career Shakespeare seems to have been especially interested in dramatizing intense family relationships.
But it would not be true to say that the brother/sister relationship wholly displaces those of the lovers. Sebastian takes
care to use an expression which carries the suggestion not
only that Olivia has married a virgin youth, but that, because
of the temperamental similarity of the twins, she is in fact
'betrothed both to a maid and man' (l. 257).[1] Although it is
true that Viola's reunion with Sebastian is given more prominence than her union with Orsino, which would normally
form the expected climax of a romantic comedy, their relationship has been so thoroughly established in 2.4 that all
that is needed now is confirmation, which is achieved in ll.
261–7; and in the process, Shakespeare moves the scene on
to its next stage by bringing Malvolio back into the action:

> The captain that did bring me first on shore
> Hath my maid's garments. He upon some action
> Is now in durance at Malvolio's suit,
> A gentleman and follower of my lady's.
>
> (ll. 268–71)

We have heard nothing of any legal action by Malvolio
against Viola's captain; this is another contrivance to effect a
smooth transition into the final business of the scene; and
since such contrivances have so far served to focus points of
characterization, it is interesting that before Malvolio emerges

---

[1] Joseph Pequigney (see p. 42 n. 1) argues that in line 257 Sebastian 'could
be referring only to himself, as a maiden man, a girl/boy, a master (to
Olivia)-mistress (to Antonio)' (p. 208).

from his imprisonment the audience is told that he in turn has imprisoned Viola's generous saviour. This may be relevant to the question of how much (or how little) sympathy Malvolio might inspire.

When he appears, he is allowed the dignity of verse for the first time, and his earlier steward's logic reappears, not this time to express delusion (as at 3.4.75–80), but to create a coherently argued case against what Olivia has apparently done to him. Olivia responds with tact and generosity, trying to let him down as lightly as possible, even promising that he shall be 'both the plaintiff and the judge | Of [his] own cause' (ll. 345–6). It begins to look as if Malvolio might be reconciled—but then, as in the Sir Topaz scene, it is Feste who turns the screw, cutting across Fabian's speech of explanation by quoting from the letter that has caused all the trouble, by mocking Malvolio's pleas of sanity to 'Sir Topaz', and by quoting (approximately) Malvolio's censure of him in their first scene together. He has nursed Malvolio's criticism in his mind—'and thus the whirligig of time brings in his revenges' (ll. 366–7). Terry Hands argues that there are two chief ways of handling Feste's line:

One can interpret [it] as: 'I've carried this burning anger and resentment [around with me], and finally my revenge has come', and a vicious line can flick out of the mouth. Or there's the person who says, 'Do you remember when we began this play? You see what happens if you take up . . . positions of cruelty or lack of caring or sensitivity. Time works its way out. Be kind.' (*Directors' Shakespeare*, p. 67)

There is at least one other way. In the rehearsals for Peter Hall's 1991 production, David Ryall developed the unemphatic, ironical manner he had used to play the Sir Topaz scene; 'thus the whirligig of time' was at once pointed and casual: he almost shrugged as if to say 'You see?'—yet the effect of the line was quite lethal, the more so for not being overstated. Eric Porter as Malvolio picked up both the point and the tone: with equal quietness and deadliness he spoke 'I'll be revenged on the whole pack of you' directly to Feste, eyeball to eyeball, followed by a rapid exit through a side door. Olivia's 'He hath been most notoriously abused' was then spoken as a direct accusation of Feste, rather than a general comment. Everything seemed to click into place. The confrontation clarified not just the Feste/Malvolio relationship but the shape of the whole Malvolio story: his first words in the play are a withering rebuke to Feste, his last ones a response to its consequences. And he appears to have learnt nothing from his experience, unlike Orsino and Olivia from theirs.[1]

There have been many other ways of handling the line, often preceded or followed by added business. For Laurence Olivier, it was 'the cry of a man unmade', followed by a tearful exit; Beerbohm Tree in 1901 angrily tore off his steward's chain; Donald Sinden returned it to his mistress with dignity; Edward Sothern in 1907 (followed by many actors since) tore the forged letter in pieces.[2] Some of these interpretations suggest frustration, some heartbreak; but in 1987, Declan Donnellan tried something quite different with his experimental company Cheek by Jowl: Malvolio 'was absorbed back into society . . . He laughed, everyone laughed with him. He enjoyed the joke on him. He started to laugh and forgave everyone on stage. It's very unsettling for the audience to see Malvolio warm-heartedly forgiving Feste and everyone else!' But then it appears that Donnellan sacrificed this unusual treatment for something more conventional: 'We froze the stage and he came up in a blackout with the final line. . . . It was quite chilling, because you felt he was biding his time.'[3]

In the same series of Stratford lectures in which Olivier talked about playing Malvolio (quoted on p. 44 above), a psychiatrist, Henry Yellowlees, also discussed the part: for all his tongue-in-cheek lightness of touch, he made some very relevant points that help to put some of these performances in perspective. He speaks of Malvolio living to some extent in a dream-world created by his own fantasies. In consequence,

---

[1] It was a pity that this revelation of the shape of the Malvolio plot was lost in performance, when Malvolio moved away from Feste upstage, and hurled his final line at the whole company in a conventional cloak-swirling exit.

[2] For Olivier, see John Russell Brown, *Shakespeare's Plays in Performance* (1966), p. 207; for Tree and Sothern, A. C. Sprague, *Shakespeare and the Actors* (Cambridge, Mass., 1944), p. 10.

[3] Quoted in Ralph Berry, *On Directing Shakespeare* (revised edn., 1989), p. 195.

I don't suppose he became really insane till long after [the play's] close. Perhaps he never became insane at all. It all depends on whether the trick played on him made his hatred of, and contempt for, his fellow men more implacable than ever, or whether, by some happy chance, it jerked him back out of dreamland by bringing him to a realization of the virtues of forgiveness and goodwill, and restoring his sense of humour.[1]

If this final scene focuses emotional realities, perhaps the reality of Malvolio's state is that he is in fact divorced from reality, a fantasist who replaces dreams of love and power with dreams of revenge; and if so, such fantasies may insulate him from too harsh a reality, so that the final line may suggest outraged bluster rather than heartbreak.

Other characters may have to face a tougher reality. In the case of Antonio, the evidence has to be deduced, since Shakespeare makes no further reference to him after his amazed question 'Which is Sebastian?' (5.1.218). Presumably his renewed friendship with Orsino's future brother-in-law and his 'kindness' to Viola (l. 60) ensure his release, but there is no reference to it, or indeed opportunity for it, in the text.[2] But this silence may be eloquent. Directors often make Antonio leave, freed but isolated, in a different direction from the lovers. Clifford Leech points out that in Antonio 'we have before us a reminder that humanity is vulnerable through its attachments, that affection puts a man in another's power'[3]— including the power to forget about him when a new relationship is established, as the stage picture at the general exit may emphasize. In John Barton's production, wrote Simon Gray, Antonio 'lingers in the memory to remind us that Illyria is after all an illusion that has been fashioned out of much potential, and some actual, pain' (*New Statesman*, 28 August 1969). Even so, too much emphasis upon Antonio at the end

---

[1] 'Medicine and Surgery in the 1955 Season's Plays', in *More Talking of Shakespeare*, ed. John Garrett (1959), 172–85; p. 180.

[2] Laurie E. Osborne, in 'The Texts of *Twelfth Night*', *ELH* 57 (1990), 37–61, points out that nineteenth-century acting versions inserted a speech for Orsino freeing Antonio and bidding him 'be ever near' Sebastian, with the result that 'a speech which seems designed to . . . recuperate [Antonio] into heterosexual comic union . . . potentially revives the homoerotic passions operating in the play' (pp. 53–4).

[3] *'Twelfth Night' and Shakespearian Comedy* (Toronto, 1965), p. 47.

can detract from the play's far more important isolation of Feste. Shakespeare *may*, by implication, have isolated Antonio at the end; he has specifically isolated Feste.

The final moments of the play set Orsino's characteristically idealistic reference to the lovers' happiness, their 'golden time' (l. 372), against the recurrent suggestion of a harsher reality in the 'wind and the rain' refrain of Feste's concluding song. Most productions insist on this contrast in one way or another. John Caird's at Stratford-upon-Avon in 1983 ended with a terrific clap of thunder and a flash of lightning, before the rain came pouring down. More wittily and less insistently, David Ryall's Feste mimed catching a few drops of rain on his tabor as the darkness fell on the late-autumnal garden of Peter Hall's 1991 staging (see fig. 9); they served as a cue for his final song. Hall's earlier version had juxtaposed Feste's isolation and the 'golden time' of the lovers by having 'all the romantic and comic characters, except Malvolio, dancing together in a golden distance behind a gauze curtain in love's now triumphant harmony, with Feste . . . seated on the fore-stage in gathering dusk, sadly remembering how the world began'.[1]

Not that Feste's song is exclusively sad: the play maintains its elusive complexity, and its individuality, to the end. The song is a kind of epilogue—at least in its last verse—but whereas the speakers of other Shakespearian epilogues like Rosalind in *As You Like It* or the King in *All's Well That Ends Well* step out of character to ask for applause, Feste simply presents the audience with a song which may or may not be a reflection of his own life. It is not certain that the words of this song, or of Feste's other songs, are by Shakespeare, though the shape of this one follows the pattern of Jaques' speech about the seven ages of man, which itself is based on commonplaces (*As You Like It* 2.7.143–66). Both speech and song present a caustic, caricatured picture of human life. On the strength of the fourth verse, Leslie Hotson in *The First Night of 'Twelfth Night'* calls the song 'a Drunkard's Progress' (p. 170). 'A Lecher's Progress' might be even more apt since, as Hotson points out, the 'foolish thing' of the first verse probably means

---

[1] Roy Walker (see p. 12 n. 1), p. 128.

9. Feste (David Ryall) catches rain-drops on his tabor at the start of his final song. Peter Hall's production, Playhouse, London, 1991.

Wee Three Loggerheads

10. This painting, probably of the seventeenth-century jesters Tom
Derry and Archie Armstrong (holding folly-stick; see note to 1.5.32),
may be an example of the trick picture referred to at 2.3.15–16, in
which the two fools invite the viewer to make up 'we three'. But
that is not quite certain, because 'loggerheads' were rounded pieces
of wood with a long handle like Armstrong's folly-stick, so arguably
there are three loggerheads in the picture already.

'penis', something of no more use than a toy to a child; as he grows 'to man's estate' in the following verses he becomes, as Hotson puts it, 'a lecherous knave and thief of love, on the prowl after other men's wives: " 'Gainst knaves and thieves men shut their gate" '—and presumably finding them, collapsing drunkenly into their 'beds' in the fourth verse. The play thus leaves us with yet another image of its central subject, love. It began with music supporting an idealized view of love; it ends with music presenting a down-to-earth, even brutish view. A more satisfying kind of love, the play has suggested, lies somewhere in between, with Viola its embodiment.

Throughout the play, Feste has tailored his songs to his hearers: 'O mistress mine' with its reminder that 'Youth's a stuff will not endure' to the knights in their cups (2.3.37–50); 'Come away death' to Orsino's melancholy and Viola's silent love (2.4.50–65); 'I am gone, sir', with its final 'Adieu, goodman devil', to the apparently possessed Malvolio (4.2.121–32). Does Feste consider, then, that a Lecher's Progress is the appropriate song for the audience? Is this the mirror he offers us? It would not be inconsistent with his statement of harsh truths during the play. In the final verse, he seems to be going further along this road, about to offer us more stern truths about the world—but then, with an evasiveness that may perhaps be a final reflection of the play's general elusiveness, he appears to change his mind, breaks off, and instead offers us a courteous farewell as he eases us out of the world of the play.

The Text

Twelfth Night first appeared in print in the First Folio of Shakespeare's works in 1623. It was entered in the Stationers' Register on 8 November 1623, together with the fifteen other plays that had not already appeared in quarto editions. It is customary to refer to the compositors of the First Folio by letter; although individual works were commonly divided up between two or more of them, *Twelfth Night* was set throughout by Compositor B, who contributed to the setting of 35 of the 36 plays in the Folio.[1] He appears to have done

---

[1] For further information, see Wells and Taylor, *Textual Companion*, pp. 39–42.

a good job on *Twelfth Night*: apart from a few obvious errors, the text is generally clean.[1]

Drawing on phrases like '*at several doors*' (2.2.0.1) and '*Malvolio within*' (4.2.20.1), John Dover Wilson suggested that the Folio text derives directly from a prompt-book,[2] but such standard theatrical terminology could just as easily have originated with the dramatist himself; and R. K. Turner has convincingly argued that F's text was printed from scribal copy.[3] The marking of the ends of Acts 1, 2, and 4 ('*Finis Actus primus*', etc.) is virtually conclusive evidence for some sort of literary transcript, rather than authorial manuscript ('foul papers') or prompt-book, though it is harder to determine what the scribe was himself copying. As there is no clear evidence to suggest that the scribe copied a prompt-book, it seems more likely that he worked from Shakespeare's own papers, perhaps in a fair copy.

Charlton Hinman[4] has shown that there was apparently some delay in securing the copy for *Twelfth Night* and *The Winter's Tale*, since setting skipped from *All's Well That Ends Well* to *King John* and part of *Richard II* before returning to complete the Comedies. *The Winter's Tale* was apparently set from a transcript by Ralph Crane, and one which shows strong signs of being later than the other four he prepared for the Folio; perhaps the copy for *Twelfth Night* was also specially prepared for the Folio, though possibly by a different (and unidentified) scribe.[5] Turner conjectures that William Jaggard, the printer of the First Folio, 'having just had a dose of foul papers in composing [*All's Well*], declined similar copy for the remaining comedies and insisted that [*Twelfth Night*] (and [*The Winter's Tale*]) be put into better shape' (p. 137),

---

[1] For B's misinterpretation of 'Viola' as 'Violenta' at 1.5.159.1, see Commentary.

[2] *Twelfth Night*, the New Shakespeare (Cambridge, 1930, 2nd edn., 1949), p. 89. He was supported by W. W. Greg, *The Shakespeare First Folio* (Oxford, 1955), p. 296.

[3] 'The Text of *Twelfth Night*', SQ 26 (1975), 128–38.

[4] *The Printing and Proof-Reading of the First Folio of Shakespeare*, 2 vols. (Oxford, 1963), 2.521.

[5] The evidence for and against identifying Crane as the scribe is assessed by Elizabeth Story Donno in her New Cambridge edition (1985), pp. 151–6. In 'Shakespeare's Earliest Editor, Ralph Crane' (*SS 44* (Cambridge, 1992), 113–29; p. 128), T. H. Howard-Hill adds a little to the evidence against.

and if so the preparation of scribal copy may explain the delay in setting these two plays. Alternatively, as Turner says, 'the transcript may have been made as a step in the preparation of the play for production', and this speculation might gain some support from the fact that the Folio texts which *Twelfth Night* most resembles, *As You Like It* and *Julius Caesar*, are close to it in date of composition.

Dover Wilson is also among those who believe that the text shows signs of revision subsequent to performance. The key scene here is 2.4. At her first appearance, Viola cites as qualifications for serving Orsino that she 'can sing, | And speak to him in many sorts of music' (1.2.54–5); yet when Orsino asks for a song in 2.4, it is Feste rather than Viola who provides it. Dover Wilson and others have conjectured that the scene was revised in response to theatrical circumstances, perhaps the breaking of a boy actor's voice. The only slight evidence for possible revision is that at the point where Feste is called for (2.4.8–12), the scene shifts from verse to prose for no apparent dramatic reason. But when verse resumes at l. 13, as Orsino asks the musician(s) to play the tune 'the while' (i.e. while Feste is summoned), and he and Viola discuss the music at length, the sequence is absolutely continuous. If the prose is an interpolation, so is everything up to the song itself (ll. 13–49), and the shift to prose in itself has no value as evidence of revision. The entire scene, in fact, is so unified that surely no one would suspect that anything was wrong unless they were looking for evidence of revision (as Dover Wilson in particular was prone to do). It is quite likely that Shakespeare originally intended to allow Viola some release of her suppressed feelings in song, but then changed his mind during the course of composition, and realized that an emotional effect as great, if not greater, could be achieved by allowing her to express her love only in the hints of ll. 24–7, in the broken-off 'Ay, but I know—' (l. 103), and in the allegory of her imaginary sister (ll. 110–15); and that introducing Feste into the scene would intensify its bittersweet mood, especially in his comparisons of Orsino's mind to an opal and to 'changeable taffeta' (ll. 73–4).

The use of Feste in this scene not only as a singer but as an ironic commentator may perhaps explain the abrupt substitution of Fabian for him as an active participant in the gulling of Malvolio in the following scene. However crudely done, this is as likely to reflect a change of mind in the process of composition as subsequent revision, and so is the apparent uncertainty about whether Orsino is 'duke' or 'count' (see Commentary to 1.1.0.1). Dover Wilson's other major piece of evidence for revision, that the use of 'Jove' in the play may be a substitute for 'God' in deference to the 1606 Act of Abuses, which prohibited the use of God's name in stage plays, is dealt a mortal blow by R. K. Turner's simple demonstration that in *Twelfth Night* the name of God appears 'about twice as often as the supposed substitute' (p. 136); and in any case the use of 'Jove' by Malvolio in particular has specific dramatic point, as already suggested (p. 50 above). In short, there is no evidence of any substance for revision.

EDITORIAL PROCEDURES

THIS edition follows the Editorial Procedures established for the series by Stanley Wells and summarized in Gary Taylor's Oxford Shakespeare edition of *Henry V* (1982), pp. 75–81; and in accordance with them, passages from Shakespeare's contemporaries quoted in the introduction and commentary are also modernized even when they are taken from editions using old spelling.

There is only one authoritative early text of *Twelfth Night*, that published in the First Folio of Shakespeare's works (F). This text is usually consistent in distinguishing between a past tense or past participle ending which is syllabic, and therefore sounded, and one which is not (1.2.9 and 39 appear to be exceptions; see commentary). We have indicated the sounded syllable by '-èd', the unsounded one by '-ed'. We have followed F's elisions in the verse (for example, 'learn'd' at 1.5.249), and in second person singular endings of verbs (for example, 'know'st' at 2.3.3) in the prose, where this clarifies the pronunciation. This procedure is a modification both of the text of *Twelfth Night* in the Oxford *Complete Works* and of Oxford Shakespeare practice in general.

Stage directions such as 'aside' or 'to' a character, or that a character speaks other than as himself, for example Feste 'as Sir Topaz', are all editorial, and are not collated; nor are act and scene divisions, which follow those of F. Speech headings are silently normalized.

Quotations from the Bible are from the Bishops' Bible of 1568; those from classical Latin works are from the Loeb editions. References to other works of Shakespeare are from the Oxford *Complete Works*, Compact Edition, 1988. References to works by Shakespeare's contemporaries are to major modern editions (wherever possible, to the Revels plays series).

Abbreviations and References

The following references are used in the introduction, in the collations and in the commentary. In all bibliographical references, the place of publication is London, unless otherwise specified.

F, Fɪ	The First Folio, 1623
F2	The Second Folio, 1632
F3	The Third Folio, 1663
Arden	J. M. Lothian and T. W. Craik, *Twelfth Night*, new Arden Shakespeare (1975)
Cambridge	W. G. Clark and W. A. Wright, *Works*, The Cambridge Shakespeare, 9 vols. (Cambridge, 1863–6)
Capell	Edward Capell, *Comedies, Histories, and Tragedies*, 10 vols. (1767–8)
Collier	John Payne Collier, *Works*, 8 vols. (1842–4)
Collier 1858	*Comedies, Histories, Tragedies, and Poems*, 'The Second Edition', 6 vols. (1858)
Collier MS	*Notes and Emendations to the Text of Shakespeare's Plays from Early Manuscript Corrections of the Folio, 1632* (1853)
Donno	Elizabeth Story Donno, *Twelfth Night*, New Cambridge Shakespeare (Cambridge, 1985)
Dyce	Alexander Dyce, *Works*, 6 vols. (1857)
Dyce 1866	Alexander Dyce, *Works*, 9 vols. (1864–7)
Hanmer	Thomas Hanmer, *Works*, 6 vols. (Oxford, 1743–4)
Harness	*Dramatic Works, with notes . . . By the Rev. William Harness*, 8 vols. (1825)
Johnson	Samuel Johnson, *Plays*, 8 vols. (1765)
Keightley	Thomas Keightley, *Plays*, 6 vols. (1864)
Mahood	M. M. Mahood, *Twelfth Night*, New Penguin Shakespeare (Harmondsworth, 1968)
Malone	Edmond Malone, *Plays and Poems*, 10 vols. (1790)
Oxford	Stanley Wells and Gary Taylor, *Complete Works* (Oxford, 1986; Compact Edition, 1988)
Pope	Alexander Pope, *Works*, 6 vols. (1723–5)
Rann	Joseph Rann, *Dramatic Works*, 6 vols. (Oxford, 1786–94)
Riverside	G. B. Evans (textual editor), *The Riverside Shakespeare* (Boston, 1974)

Rowe   Nicholas Rowe, *Works*, 6 vols. (1709)
Rowe 1714   Nicholas Rowe, *Works*, 8 vols. (1714)
Steevens   Samuel Johnson and George Steevens, *Plays*, 10 vols. (1773)
Theobald   Lewis Theobald, *Works*, 7 vols. (1733)
Theobald 1740   Lewis Theobald, *Works*, 8 vols. (1740)
Warburton   Alexander Pope and William Warburton, *Works*, 8 vols. (1747)
Wilson   John Dover Wilson, *Twelfth Night*, the New Shakespeare (Cambridge, 1930; 2nd edn., 1949)

OTHER WORKS

Abbott   E. A. Abbott, *A Shakespearian Grammar*, 2nd edn. (1870)
Berger/Bradford Thomas L. Berger and William C. Bradford, Jnr., *An Index of Characters in English Printed Drama to the Restoration* (Eaglewood, Colorado, 1975)
Bullough   Geoffrey Bullough, *Narrative and Dramatic Sources of Shakespeare*, 8 vols. (1957–75)
COD   *The Concise English Dictionary*, 7th edn. (Oxford, 1982)
Daniel   P. A. Daniel, *Notes and Conjectural Emendations of Certain Doubtful Passages in Shakespeare's Plays* (1870)
Dent   R. W. Dent, *Shakespeare's Proverbial Language: An Index* (1981)
Directors' Shakespeare   *Directors' Shakespeare: Approaches to 'Twelfth Night'*, ed. Michael Billington (1990)
EC   *Essays in Criticism*
ELR   *English Literary Renaissance*
T. R. Henn   T. R. Henn, *The Living Image* (1972)
Henslowe's Diary   *Henslowe's Diary*, ed. R. A. Foakes and R. T. Rickert (Cambridge, 1961)
Hotson   Leslie Hotson, *The First Night of 'Twelfth Night'* (1954)
Hunter   Joseph Hunter, *New Illustrations of the Life, Studies, and Writings of Shakespeare*, 2 vols. (1845)
Mason   John Monck Mason, *Comments on the Last Edition of Shakespeare's Plays* (Dublin, 1785)
Nashe, *Works* *The Works of Thomas Nashe*, ed. R. B. McKerrow (1904–10), revised by F. P. Wilson, 5 vols. (Oxford, 1958)

NQ	*Notes and Queries*
ODEP	*Oxford Dictionary of English Proverbs*, 3rd edn., revised by F. P. Wilson (Oxford, 1970)
OED	*The Oxford English Dictionary*, 2nd edn., 20 vols. (Oxford, 1989)
Onions	C. T. Onions, *A Shakespeare Glossary*, 2nd edn. (Oxford, 1922)
PQ	*Philological Quarterly*
Re-Editing	Stanley Wells, *Re-Editing Shakespeare for the Modern Reader* (Oxford, 1984)
RES	*Review of English Studies*
Schmidt	Alexander Schmidt, *Shakespeare-Lexicon*, 2 vols. (Berlin and Leipzig, 1923)
SQ	*Shakespeare Quarterly*
SSt	*Shakespeare Studies*
SS	*Shakespeare Survey*
Thirlby	Styan Thirlby's unpublished conjectures (mainly manuscript annotations in his copies of contemporary editions)
Tilley	M. P. Tilley, *A Dictionary of the Proverbs in England in the Sixteenth and Seventeenth Centuries* (Ann Arbor, 1950)
Turner	R. K. Turner, Jnr., 'The Text of *Twelfth Night*', *Shakespeare Quarterly* 26 (1975), 128–38
Tyrwhitt	Thomas Tyrwhitt, *Observations and Conjectures upon Some Passages of Shakespeare* (Oxford, 1766)

Wells and Taylor, *Textual Companion*   Stanley Wells and Gary Taylor with John Jowett and William Montgomery, *William Shakespeare: A Textual Companion* (Oxford, 1987)

Twelfth Night, or What You Will

THE PERSONS OF THE PLAY

ORSINO, Duke of Illyria

CURIO
VALENTINE } attending on Orsino

FIRST OFFICER

SECOND OFFICER

VIOLA, later disguised as Cesario

A Sea-CAPTAIN

SEBASTIAN, her twin brother

ANTONIO, another sea-captain

OLIVIA, a Countess

MARIA, her waiting-gentlewoman

SIR TOBY Belch, Olivia's kinsman

SIR ANDREW Aguecheek, companion of Sir Toby

MALVOLIO, Olivia's steward

FABIAN, a member of Olivia's household

FESTE the Clown, her jester

A PRIEST

A SERVANT of Olivia

Musicians, sailors, lords, attendants

Twelfth Night, or What You Will

1.1   *Music. Enter Orsino Duke of Illyria, Curio, and other lords*

ORSINO

If music be the food of love, play on,
Give me excess of it, that surfeiting,
The appetite may sicken and so die.
That strain again, it had a dying fall.
O, it came o'er my ear like the sweet sound   5
That breathes upon a bank of violets,

1.1.0.1 *Music*] CAPELL (*subs.*); *not in* F   1, etc. ORSINO] F (*Duke.*)   5 sound] F; south POPE

1.1.0.1 **Music** In the Folio text of this scene there are no music cues, which must be deduced from the lines. In early performances, music was presumably played by an ensemble, perhaps by a consort of viols, or by a single lutenist, before Orsino entered. See Appendix for further discussion.
Orsino The name, of a prominent Italian family, the dukes of Bracciano in Tuscany, means 'little bear'. See Introduction, p. 4, for an Orsino contemporary with Shakespeare.
Duke In the Folio stage directions and speech prefixes Orsino is always *Duke*; but in the dialogue he is 'Duke' only four times (1.2.23, 43, 52, 1.4.1), 'Count' thirteen times. Since all the references to 'Duke' occur in early scenes, Shakespeare's conception may have changed during composition, as Turner suggests (p. 131); the scribe who prepared the Folio text may have imposed consistency in the directions and prefixes (see Introduction, p. 74).
Illyria Illyria (from Latin *Illyricum*) was the ancient name of an area of the Dalmatian coast; see Introduction, pp. 8–14 for further discussion.
Curio An apt name for a courtier, from Italian *curia*, court, and its first use in

English drama of the period, according to Berger and Bradford's *Index*.
1–15 Like much of the lyrical language of the play, this celebrated speech depends less on paraphrasable detail than on metaphorical implication. The general drift is clear: Orsino wants music to feed his love to the point where he becomes literally sick of it, so that his pains of love may be eased. He seizes enthusiastically upon an appropriately *dying fall*, but then tires of it—which prompts the reflection that the spirit of love is so all-consuming that it can rob beautiful things (like the music) of their value.
1 **If music . . . love** Orsino's *if* sounds as though he is drawing upon a common saying, but if so there is no record of it. Shakespeare uses the phrase again at *Antony* 2.5.1–2: 'music, moody food | Of us that trade in love.'
4 **dying fall** expressive cadence which falls to its resolution, perhaps combined with poignant harmony (with metaphorical implications: *dying* suggests 'swooning' (in the act of love))
5 **sound** There is no need to adopt Pope's emendation 'south', i.e. 'south wind', since *sound*, meaning 'sound of a breeze', incorporates the idea anyway.

Stealing and giving odour. Enough, no more,
'Tis not so sweet now as it was before.
⌈ *Music ceases* ⌉
O spirit of love, how quick and fresh art thou,
That notwithstanding thy capacity   10
Receiveth as the sea, naught enters there,
Of what validity and pitch so e'er,
But falls into abatement and low price
Even in a minute! So full of shapes is fancy
That it alone is high fantastical.   15

8.1 *Music ceases*] COLLIER 1858   10 capacity‸] ROWE 1714; ~, F   11 sea, naught] ROWE
1714; Sea. Nought F

7 **Stealing and giving** i.e. taking the
scent from some flowers, then bestow-
ing it on others
no more The music ceases either at
once or at the end of the couplet.
8 **'Tis not . . . before** For the idea that
something good disappoints the second
time round, compare Sonnet 102,
about the nightingale's song: 'Not that
the summer is less pleasant now │
Than when her mournful hymns did
hush the night, │ But that wild music
burdens every bough, │ And sweets
grown common lose their dear delight'
(9–12).
9–14 **O spirit . . . minute** This edition, like
most others, adopts Rowe's repunctu-
ation of the Folio, which affects the
sense. Barry B. Adams defends the
Folio, and interprets: the spirit of love,
perhaps specifically Cupid, though its /
his capacity is smaller than the sea's,
contains as much ('Orsino and the
Spirit of Love', *SQ* 29 (1978), 52–9).
In this interpretation, *notwithstanding*
contrasts the capacity of love and the
sea in size. But in Rowe's version the
capacities are the same, and *notwithstanding* implies a contrast between
love which devalues everything and
the sea which transforms everything,
an implication supported by *Tempest*
1.2.403–4, where Alonso's body is
said to 'suffer a sea-change │ Into
something rich and strange'.
9–11 **quick . . . fresh . . . capacity . . . Receiveth** These words develop the idea of

feeding and appetite from ll. 1–3.
9 **quick** keen. Compare *Pericles* Sc.
15.79–80, 'The air is piercing there,
│ And quick; it sharps the stomach',
another context involving both the
breeze and the appetite.
fresh eager, and so hungry (*OED a.* 11)
11 **Receiveth** swallows (*OED v.* 6, citing
Pericles Sc. 2.72–3: 'a potion . . . │
That thou wouldst tremble to receive
thyself')
as the sea i.e. without limit. Compare
2.4.99–100, where Orsino claims that
his love is 'all as hungry as the sea, │
And can digest as much', and *Romeo*
2.1.175–6: 'My bounty is as boundless
as the sea, │ My love as deep.'
12 **what . . . so e'er** whatever, however
great
validity value
pitch height, excellence. A metaphorical use of a technical term from falconry, meaning the highest point to
which a falcon flies, as at *Richard II*
1.1.109: 'How high a pitch his resolution soars!'
13 **abatement** depreciation
14–15 **So full . . . high fantastical** in the
same way love consumes so many im-
agined forms that it is uniquely and
supremely imaginative. Compare *LLL*
5.2.755–7, where love is 'Full of
strange shapes, of habits and of forms,
│ Varying in subjects as the eye doth
roll │ To every varied object in his
glance'. Originally a contraction of
'fantasy' (*OED sb.*), *fancy* when used to

CURIO

Will you go hunt, my lord?

ORSINO   What, Curio?

CURIO   The hart.

ORSINO

Why so I do, the noblest that I have.
O, when mine eyes did see Olivia first
Methought she purged the air of pestilence;
That instant was I turned into a hart,   20
And my desires, like fell and cruel hounds,
E'er since pursue me.
          Enter Valentine
                    How now, what news from her?

VALENTINE

So please my lord, I might not be admitted,
But from her handmaid do return this answer:
The element itself till seven years' heat   25

---

22 *Enter Valentine*] F (*after* 'her')   25 years' heat] HARNESS; yeares heate F; years hence
ROWE 1714

---

mean 'love' often has overtones of deception or illusion in Shakespeare, as at *Merchant* 3.2.67–9: 'It is engendered in the eyes, | With gazing fed; and fancy dies | In the cradle where it lies.' The choice of word here may imply either criticism of Orsino or self-criticism. For a further discussion of Orsino's language, see Introduction, pp. 25–8.

17 **the noblest** i.e. heart, punning on the *hart* of the previous line. By l. 20, Orsino has himself become the *hart* (stag).

18 **Olivia** For a possible source of the name, see note to 1.2.0.1.

19 **pestilence** plague—an ever-present reality to the Elizabethans, who thought that illnesses were caused by bad air

20–2 **was I turned . . . pursue me** These lines allude to the classical legend of the huntsman Actaeon who, having seen the goddess Diana naked, was turned by her into a stag and torn to pieces by his own hounds (Ovid, *Metamorphoses* 3. 138–252). See fig. 3. This

is a vivid way of expressing the ferocity of Orsino's frustrated desire for Olivia and may have been suggested by Samuel Daniel's sonnet sequence *Delia* (1592), which seems to have been in Shakespeare's mind while he was writing the lyrical episodes of this play: Delia 'turned my sport into a hart's despair, | Which still is chased, whilst I have any breath, | By mine own thoughts. Set on me by my fair, | My thoughts like hounds pursue me to my death' (*Delia* 5. 9–12); see also notes to 1.5.262 and 2.4.37–40.

21 **fell** savage

22 *Valentine* He is an aptly named servant for a love-sick master, since Valentine was the patron saint of lovers. The names Orsino and Valentine are associated in the anonymous lost play *Valentine and Orson*, entered in the Stationers' Register on 23 May 1595.
    How now A colloquial greeting, an abbreviation of 'how is it now?'

25 **element** sky. The other uses of this word in the play (3.1.58, 3.4.119)

Shall not behold her face at ample view,
But like a cloistress she will veilèd walk
And water once a day her chamber round
With eye-offending brine—all this to season
A brother's dead love, which she would keep fresh   30
And lasting in her sad remembrance.

ORSINO

O, she that hath a heart of that fine frame
To pay this debt of love but to a brother,
How will she love when the rich golden shaft
Hath killed the flock of all affections else   35
That live in her—when liver, brain, and heart,
These sovereign thrones, are all supplied, and filled

37 supplied,] ROWE; ~∧ F

suggest that it may have been a fashionable affectation. Although Valentine is reporting an *answer* given by Olivia's *handmaid*, the language is obviously not Maria's, but Olivia's own, perhaps under Malvolio's influence. See the following notes.
till seven years' heat for seven hot summers. For the expression, compare Sonnet 104.7: 'Three April perfumes in three hot Junes burned'.

26 **ample** full
27 **cloistress** nun (of an enclosed order). *OED* gives only this example, saying that the word is both obsolete and rare. Perhaps, therefore, it is intended to suggest a mannered effect, as with *element* (l. 25).
28 **water . . . her chamber round** walk tearfully around her room. For the idiom, compare *Lucrece* 1499: 'She throws her eyes about the painting round'.
29 **eye-offending brine** stinging tears
    season preserve (as if in *brine*). Shakespeare frequently compares tears to seasoning in brine, sometimes critically, as at *Romeo* 2.2.69–72: 'what a deal of brine | Hath washed thy sallow cheeks for Rosaline! | How much salt water thrown away in waste | To season love, that of it doth not taste!'

The appropriateness of *season* in a context of death would have been more apparent in Shakespeare's time, when in the winter months there was no fresh meat owing to the absence of winter feed, only the flesh of animals killed the previous autumn and preserved by seasoning.

30 **brother's dead love** A quibble: her love for her dead brother, and her dead brother's love for her.
31 **remembrance** memory. The verse line requires four syllables: 'remembe-rance'.
32 **of that fine frame** so exquisitely made
34–8 **How will . . . self king** How will she love when Cupid's arrow has killed off all her other feelings (*affections*) except love; when *liver, brain, and heart,* the seats of passion, judgement, and sentiment, are all occupied (*supplied*) by only one emotion, love; and when her *sweet perfections* are similarly all occupied (*filled*), and so made complete, by the object of that love, one and the same (*one self*) king—Orsino himself.
34 **rich golden shaft** Cupid had two arrows, a sharp golden one to cause love, and a blunt one to destroy it (Ovid, *Metamorphoses* 1. 468–71).

Her sweet perfections with one self king!
Away before me to sweet beds of flowers:
Love-thoughts lie rich when canopied with bowers.   40

Exeunt

1.2   *Enter Viola, a Captain, and sailors*

VIOLA

What country, friends, is this?

CAPTAIN   This is Illyria, lady.

VIOLA

And what should I do in Illyria?
My brother he is in Elysium.
Perchance he is not drowned. What think you sailors?

CAPTAIN

It is perchance that you yourself were saved.   5

VIOLA

O my poor brother! And so perchance may he be.

CAPTAIN

True madam, and to comfort you with chance,
Assure yourself, after our ship did split,
When you and those poor number saved with you

1.2.9 saved] saued F (*see commentary*)

1.2.0.1 **Viola** The names Violetta and Olivia occur in Emanuel Forde's prose
narrative *Parismus* (1598), which has
some similarities with *Twelfth Night*
(see the discussion of the sources, pp.
18–19). *Viola* means 'violet' in Italian
and in some pre-Shakespearian English
examples cited by *OED*. A poem called
'A Nosegay Always Sweet', first published in Clement Robinson's *A Handful
of Pleasant Delights* (1584), points out
that the 'Violet is for faithfulness'; it
was also claimed to purge melancholy
by Renaissance medical works (see
Winfried Schleiner, 'Orsino and Viola',
SSt 16 (1983), 135–41). The name is
therefore apt to a faithful servant who
purges her master of melancholy. It is
not, however, used in the dialogue
until 5.1.235, where the metre requires the pronunciation '*Vy*-ola' (stress

on the first syllable). F's stage direction thus falsifies an audience's experience: they meet, not an identified
heroine, but (in some productions)
a destitute victim of shipwreck, or
(in others) a mysterious figure rising
like Venus from the sea, who only assumes an identity as the page Cesario
in her next scene (1.4).

3 **Elysium** the heaven of classical mythology. The similarity in initial sound
with *Illyria* helps, paradoxically, to
point the contrast between the places.

4–7 **Perchance** Viola first uses this to
mean 'perhaps'; the Captain uses it in
the sense 'by mere accident' (l. 5);
Viola echoes this sense (l. 6); and then
the Captain varies the word-play with
chance, meaning 'the thought of what
may happen' (l. 7).

9 **saved** In general, the First Folio is

Hung on our driving boat, I saw your brother,   10
Most provident in peril, bind himself—
Courage and hope both teaching him the practice—
To a strong mast that lived upon the sea,
Where like Arion on the dolphin's back,
I saw him hold acquaintance with the waves   15
So long as I could see.

VIOLA (*giving money*)   For saying so, there's gold.
Mine own escape unfoldeth to my hope,
Whereto thy speech serves for authority,
The like of him. Know'st thou this country?

CAPTAIN

Ay madam, well, for I was bred and born   20
Not three hours' travel from this very place.

VIOLA Who governs here?

---

14 Arion] POPE; *Orion* F   16 *giving money*] OXFORD; *not in* F

---

consistent in distinguishing typo-
graphically between a past tense or
past participle ending which is syllabic,
and therefore sounded (*-ed* in F), and
one which is not (*-'d* in F). But this
line may be an exception, since it is
perfectly regular if *saved* is one syllable,
and so may l. 39.

10 **driving** being driven (by the wind). A
nautical term; compare *Pericles* Sc.
10.50: 'up and down the poor ship
drives'.
    boat i.e. the ship's life-boat
12 **practice** method
13 **To a strong mast** The details of this
shipwreck rework Egeon's narrative in
Shakespeare's earlier play about twins,
The Comedy of Errors, where the par-
ents tie themselves, with one pair of
twins each, 'at either end the mast'
(1.1.85).
    lived remained afloat. A nautical term;
OED v.[1] 10 cites a phrase of 1615: 'to
row in waters wherein (to use the
seafaring phrase) they cannot live'.
14 **Arion** A legendary Greek musician
who saved himself from being mur-
dered on a voyage by jumping over-
board; he was carried to land by a

dolphin who had been enchanted by
his singing (Ovid, *Fasti* 2. 79–118). A
striking Elizabethan version of the
story comes in Robert Laneham or
Langham's account of the 'Princely
Pleasures' presented before Elizabeth I
by her favourite Leicester at Kenilworth Castle in 1575, which included
a water-pageant with Arion 'riding
aloft upon his old friend the dolphin'
(*A Letter*, ed. R. J. P. Kuin (Leiden,
1983), p. 57). The tone of easy familiarity ('his old friend') also occurs in
the Captain's image of Sebastian
hold[ing] *acquaintance with the waves*
(i.e. remaining afloat). The verse requires the pronunciation 'A-ry-on'
(stress on the second syllable).
17–19 **unfoldeth to my hope . . . the like
of him** encourages me to hope . . . that
he, too, has escaped
17 **unfoldeth** opens up, makes plain
18 **authority** support, sanction
20 **Ay** yes. *OED* says that 'ay' appeared
suddenly about 1575, of unknown
origin. It was usually spelt 'I' (as in
the Folio text here), which indicates
the pronunciation. It survives in English dialects and regional accents.

CAPTAIN
A noble duke, in nature as in name.
VIOLA
What is his name?
CAPTAIN   Orsino.
VIOLA
Orsino. I have heard my father name him.   25
He was a bachelor then.
CAPTAIN
And so is now, or was so very late,
For but a month ago I went from hence,
And then 'twas fresh in murmur—as you know,
What great ones do the less will prattle of—   30
That he did seek the love of fair Olivia.
VIOLA What's she?
CAPTAIN
A virtuous maid, the daughter of a count
That died some twelvemonth since, then leaving her
In the protection of his son, her brother,   35
Who shortly also died, for whose dear love,
They say, she hath abjured the sight
And company of men.
VIOLA   O that I served that lady,
And might not be delivered to the world
Till I had made mine own occasion mellow,   40

37–8 sight | And company] F; company | And sight HANMER

---

27 **late** lately
28 **but** only
29 **fresh in murmur** newly rumoured
32 **What's she** of what quality or rank is
she? (Abbott 254)
36 **Who ... died** Shakespeare presents
both his heroines in the same emotional situation, bereaved of their brothers, partly to contrast their reactions
to that loss. Viola's interest in Olivia,
and urge to serve her in the next line,
derives partly from sympathy for someone who has suffered a similar bereavement.
39 **delivered to the world** revealed (literally 'born'), perhaps carrying the sug-

gestion that she wants Sebastian to be
reborn in herself (see Introduction, p.
21). For the verse line, see the note to
l. 9.
40–1 **Till I ... estate is** The general
meaning is 'until I was ready to reveal
what my true situation and social
standing is'.
40 **made mine own occasion mellow**
brought my own situation to the point
of readiness. The same expression is
used by Holofernes in *LLL* 4.2.70–1 to
describe the birth of his ideas: 'delivered upon the mellowing of occasion' (i.e. born when the time is ripe).

What my estate is.

CAPTAIN   That were hard to compass,
Because she will admit no kind of suit,
No, not the Duke's.

VIOLA

There is a fair behaviour in thee, captain,
And though that nature with a beauteous wall   45
Doth oft close in pollution, yet of thee
I will believe thou hast a mind that suits
With this thy fair and outward character.
I pray thee—and I'll pay thee bounteously—
Conceal me what I am, and be my aid   50
For such disguise as haply shall become
The form of my intent. I'll serve this duke.
Thou shalt present me as an eunuch to him.
It may be worth thy pains, for I can sing,
And speak to him in many sorts of music   55
That will allow me very worth his service.
What else may hap, to time I will commit,
Only shape thou thy silence to my wit.

49 pray thee] OXFORD; prethee F

41 **compass** bring about
42 **suit** petition
43 **not** not even
44 **behaviour** outward appearance (including 'conduct')
45–6 **a beauteous wall . . . pollution** Perhaps echoes the biblical description of the scribes and Pharisees: 'ye are like unto painted sepulchres, which indeed appear beautiful outward, but are within full of . . . all filthiness' (Matthew 23: 27).
48 **character** appearance (including moral qualities)
49 **pray thee** Oxford emends F's 'prethee' on the grounds that Compositor B regularly imposed his preferred form 'prethee', thus possibly obscuring a symmetry between 'pray thee' and 'pay thee'.
50 **Conceal me what I am** i.e. conceal the fact that I am a woman. *Me* is here a redundant object, as often in Shakes-

peare (Abbott 414).
51 **haply** by chance
    become be fitting for
52 **The form of my intent** carrying out my purpose (literally, 'the shape of what I intend')
53 **eunuch** castrated male. Pubescent youths were castrated to maintain their high singing voices, and Viola chooses this disguise partly to account for her high-pitched voice.
55 **speak to** This figurative use seems to anticipate the sense 'appeal to, influence, affect, or touch', first noted in *OED* (13c) at *Othello* 1.2.23: 'speak unbonneted to as proud a fortune'.
    sorts of music kinds of song (or perhaps instrumental as well as vocal music)
56 **allow** prove
    worth worthy of
57 **hap** happen, come about by chance
58 **wit** imagination, plan

CAPTAIN
Be you his eunuch, and your mute I'll be.
When my tongue blabs, then let mine eyes not see.   60
VIOLA
I thank thee. Lead me on.   *Exeunt*

I.3   *Enter Sir Toby Belch and Maria*
SIR TOBY What a plague means my niece to take the death
of her brother thus? I am sure care's an enemy to life.
MARIA By my troth, Sir Toby, you must come in earlier
a-nights. Your cousin, my lady, takes great exceptions
to your ill hours.   5
SIR TOBY Why, let her except, before excepted.
MARIA Ay, but you must confine yourself within the mod-
est limits of order.
SIR TOBY Confine? I'll confine myself no finer than I am.
These clothes are good enough to drink in, and so be   10

1.3.0.1 *Belch*] MALONE; *not in* F

59 **mute** Eunuchs were often guards in
Turkish harems, attended by mutes.
Compare *Henry V* 1.2.231–2: 'our
grave, | Like Turkish mute, shall have
a tongueless mouth'.
60 **let mine eyes not see** Perhaps an allusion to the punishment of blinding for
betraying secrets reputedly used in harems (see the previous note).
1.3.1 **What a plague** A frequent impreca-
tion in Shakespeare, and apparently a
favourite with Sir Toby (see 1.5.115).
A modern equivalent might be 'What
the hell' (but for the sinister overtone,
see the note to 1.1.19).
niece Like *cousin* in l. 4, this was used
less precisely in Shakespeare's day than
now, to denote general kinship. Even
so, Sir Toby may well be the younger
brother of Olivia's dead father, so that
his position in her household is a delicate one, tolerated yet precarious, as
Maria's following warnings emphasize.
2 **care's an enemy to life** Proverbial
(Tilley C82).

3 **By my troth** by my faith (a mild oath).
In *As You Like It* Rosalind says that it
is one of the 'pretty oaths that are not
dangerous' (4.1.178–80).
4 **a-nights** at night. *OED prep.*[1] 8 says
that 'a' was sometimes 'prefixed to
OE adverbial genitive . . . *nihtes*, giving
a nights'.
6 **except, before excepted** Playing on the
legal phrase *exceptis excipiendis* ('with
the stated—before-mentioned—exceptions'). Sir Toby refuses to take Olivia's
displeasure (*exceptions*) seriously.
8 **modest . . . order** bounds of reasonable
behaviour
9 **confine . . . finer** Sir Toby takes Maria's
meaning of *confine* ('restrict') and applies it both to his size ('I won't make
myself smaller than I am') and to more
refined behaviour ('I won't be more
than I am'). However much they dis-
agree in other things, uncle and niece
share a proud reluctance to appear
grander than they are (compare
ll. 102–4).

these boots too; an they be not, let them hang themselves in their own straps.

MARIA   That quaffing and drinking will undo you. I heard
my lady talk of it yesterday, and of a foolish knight that
you brought in one night here to be her wooer.   15

SIR TOBY   Who, Sir Andrew Aguecheek?

MARIA   Ay, he.

SIR TOBY   He's as tall a man as any's in Illyria.

MARIA   What's that to th' purpose?

SIR TOBY   Why, he has three thousand ducats a year.   20

MARIA   Ay, but he'll have but a year in all these ducats.
He's a very fool, and a prodigal.

SIR TOBY   Fie that you'll say so! He plays o'th' viol-de-gamboys, and speaks three or four languages word for word
without book, and hath all the good gifts of nature.   25

MARIA   He hath indeed, almost natural, for besides that
he's a fool, he's a great quarreller, and but that he hath
the gift of a coward to allay the gust he hath in quarrel-

---

11 **an** if (a common Elizabethan usage)

11–12 **hang ... straps** Playing on the
proverb 'He may go hang himself in
his own garters' (Tilley G42).

13 **quaffing** drinking deep
   undo ruin

16 **Aguecheek** Hotson thinks that this
represents Spanish *Agu-chica*, 'Little-
wit', 'shortened from *agucia chica* or
agudeza chica' (p. 115). It is more likely
to derive from 'ague', fever, which for
Shakespeare evokes paleness and thin-
ness, most strikingly at *King John*
3.4.85, 'As dim and meagre as an
ague's fit'. At 5.1.200, Sir Toby calls
Sir Andrew 'a thin-faced knave', so
Aguecheek probably implies 'lean-face',
hence Sir Toby's 'Agueface' at l. 40.

18 **tall** Sir Toby uses the Elizabethan sense
'valiant'; Maria takes it in the modern
one in her reply.
   any's any (man who) is

20 **three thousand ducats** A *ducat* was a
gold coin of varying value, in use in
most European countries but origin-
ating in Venice, so it is appropriately
used in Illyria, a Venetian dependency.
It is notoriously difficult to express the
value of money of the past in modern

terms; but in the late sixteenth century, the annual income of a well-off
Italian nobleman was roughly one
thousand ducats (J. C. Davis, *A Venetian Family and its Fortune, 1500–
1900* (Philadelphia, 1975), pp. 41,
56), so Sir Andrew's income is clearly
substantial.

21 **he'll have ... in** he'll only have possession of them for a year (i.e. he'll use
up all his estate in one year)

22 **very** absolute

23–4 **viol-de-gamboys** A facetious corruption of 'viola da gamba', a bass viol
played held between the legs.

25 **without book** from memory. Sir Andrew's linguistic prowess clearly does
not extend to French, since he has
difficulty with *Pourquoi* at l. 87, and
with Viola's *Et vous aussi, votre serviteur* at 3.1.71–2; and in any case such
accomplishments are products of 'nur-
ture', not *gifts of nature*.

26 **almost natural** almost to the point of
being an idiot (a 'natural')

28–30 **gift ... gift** The sense shifts from
'talent' to 'present'.

28 **gust ... in** relish ... for

ling, 'tis thought among the prudent he would quickly
have the gift of a grave.   30

SIR TOBY By this hand, they are scoundrels and substractors that say so of him. Who are they?

MARIA They that add, moreover, he's drunk nightly in
your company.

SIR TOBY With drinking healths to my niece. I'll drink to   35
her as long as there is a passage in my throat and drink
in Illyria. He's a coward and a coistrel that will not drink
to my niece till his brains turn o'th' toe, like a parish
top. What wench, *Castiliano vulgo*, for here comes Sir
Andrew Agueface.   40

    Enter Sir Andrew Aguecheek

SIR ANDREW Sir Toby Belch! How now, Sir Toby Belch?

SIR TOBY Sweet Sir Andrew.

SIR ANDREW (*to Maria*) Bless you, fair shrew.

MARIA And you too sir.

SIR TOBY Accost, Sir Andrew, accost.   45

SIR ANDREW What's that?

SIR TOBY My niece's chambermaid.

40.1 *Aguecheek*] MALONE; *not in* F

31–2 **substractors** This Shakespearian
coinage is Sir Toby's perversion of 'de-
tractors'. In her reply, Maria's *add* (l.
33) puns on 'substract' meaning 'sub-
tract' (*OED, substract, v.* 2).

37 **coistrel** knave (literally 'groom' (*OED*
1)). It is used abusively of the cowardly servant Michael in the anonymous
Arden of Faversham (published 1592)
Sc. 5.41, 59, and of the brothel cus-
tomers in *Pericles* Sc. 19.190.

38 **o'th' toe** head-over-heels

38–9 **parish top** a whipping-top provided
for exercise and entertainment

39 *Castiliano vulgo* Not satisfactorily explained. Of various interpretations, the
one that fits the context best is 'Speak
of the Devil', since Spaniards ('Castil-
ians') were thought to be devilish and
vulgo in Latin means 'in the common
(parlance)'. And a devil adopts the
name Castiliano in the play *Grim the
Collier of Croydon* (1600 or earlier).

43 **shrew** Possibly Sir Andrew confuses
one meaning of *shrew*—ill-tempered
woman—with another—the small an-
imal known as 'shrew-mouse' (*OED sb.*
1)—in an attempt to produce an endearment such as Feste uses at 1.5.57–
8: 'Good my mouse of virtue'.

45 **Accost** Much play is made with the
meaning of this word in what follows.
It was originally a naval term, 'ac-
coast', 'go alongside' (*OED v.* 1), and
Sir Toby sustains some of the naval
implication in his glosses *front her,
board her*, finally explaining the sexual
significance in *woo her, assail her*
(ll. 52–3).

46 **What's that** Sir Andrew is asking what
'accost' means, but Sir Toby (deliberately?) takes him to mean 'Who is that
woman?', hence his reply, and Sir Andrew's subsequent misunderstanding
of *accost* as a name.

47 **chambermaid** lady-in-waiting, not, as

SIR ANDREW Good Mistress Accost, I desire better acquaintance.

MARIA My name is Mary, sir.   50

SIR ANDREW Good Mistress Mary Accost.

SIR TOBY You mistake, knight. 'Accost' is front her, board
her, woo her, assail her.

SIR ANDREW By my troth, I would not undertake her in
this company. Is that the meaning of 'accost'?   55

MARIA Fare you well, gentlemen.

SIR TOBY An thou let part so, Sir Andrew, would thou
mightst never draw sword again.

SIR ANDREW An you part so, mistress, I would I might
never draw sword again. Fair lady, do you think you   60
have fools in hand?

MARIA Sir, I have not you by th' hand.

SIR ANDREW Marry, but you shall have, and here's my
hand.

MARIA (*taking his hand*) Now sir, thought is free. I pray   65
you, bring your hand to th' buttery-bar, and let it drink.

48 SIR ANDREW] F2 (*An.*); *Ma.* F1   51 Mary Accost] ROWE; *Mary*, accost F   65 *taking his hand*] OXFORD; *not in* F

the word came later to mean, bed-
maker and cleaner. She is elsewhere
called *gentlewoman* (1.5.156). Reviewers
often become indignant when the part
is played as a menial; but this well-es-
tablished stage tradition serves to bring
out an important distinction between
Maria and gentlewomen in Shakespeare's other comedies: she is never
shown on intimate terms—indeed, on
hardly any terms at all—with Olivia,
as Lucetta is with Julia in *Two
Gentlemen*, Nerissa with Portia in *Merchant*, or Margaret and Ursula with
Hero in *Much Ado*. This helps to keep
Olivia isolated, and so more dependent
on Malvolio and more susceptible to
Viola/Cesario.

54 **undertake her** take her on (with sexual innuendo)

55 **this company** in public (perhaps the
audience)

57 **An thou let part so** i.e. if you let her

go without 'accosting' her. *OED v.*[1] 23
implies that 'let pass' as a combination
was becoming obsolete, and the Third
Folio (followed by the Fourth) clearly
had trouble with the phrase, reading
'let her part so'.

58 **never draw sword again** i.e. no longer
be a gentleman. Compare Middleton,
The Changeling (1622?) 5.2.20–1:
'Never to use that sword again in fight,
| In way of honest manhood'.

61 **in hand** to deal with. Maria takes him
literally in her reply.

63 **Marry** a mild oath, originally 'by the
Virgin Mary'

65 **thought is free** The customary reply to
'Do you think I'm a fool?', as in Lyly's
Euphues (1580): 'quoth he, "Dost thou
think me a fool?" "Thought is free, my
lord", quoth she' (*Works*, ed. R. W.
Bond (1902), 2. 60). The phrase was
proverbial (Tilley T244).

66 **buttery** store-room for liquor (from Old
French *boterie*, bottle), later for provi-

SIR ANDREW Wherefore, sweetheart? What's your metaphor?

MARIA It's dry, sir.

SIR ANDREW Why, I think so. I am not such an ass but I   70
can keep my hand dry. But what's your jest?

MARIA A dry jest, sir.

SIR ANDREW Are you full of them?

MARIA Ay sir, I have them at my fingers' ends. Marry,
now I let go your hand I am barren.   *Exit*   75

SIR TOBY O knight, thou lack'st a cup of canary. When did
I see thee so put down?

SIR ANDREW Never in your life, I think, unless you see
canary put me down. Methinks sometimes I have no
more wit than a Christian or an ordinary man has; but   80
I am a great eater of beef, and I believe that does harm
to my wit.

SIR TOBY No question.

SIR ANDREW An I thought that, I'd forswear it. I'll ride
home tomorrow, Sir Toby.   85

SIR TOBY *Pourquoi*, my dear knight?

75 *Exit*] F (*Exit Maria*)

sions generally (perhaps by association
with 'butter')

buttery-bar The top half of the buttery
door opened outwards to create a ledge
or bar. Presumably, as in most performances, Maria means her breasts, and
on this *metaphor* (ll. 67–8), the following jokes depend.

69 **dry** A dry hand was thought to show
weakness, possibly impotence, in contrast to a 'moist' one, which 'argues
fruitfulness and liberal heart' (*Othello*
3.4.36–8).

71 **hand dry** Alluding to the proverb
'Fools have wit enough to keep themselves out of the rain' (Tilley F537).

72 **dry jest** (a) stupid joke, also glancing
at Sir Andrew's stupidity (b) ironical
quip (*OED a.* 14, citing Puttenham's
Art of English Poesie (1589) 3.18: 'The
figure Ironia, which we call the dry

mock')

74 **at my fingers' ends** (a) always ready
(b) holding Sir Andrew, the inspirer of
her jests, *by th' hand* (l. 62)

75 **barren** empty of jokes (compare *Hamlet*
3.2.41: 'barren spectators') because
she has let go the hand of Sir Andrew
who enabled her to be *full of them*
(l. 73)

76 **canary** a sweet wine, originally from
the Canary Islands

77–9 **put down** Sir Toby means 'defeated
in repartee'; Sir Andrew takes up the
meaning 'drunk'.

80 **Christian** i.e. a normal man, the man
in the street, as Sir Andrew goes on to
explain

81 **eater of beef** Contemporary medicine
held that beef dulled the intellect. Compare *Troilus* 2.1.13, 'beef-witted lord',
describing the 'blockish' Ajax.

86 *Pourquoi* why (French)

SIR ANDREW What is 'Pourquoi'? Do, or not do? I would I
  had bestowed that time in the tongues that I have in
  fencing, dancing, and bear-baiting. O had I but followed
  the arts!   90
SIR TOBY Then hadst thou had an excellent head of hair.
SIR ANDREW Why, would that have mended my hair?
SIR TOBY Past question, for thou seest it will not curl by
  nature.
SIR ANDREW But it becomes me well enough, does't not?   95
SIR TOBY Excellent, it hangs like flax on a distaff, and I
  hope to see a housewife take thee between her legs and
  spin it off.
SIR ANDREW Faith, I'll home tomorrow, Sir Toby. Your
  niece will not be seen, or if she be, it's four to one she'll   100
  none of me. The Count himself here hard by woos her.
SIR TOBY She'll none o'th' Count. She'll not match above
  her degree, neither in estate, years, nor wit, I have
  heard her swear't. Tut, there's life in't, man.
SIR ANDREW I'll stay a month longer. I am a fellow o'th'   105
  strangest mind i'th' world. I delight in masques and revels sometimes altogether.

93 curl by] THEOBALD; coole my F   95 me] F2; we F1   does't] F (dost)   97 housewife]
F (huswife)

88 **tongues** foreign languages. Toby takes
  him to mean 'curling-tongs': *tongues*
  was pronounced 'tongs' at the time,
  and still is in some English regional
  accents.
92 **mended** improved (amended)
94 **nature** (as opposed to *arts* (l. 90))
96 **flax** Flaxen-haired men were thought
  to be 'chicken-hearts, and yet great
  quarrellers' (Dekker (or Middleton?),
  Blurt Master Constable (1602?) 2.2.128–
  30). Sir Andrew is both (ll. 27–8).
  distaff In spinning, *flax* would hang in
  long, thin, yellowish strands on a *distaff*, a pole held between the knees.
  This inevitably sets off the sexual punning that follows.
97 **housewife** Housewives spun *flax*. F's
  spelling 'huswife' suggests both the
  pronunciation 'hussif' and the word
  'hussy', a phonetic reduction of 'house-

wife' (*OED*, *hussy*, *sb.*) with the implication 'prostitute'.
98 **spin it off** If the housewife/hussy takes
  the *distaff* (penis) between her legs and
  spins it off, she will probably give him
  venereal disease, resulting in his loss
  of hair.
100–1 **she'll none of me** she will have
  nothing to do with me
103 **degree** rank
  estate status; perhaps possessions too
  years presumably implies that Sir
  Andrew is no older than Olivia (see
  Introduction, p. 55)
  wit intelligence
104 **Tut** an exclamation of impatience
  life in't Proverbial (Tilley L265).
106–7 **masques and revels** formal courtly entertainments in which dancing
  played a central part, hence the discussion that follows

SIR TOBY Art thou good at these kickshawses, knight?

SIR ANDREW As any man in Illyria, whatsoever he be, under the degree of my betters; and yet I will not com- 110
pare with an old man.

SIR TOBY What is thy excellence in a galliard, knight?

SIR ANDREW Faith, I can cut a caper.

SIR TOBY And I can cut the mutton to't.

SIR ANDREW And I think I have the back-trick simply as 115
strong as any man in Illyria.

SIR TOBY Wherefore are these things hid? Wherefore have these gifts a curtain before 'em? Are they like to take dust, like Mistress Mall's picture? Why dost thou not go to church in a galliard, and come home in a coranto? 120
My very walk should be a jig. I would not so much as make water but in a cinquepace. What dost thou mean? Is it a world to hide virtues in? I did think by the excellent constitution of thy leg it was formed under the star of a galliard. 125

---

122 cinquepace] F (Sinke-a-pace)

---

108 **kickshawses** trifles, trivialities (a corruption of French *quelque chose*, 'something', though virtually reversing its meaning to 'nothing')

110 **betters** social superiors

111 **old man** expert; probably an attempt to compliment Sir Toby on his experience, but ineptly stressing his age

112 **galliard** a lively dance of five steps, the fifth a caper (see the next note), sustaining the topic of *masques and revels* from ll. 106–7

113 **caper** Sir Andrew means 'leap'; Sir Toby in his reply puns on the sense 'pickled flower-buds', used for a sauce to season *mutton*.

114 **mutton** with quibble 'prostitute', which may contribute to the next phrase (*OED* 4)

115 **back-trick** This is almost certainly one of the *capers* referred to in l. 113, a vigorous kick of the foot behind the body. It may also suggest sexual prowess.

118 **curtain** (used to protect paintings from fading)

119 **Mistress Mall's picture** Mall, like Moll, was a nickname for Mary. Various Malls have been suggested for this allusion (if it is one). The likeliest is Mary Fitton, one of Elizabeth I's maids of honour, disgraced for bearing the Earl of Pembroke's child in 1601 (see Hotson, pp. 103–6).

120–2 **coranto ... jig ... cinquepace** More lively dances. A *coranto* (from French *courante*, a running dance) was even faster than a *galliard*. A *cinquepace* (French 'five steps') was equivalent to a galliard, here used to pun on 'sink' meaning 'sewer'. F's spelling *Sinke-a-pace* may be intended to point the pun, but *OED* records *sinkapace* in Harington (1596) with no pun.

124–5 **star of a galliard** astrological influence favourable to dancing. Compare *Much Ado* 2.1.314, where the lively Beatrice says 'there was a star danced, and under that was I born'.

SIR ANDREW Ay, 'tis strong, and it does indifferent well in
   a divers-coloured stock. Shall we set about some revels?
SIR TOBY What shall we do else—were we not born under
   Taurus?
SIR ANDREW Taurus? That's sides and heart.   130
SIR TOBY No sir, it is legs and thighs: let me see thee caper.
   ⌈*Sir Andrew capers*⌉
   Ha, higher! Ha ha, excellent.   *Exeunt*

1.4   *Enter Valentine, and Viola (as Cesario) in man's
         attire*

VALENTINE If the Duke continue these favours towards
   you, Cesario, you are like to be much advanced. He
   hath known you but three days, and already you are no
   stranger.
VIOLA You either fear his humour or my negligence, that   5

---

127 divers] OXFORD; dam'd F; flame ROWE 1714; dun COLLIER MS   set] ROWE 1714; sit F
130 That's] F3; That F1   131.1 *Sir Andrew capers*] OXFORD; *not in* F
   1.4.0.1 *(as Cesario)*] OXFORD; *not in* F

---

126 **indifferent** moderately
127 **divers-coloured** This is Wells's tent-
   ative emendation of F's 'damned' (*Re-
   Editing*, pp. 33–4). Among many other
   emendations, Barbara Everett proposes
   'lemon-coloured' ('Two Damned
   Cruces: *Othello* and *Twelfth Night*', *RES*
   146 (1986), 184–97). This is attractive, as Sir Andrew would then propose
   to woo Olivia wearing *a colour she
   abhors* (2.5.189; and see note). But
   Warren argues that F makes sense if
   'damned' is an intensifier: compare
   'damned epicurean rascal' (*Merry
   Wives* 2.2.277), 'damned tripe-visaged
   rascal' (*2 Henry IV* 5.4.8), 'damnèd
   furious wight' (*Henry V* 2.1.58), all
   spoken by eccentric characters in plays
   written close in date (1597–9) to
   Twelfth Night.
   stock stocking
129–31 **Taurus ... thighs** Astrological
   signs were thought to govern human
   behaviour. *Taurus*, the Bull, governed
   neck and throat, appropriate to heavy
   drinkers, which is why Sir Toby refers
   to it at l. 129. Sir Andrew misat-
   tributes *Taurus* at l. 130 through ignorance, so Sir Toby makes the deliberate mistake at l. 131, to get him
   back to the dancing again.
1.4.0.1 *Cesario* This name may have
   been suggested by Curzio Gonzaga's
   comedy *Gl'Inganni* (published 1592),
   which John Manningham (see Introduction, p. 1) compared to *Twelfth
   Night*, and in which the heroine disguises herself as a page called Cesare.
   Since Viola has not been named in the
   dialogue, she first begins to take on an
   identity for an audience as 'Cesario',
   and retains this almost to the end.
2 **advanced** promoted
3 **three days** A double time scheme oper-
   ates in the play. *Three days* emphasizes
   the vital dramatic fact that Orsino is
   immediately attracted to Viola/Cesario;
   but in the last scene *three months* are
   said to have elapsed (5.1.89, 94), in
   order to emphasize their maturing
   affection.
5 **humour** disposition (perhaps implying
   capriciousness, as at *As You Like It*
   1.2.256: 'The Duke is humorous', i.e.
   changeable)

you call in question the continuance of his love. Is he
inconstant, sir, in his favours?
VALENTINE No, believe me.
    Enter Duke Orsino, Curio, and attendants
VIOLA I thank you. Here comes the Count.
ORSINO Who saw Cesario, ho?   10
VIOLA On your attendance, my lord, here.
ORSINO *(to the courtiers)*
  Stand you a while aloof. *(To Viola)* Cesario,
  Thou know'st no less but all: I have unclasped
  To thee the book even of my secret soul.
  Therefore good youth, address thy gait unto her,   15
  Be not denied access, stand at her doors,
  And tell them there thy fixèd foot shall grow
  Till thou have audience.
VIOLA   Sure, my noble lord,
  If she be so abandoned to her sorrow
  As it is spoke, she never will admit me.   20
ORSINO
  Be clamorous, and leap all civil bounds,
  Rather than make unprofited return.
VIOLA
  Say I do speak with her, my lord, what then?
ORSINO
  O then unfold the passion of my love,
  Surprise her with discourse of my dear faith.   25
  It shall become thee well to act my woes.

8.1 *Orsino*] not in F

8.1–9 ***Duke ... Count*** See note to
   I.I.0.I.
13 **but all** than everything
   unclasped Ornate book-covers were
   often fastened with clasps. The unclas-
   ping of a book is a favourite image in
   Shakespeare for expressing intimate
   communications. Compare *1 Henry IV*
   1.3.186, 'I will unclasp a secret book',
   and *Much Ado* 1.1.306: 'in her bosom
   I'll unclasp my heart'. Here, it emphasizes Orsino's immediate trust and

confidence in Viola/Cesario, an impression reinforced by his use of the
familiar *thou* instead of the formal *you*
used to the rest of the court.
15 **address thy gait** direct your steps
16 **access** The stress is on the second syllable.
17 **grow** i.e. take root
21 **civil bounds** constraints of polite behaviour
25 **Surprise** capture by unexpected attack
   (a military expression)

She will attend it better in thy youth
Than in a nuncio's of more grave aspect.
VIOLA
I think not so, my lord.
ORSINO   Dear lad, believe it;
For they shall yet belie thy happy years   30
That say thou art a man: Diana's lip
Is not more smooth and rubious; thy small pipe
Is as the maiden's organ, shrill and sound,
And all is semblative a woman's part.
I know thy constellation is right apt   35
For this affair. (*To the courtiers*) Some four or
      five attend him,
All if you will, for I myself am best
When least in company. (*To Viola*) Prosper well in this
And thou shalt live as freely as thy lord,
To call his fortunes thine.
VIOLA   I'll do my best   40
To woo your lady. ⌈*Aside*⌉ Yet a barful strife,
Whoe'er I woo, myself would be his wife.
                              Exeunt severally

1.5   *Enter Maria and Feste, the clown*
MARIA Nay, either tell me where thou hast been or I will
    not open my lips so wide as a bristle may enter in way of

---

28 nuncio's] F (Nuntio's); nuntius (*conj.* Oxford)   42.1 *severally*] *not in* F
  1.5.0.1 *Feste, the*] *not in* F

28 **nuncio's** messenger's. The genitive
   case is illogical but not necessarily un-
   Shakespearian. Nevertheless he may
   have written 'nuntius' (*OED*'s first
   reference is from 1605) or 'nuncius'
   (*OED* 1613–16).
   aspect appearance (stressed on the second syllable)
32 **rubious** ruby-red (a Shakespearian
   coinage)
   pipe voice
33 **shrill and sound** high-pitched and un-
   broken. For the significance of *sound*,
   compare *Hamlet* 2.2.430–1, where
   Hamlet hopes that the boy player's
   voice, 'like a piece of uncurrent gold,

be not cracked within the ring'.
34 **semblative a woman's part** i.e. as if
   Cesario were playing a woman's role.
   Semblative means 'like', and is a Shakespearian coinage.
35 **constellation** character and abilities
   (formed supposedly by the stars, as at
   1.3.129–31)
39 **freely** independently
41 **barful strife** a conflict within herself
   full of bars, or difficulties
42.1 *severally* separately (a standard
   phrase in Elizabethan directions,
   though here editorial)
1.5.0.1 *Feste* Only mentioned in the dialogue at 2.4.11, the name, from Latin

thy excuse. My lady will hang thee for thy absence.

FESTE Let her hang me. He that is well hanged in this
world needs to fear no colours.   5

MARIA Make that good.

FESTE He shall see none to fear.

MARIA A good lenten answer. I can tell thee where that
saying was born, of 'I fear no colours'.

FESTE Where, good Mistress Mary?   10

MARIA In the wars, and that may you be bold to say in
your foolery.

FESTE Well, God give them wisdom that have it; and those
that are fools, let them use their talents.

MARIA Yet you will be hanged for being so long absent, or   15
to be turned away—is not that as good as a hanging to
you?

FESTE Many a good hanging prevents a bad marriage;
and for turning away, let summer bear it out.

MARIA You are resolute then?   20

FESTE Not so neither, but I am resolved on two points.

4 FESTE] F ('*Clo.*' *throughout*)

or Italian *festa*, feast or festival, is appropriate to the character's profession,
if not to his barbed and melancholy
personality. It is pronounced 'Fest-ay'.

1 **where thou hast been** This prepares
the audience for Feste's detachment
from the action, and for the fact that,
though employed by Olivia, he also
spends time at Orsino's court.

2 **in way** by way

4–5 **He that is ... fear no colours** whoever is well hanged needs to fear nothing (because he is dead). To *fear no
colours* is proverbial (Tilley C520), and
derives from the military meaning of
colours, flags or standards (*OED sb.* 7).
That is the primary sense; but Hotson,
citing contemporary examples, sees a
pun on *well hanged*, sexually endowed,
as in modern sexual slang 'well hung':
a virile man does not fear the enemy
or his colours (p. 168).

6 **Make that good** prove that

8 **lenten** thin, meagre-witted (because
Lent is a time of fasting)

11–12 **be bold ... foolery** Is Maria twitting Feste with cowardice, implying
that he is bold enough to joke about
the wars but not to take part in them?

13–14 **God give ... their talents** i.e. let
wise men make the most of their wisdom, and fools of their professional folly.
The mock-religious phrasing is one of
Feste's *talents*, which reaches its climax in his impersonation of Sir Topaz
(4.2). Here he echoes St Matthew 25:
29, 'unto every one that hath shall be
given', the moral of the parable of the
talents, which argues that we should
make the most of what we are given.

16 **turned away** dismissed (quibbling on
'turning off', hanging)

18 **Many ... marriage** Alluding to
proverbs like 'Better be half hanged
than ill wed' (Tilley H130).
hanging (a) execution (b) sexual en-
dowment. See note to ll. 4–5.

19 **bear it out** make it endurable

21 **points** matters. He does not have the
chance to say what these are, since
Maria intervenes with her pun upon

MARIA That if one break, the other will hold; or if both break, your gaskins fall.

FESTE Apt, in good faith, very apt. Well, go thy way. If Sir Toby would leave drinking thou wert as witty a piece of   25 Eve's flesh as any in Illyria.

MARIA Peace, you rogue, no more o' that. Here comes my lady: make your excuse wisely, you were best.   *Exit*
     Enter Lady Olivia, with Malvolio and attendants

FESTE Wit, an't be thy will, put me into good fooling! Those wits that think they have thee do very oft prove   30 fools, and I that am sure I lack thee may pass for a wise man. For what says Quinapalus? 'Better a witty fool than a foolish wit.' (*To Olivia*) God bless thee, lady.

---

28. Exit] POPE; *not in* F   28.1 *and attendants*] CAPELL (*Enter Olivia attended*); *not in* F

'points' meaning laces holding up breeches. Compare the pun at 1 *Henry IV* 2.5.218–19: 'Their points [swords] being broken— | Down fell their hose.'

23 **gaskins** wide knee-breeches
24 **Apt** Probably ironical, in view of Maria's interruption of his *points* at l. 22.
25 **witty** clever.
25–6 **piece of Eve's flesh** i.e. woman, perhaps suggesting Eve's temptation of Adam. Feste implies that Sir Toby and Maria could make a good match.
28 **you were best** you had better
28.1 *Enter . . . attendants* As befits her rank, *Lady* Olivia enters with other male attendants besides her steward Malvolio: Feste addresses them at ll. 35 (*fellows*) and 67 (*gentlemen*). She probably also has female attendants (see note to l. 160).
     Malvolio The name means 'ill-will', formed from Italian *mal* (bad) and *voglia* (desire). For a discussion of its significance, see Introduction, p. 45.
29–33 **Wit . . . a foolish wit** This appears to be a soliloquy, but Feste may intend Olivia to hear some or all of it. If she does, this has the dramatic advantage of giving a clear focus on which the audience can concentrate, with everyone listening to Feste; otherwise there is a danger that the focus is split between Feste's speech and the entry of two new characters, one of whom has been much talked about since the start of the play, so that interest in her is bound to be considerable.

29 **Wit . . . will** In invoking the spirit of intelligence to help him if it is prepared to do so, Feste is playing on the traditional opposition of *wit* (intelligence) and *will* (passion, desire). Compare *Lucrece* 1298–9: 'Conceit and grief an eager combat fight; | What wit sets down is blotted straight with will'.
30–1 **Those wits . . . prove fools** Feste echoes the proverb 'He that is wise in his own conceit is a fool' (Tilley C582), which itself echoes Proverbs 26:5: 'make the fool an answer to his foolishness, lest he be wise in his own conceit'. More Festian mock-clericalism?
32 **Quinapalus** Feste invents an authority. Hotson thinks that the name may be pseudo-Italian, meaning 'there on the stick', and referring to the figure of a jester on the bauble or folly-stick often carried by fools (p. 157). Terry Hands thinks it may be French. When he was directing the play at the Comédie Française in 1976, his French actor naturally pronounced the word 'qui n'a pas lu'—'who has not read' (*Directors' Shakespeare*, p. 123). Or the joke may

OLIVIA (*to attendants*) Take the fool away.

FESTE Do you not hear, fellows? Take away the lady.   35

OLIVIA Go to, you're a dry fool. I'll no more of you.
Besides, you grow dishonest.

FESTE Two faults, madonna, that drink and good counsel
will amend: for give the dry fool drink, then is the fool
not dry; bid the dishonest man mend himself: if he   40
mend, he is no longer dishonest; if he cannot, let the
botcher mend him. Anything that's mended is but
patched: virtue that transgresses is but patched with
sin, and sin that amends is but patched with virtue. If
that this simple syllogism will serve, so; if it will not,   45
what remedy? As there is no true cuckold but calamity,
so beauty's a flower. The lady bade take away the fool,
therefore I say again, take her away.

OLIVIA Sir, I bade them take away you.

FESTE Misprision in the highest degree! Lady, *Cucullus non*   50

simply be that Feste asks the *audience* about someone they have never heard of, and having waited in vain for a reply, provides the punch-line as if it was so obvious that the audience should have known all the time.

36 **Go to** an expression of impatience (like modern 'come come')
dry dull. Feste plays on the meaning 'thirsty' (ll. 38–40). Compare the same joke at *LLL* 5.2.372–3: 'fools would fain have drink. | This jest is dry to me.'

37 **dishonest** undutiful (because of his absences)

38 **madonna** my lady (Italian). Feste is the only character in Shakespeare to use the word; he surely chooses it because its Catholic overtones—referring to the Virgin Mary—will antagonize the puritan Malvolio, although *OED*'s first examples of 'madonna' that unmistakably allude to the Virgin Mary are from 1644 and 1645 (2a).

40 **mend** reform; but later in the speech Feste modulates into the modern sense (ll. 42–4).

42 **botcher** clothes-mender or cobbler

43–4 **virtue ... with virtue** i.e. nothing is absolutely good or bad, but a mixture.

Compare *All's Well* 4.3.74–5: 'The web of our life is of a mingled yarn, good and ill together.'

45 **syllogism** formal reasoning (in which a conclusion is drawn from two premisses: here, the two phrases about *virtue* and *sin*)

46 **what remedy** it can't be helped
there is no true cuckold but calamity i.e. one wedded to calamity is always faithless

47 **beauty's a flower** i.e. and so will fade. An image of transience, like Nashe's celebrated 'Beauty is but a flower, | Which wrinkles will devour' (*Summer's Last Will and Testament* (1600), ll. 1588–9). Feste is urging Olivia to make the most of her beauty and to marry, not to shut herself away for seven years. To do so is to be a fool—hence his next phrase.

50 **Misprision** (a) wrongful arrest, alluding to Olivia's order to remove him (b) misapprehension, the more usual sense in Shakespeare, as at *Much Ado* 4.1.187: 'There is some strange misprision in the princes.'

50–1 *Cucullus non facit monachum* A Latin tag, 'the cowl does not make the monk', which Feste goes on to explain.

facit monachum—that's as much to say as I wear not
motley in my brain. Good madonna, give me leave to
prove you a fool.

OLIVIA   Can you do it?

FESTE   Dexteriously, good madonna.   55

OLIVIA   Make your proof.

FESTE   I must catechize you for it, madonna. Good my
mouse of virtue, answer me.

OLIVIA   Well sir, for want of other idleness I'll bide your
proof.   60

FESTE   Good madonna, why mourn'st thou?

OLIVIA   Good fool, for my brother's death.

FESTE   I think his soul is in hell, madonna.

OLIVIA   I know his soul is in heaven, fool.

FESTE   The more fool, madonna, to mourn for your   65
brother's soul being in heaven. Take away the fool,
gentlemen.

66 soul being] ROWE; soule, being F

51 **That's as much to say as** Elsewhere,
Shakespeare uses both this construction (compare 'which is as much to
say as "Let the magistrates be labour-
ing men"' (*Contention* 4.2.18–19))
and the more familiar modern one
(compare 'That's as much as to say
"Can she so?"' (*Two Gentlemen*
3.1.300)), which Rowe reads here,
and which is probably clearer for a
modern audience.

52 **motley** the fool's parti-coloured garment. There is no consensus of opinion
as to whether *motley* described a var-
iegated weave or patches of different
colours sewn on to the costume.

55 **Dexteriously** dextrously, cleverly. This
is not a fool's play on 'dextrously', but
a variant Elizabethan form. J. O.
Wood, *NQ* 211 (1966), 253–4, cites
an earlier use (1597) than Feste's,
which is *OED*'s first example. Feste
presumably chooses this form of the
word for the relish with which it can
be spoken.

57 **catechize** question. The catechism,
which tests the orthodoxy of religious

belief, is set out as a series of formal
questions and answers, like Feste's in-
terrogation of Olivia here. Once again,
he enjoys playing the mock-priest, no
doubt because it will further scandalize
Malvolio.

57–8 **Good my mouse of virtue** my good
virtuous mouse. Abbott, 13, says that
the construction is formed on analogy
with such phrases as 'Good my lord'.
Mouse is a term of endearment, as at
Hamlet 3.4.167, 'call you his mouse',
rather than implying that Olivia has
little virtue.

59 **idleness** pastime
bide await (perhaps with secondary
meaning 'endure, put up with'; com-
pare 'no woman's sides | Can bide the
beating of so strong a passion'
(2.4.92–3))

66 **soul being** F's punctuation 'soul,
being' must be wrong, since it implies
that the soul's being in heaven is in-
cidental, whereas the whole point of
Feste's 'proof' *depends* upon the fact
that the soul is in heaven: that is why
Olivia is a fool to mourn.

OLIVIA What think you of this fool, Malvolio? Doth he not
     mend?
MALVOLIO Yes, and shall do, till the pangs of death shake   70
     him. Infirmity, that decays the wise, doth ever make the
     better fool.
FESTE God send you, sir, a speedy infirmity for the better
     increasing your folly. Sir Toby will be sworn that I am
     no fox, but he will not pass his word for twopence that   75
     you are no fool.
OLIVIA How say you to that, Malvolio?
MALVOLIO I marvel your ladyship takes delight in such a
     barren rascal. I saw him put down the other day with
     an ordinary fool that has no more brain than a stone.   80
     Look you now, he's out of his guard already. Unless you
     laugh and minister occasion to him, he is gagged. I pro-
     test I take these wise men that crow so at these set kind
     of fools no better than the fools' zanies.
OLIVIA O, you are sick of self-love, Malvolio, and taste   85
     with a distempered appetite. To be generous, guiltless,
     and of free disposition is to take those things for bird-
     bolts that you deem cannon bullets. There is no slander
     in an allowed fool, though he do nothing but rail; nor
     no railing in a known discreet man, though he do noth-   90
     ing but reprove.

69–72 **mend . . . better fool** Olivia asks if
     Feste does not improve; Malvolio re-
     plies that he does, in the sense of
     becoming more foolish (*the better fool*).
71 **Infirmity** (old) age
75 **no fox** not cunning
     pass pledge (*OED v.* 48). Compare *Titus*
     1.1.465–6: 'I have passed | My word
     and promise'.
79 **barren** (of wit)
80 **ordinary fool** (a) unexceptional fool (b)
     fool performing in an inn (*ordinary*)
     stone Perhaps alluding to Stone, an
     Elizabethan fool who performed in ta-
     verns, though the line makes perfect
     sense as it stands, and 'he has no more
     wit than a stone' was proverbial (Tilley
     W550).
81 **he's out of his guard** he has no defence
     (from the fencing term 'off guard')
82 **minister occasion** offer an opportunity
83 **crow** laugh uproariously

set not spontaneous
84 **zanies** stooges or 'straight men' to
     fools. The *zanni* were the comic ser-
     vants in the *commedia dell'arte*, but the
     word seems to have come to mean
     someone who assists the performer to
     get his effects. That is certainly how
     Malvolio uses it here, and Jonson in
     Volpone (1606) 2.2.28, where Vol-
     pone, disguised as a mountebank, calls
     his assistant 'zany'.
85–91 **O . . . reprove** Olivia points out
     that a magnanimous (*free*) nature
     plays down faults rather than empha-
     sizing them, and can overlook the criti-
     cisms of a licensed (*allowed*) fool in
     exactly the same way as the *railing* of
     a *known discreet man* (Malvolio).
86 **distempered** sick, unbalanced
87–8 **birdbolts** blunt arrows for shooting
     birds

FESTE Now Mercury endue thee with leasing, for thou
   speak'st well of fools.
      Enter Maria
MARIA Madam, there is at the gate a young gentleman
   much desires to speak with you.   95
OLIVIA From the Count Orsino, is it?
MARIA I know not, madam, 'tis a fair young man, and
   well attended.
OLIVIA Who of my people hold him in delay?
MARIA Sir Toby, madam, your kinsman.   100
OLIVIA Fetch him off, I pray you, he speaks nothing but
   madman. Fie on him.
                                             ⌈*Exit Maria*⌉
   Go you, Malvolio. If it be a suit from the Count, I am
   sick, or not at home—what you will to dismiss it.
                                             Exit Malvolio
   Now you see, sir, how your fooling grows old, and   105
   people dislike it.
FESTE Thou hast spoke for us, madònna, as if thy eldest
   son should be a fool, whose skull Jove cram with brains,
   for—here he comes—
      Enter Sir Toby
   one of thy kin has a most weak *pia mater*.   110

102 *Exit Maria*] CAPELL; *not in* F   109 for—here he comes—] CAMBRIDGE (*subs.*); for heere
he comes. F

92 **Mercury . . . leasing** *Endue* in the sixteenth and seventeenth centuries 'had
   all the senses of ENDOW' according to
   OED v. 8c, which cites *Coriolanus*
   2.3.139–40: 'the tribunes | Endue
   you with the people's voice.' *Leasing*
   was a common alternative for 'lying'.
   In addition to *OED*'s examples, it occurs in one of the main sources of the
   play, *Riche his Farewell to Military Profession* (see Introduction, pp. 16–18).
   So the whole phrase means 'May the
   god of deception teach you the art of
   lying (in praising fools)'. Mercury was
   also the god of concealed, hermetic
   (from Hermes, the Greek version of the
   name) wisdom, which makes him a
   suitable patron saint for a wise fool.
95 **much desires** i.e. who much desires. The

omission of the relative is a common
   Elizabethan abbreviation (Abbott 244).
102 **madman** madman's language
   Exit Maria F gives her no exit, yet
   brings her on again at l. 157. It seems
   clear that Olivia sends Maria to *fetch
   off* Sir Toby, and Malvolio to deal with
   Orsino's messenger.
105 **old** stale
109 **for—here he comes** *He* is of course
   Sir Toby. The change of subject from
   Olivia's yet-to-be-born eldest son (ll.
   107–8) is rather abrupt, but the connection is that Feste hopes that Olivia's
   first-born son will have more brains
   than another example *of thy kin* (l.
   110) who is now approaching.
110 *pia mater* brain (literally, a mem-
   brane enclosing it)

OLIVIA By mine honour, half-drunk. What is he at the
gate, cousin?

SIR TOBY A gentleman.

OLIVIA A gentleman? What gentleman?

SIR TOBY 'Tis a gentleman here. (*He belches*) A plague o'   115
these pickle herring! (*To Feste*) How now, sot?

FESTE Good Sir Toby.

OLIVIA Cousin, cousin, how have you come so early by
this lethargy?

SIR TOBY Lechery? I defy lechery. There's one at the gate.   120

OLIVIA Ay, marry, what is he?

SIR TOBY Let him be the devil an he will, I care not. Give
me faith, say I. Well, it's all one.   *Exit*

OLIVIA What's a drunken man like, fool?

FESTE Like a drowned man, a fool, and a madman: one   125
draught above heat makes him a fool, the second mads
him, and a third drowns him.

OLIVIA Go thou and seek the coroner, and let him sit o'
my coz, for he's in the third degree of drink, he's
drowned. Go look after him.   130

FESTE He is but mad yet, madonna, and the fool shall look
to the madman.   *Exit*

    Enter Malvolio

MALVOLIO Madam, yon young fellow swears he will speak
with you. I told him you were sick—he takes on him to
understand so much, and therefore comes to speak with   135
you. I told him you were asleep—he seems to have a

---

115 *He belches*] OXFORD; *not in* F   132 *Exit*] ROWE; *not in* F

116 **pickle herring** Herrings induce fla-
tulence; Sir Toby justifies his surname.
'Pickleherring' became a typename for
the clown in German comedies of the
period, perhaps through the influence
of English actors on the Continent
(*OED* 2; see also Willem Schrickx,
' "Pickleherring" and English Actors in
Germany', *SS 36* (Cambridge, 1983),
135–47).
   sot (a) fool (b) drunkard
120 **one** someone
122–3 **Give me faith** Protestants believed

that grace (e.g. to defy the devil) could
be achieved by faith alone.
123 **it's all one** it doesn't matter. The
expression recurs several times in the
final scene: Sir Toby uses it at l. 190,
and Feste at ll. 364 and 397.
126 **above heat** beyond the quantity that
would warm him
127 **drowns him** makes him insensible
128 **sit** hold an inquest
129 **coz** familiar abbreviation of 'cousin'
135 **therefore** for that very reason

foreknowledge of that too, and therefore comes to speak
with you. What is to be said to him, lady? He's fortified
against any denial.

OLIVIA Tell him he shall not speak with me.   140

MALVOLIO 'Has been told so, and he says he'll stand at
your door like a sheriff's post, and be the supporter to a
bench, but he'll speak with you.

OLIVIA What kind o' man is he?

MALVOLIO Why, of mankind.   145

OLIVIA What manner of man?

MALVOLIO Of very ill manner: he'll speak with you, will
you or no.

OLIVIA Of what personage and years is he?

MALVOLIO Not yet old enough for a man, nor young   150
enough for a boy: as a squash is before 'tis a peascod, or
a codling when 'tis almost an apple. 'Tis with him in
standing water between boy and man. He is very well-
favoured, and he speaks very shrewishly. One would
think his mother's milk were scarce out of him.   155

OLIVIA
Let him approach. Call in my gentlewoman.

MALVOLIO Gentlewoman, my lady calls.   *Exit*
        Enter Maria

OLIVIA
Give me my veil, come throw it o'er my face.
We'll once more hear Orsino's embassy.
        Enter Viola as Cesario

---

141 'Has] F (Ha's)   152 in] F; e'en CAPELL *(after* F)   159.1 *Enter Viola as Cesario*] *Enter
Viola* F2; *Enter Violenta.* F1

---

141 **'Has** F's *Has* appears to stand for 'a
   [the unaccented form of "he"] has' =
   'he has'.
142 **sheriff's post** conspicuous, decorative
   post set before the door of a sheriff or
   mayor, denoting authority
145 **of mankind** i.e. just like any other
149 **personage** appearance
151 **squash** undeveloped pea-pod (*peascod*)
152 **codling** unripe apple
152–3 **in standing water** at the turn of
   the tide

153–4 **well-favoured** handsome
154 **shrewishly** Perhaps this means, as in
   all *OED*'s examples, 'sharply'. But, especially in view of Malvolio's following
   line, it is likelier to mean 'high-
   pitched', like the squeaking of the
   common shrew; see the evidence as-
   sembled in Brian Morris's new Arden
   Shrew (1981), pp. 120–2. And compare *shrill* (1.4.33).
159.1 **Viola** F's 'Violenta' is probably a
   compositorial error: F's Compositor B
   may have expanded 'Vio.' to the form

VIOLA The honourable lady of the house, which is she?   160
OLIVIA Speak to me, I shall answer for her. Your will.
VIOLA Most radiant, exquisite, and unmatchable beauty
—I pray you tell me if this be the lady of the house, for I
never saw her. I would be loath to cast away my speech,
for besides that it is excellently well penned, I have taken   165
great pains to con it. Good beauties, let me sustain no
scorn; I am very 'countable, even to the least sinister
usage.
OLIVIA Whence came you, sir?
VIOLA I can say little more than I have studied, and that   170
question's out of my part. Good gentle one, give me
modest assurance if you be the lady of the house, that I
may proceed in my speech.
OLIVIA Are you a comedian?
VIOLA No, my profound heart; and yet—by the very fangs   175

---

162 beauty—] ROWE; beautie. F   167 'countable] F (comptible)   172 I] F (*catchword;
not in text*)

160 **which is she** Productions sometimes
confront Viola with several veiled
figures (including Maria and ladies-in-
waiting), suitably enough for a household in mourning, so that Viola's question reflects genuine perplexity. If
Olivia alone is veiled, there is no problem of identification: this must be the
retired lady of the house—in which
case Viola is deliberately mistaking
her, going on the offensive in dealing
with Orsino's cruel beloved.

162–3 **Most radiant . . . tell me** Viola begins her prepared speech in praise of
Olivia, then breaks off with her prosaic
factual question, reinforcing her earlier
one. She is also drawing a sharp distinction between her own words and
those she has learnt, a distinction that
develops as the scene proceeds, where
much of the language has specifically
theatrical connotations, for example *con*,
studied, comedian. See the following notes.

164 **cast away** waste

he had recently set in the opening
stage direction of *All's Well* 3.5 (see
Turner, p. 130).

165 **excellently well penned** exceedingly
well written
166 **con** memorize
sustain suffer
167 **'countable** accountable, i.e. sensitive.
OED lists F's 'comptible' as a spelling
of 'countable', 'often aphetic for "accountable" '. Hotson suggests that
Viola means 'I am very accountable to
Orsino for any insult offered to his
ambassador' (p. 135).
170 **studied** learnt by heart. Compare
Hamlet 2.2.543: 'study a speech of
some dozen or sixteen lines'.
172 **modest** adequate
174 **comedian** actor (perhaps with the
mocking overtone 'actor in a comedy',
which would be in keeping with the
tone of witty banter that pervades their
dialogue)
175 **my profound heart** probably an
oath—'upon my soul'—rather than an
address to Olivia
175–6 **by the . . . I swear** Viola swears by
something that might threaten her (by
hinting at her identity?), comparable
perhaps to the modern slang 'Cross my
heart and hope to die'. *By the very*

of malice I swear—I am not that I play. Are you the lady
of the house?

OLIVIA If I do not usurp myself, I am.

VIOLA Most certain if you are she you do usurp yourself,
for what is yours to bestow is not yours to reserve. But   180
this is from my commission. I will on with my speech in
your praise, and then show you the heart of my message.

OLIVIA Come to what is important in't, I forgive you the
praise.   185

VIOLA Alas, I took great pains to study it, and 'tis poetical.

OLIVIA It is the more like to be feigned, I pray you keep it
in. I heard you were saucy at my gates, and allowed
your approach rather to wonder at you than to hear   190
you. If you be not mad, be gone. If you have reason, be
brief. 'Tis not that time of moon with me to make one in
so skipping a dialogue.

MARIA Will you hoist sail, sir? Here lies your way.

VIOLA No, good swabber, I am to hull here a little longer.   195

191 not mad] F; mad RANN (conj. Mason)

fangs of malice may be an example of
what Sir Toby calls 'swear[ing] horrible', 'a terrible oath' (3.4.172–3).

176 **that I play** the character I perform
178–9 **usurp ... usurp** Olivia means
'counterfeit'; Viola takes her to mean
'wrongfully supplant'.
181 **from my commission** not part of my
errand, my charge
   from at variance with (Abbott 158)
   I will on 'Go' is understood (Abbott
   405).
184 **forgive** excuse. Olivia is as impatient
as Viola with cliché.
186–8 **poetical ... feigned** The words
poetical and *poetry* sometimes have pe-
jorative overtones in Shakespeare, especially in the context of lovers'
speeches. In *As You Like It*, for instance, Touchstone says that 'lovers
are given to poetry; and what they
swear in poetry it may be said, as
lovers, they do feign' (3.3.17–18).

188–9 **keep it in** keep it to yourself
189 **saucy** cheeky, impatient
191–2 **If you be not mad ... be brief**
There is no need to emend F's *not mad*
to 'mad'. F makes good sense: 'if you
have any sense, go; if (also) you have
anything reasonable to say [*OED, reason, sb.*¹ 18b], say it quickly (before
going)'.
192 **'Tis not that time of moon with me**
i.e. I am not lunatic. Lunacy was associated with changes of the moon.
193 **skipping** inconsequential (because a
dialogue with someone apparently
mad)
194–5 **hoist sail ... swabber ... hull** Nautical phrases. A *swabber* cleans decks.
Hull means to be anchored with furled
sails, hence stay put. *OED v.*² 1 cites
Captain Smith's *Seaman's Grammar*
(1627), 9. 40: 'They call it hulling ...
when they strike their sails lest [a
storm] should beat them in pieces
against the mast'.

(*To Olivia*) Some mollification for your giant, sweet lady.
Tell me your mind, I am a messenger.

OLIVIA Sure you have some hideous matter to deliver
when the courtesy of it is so fearful. Speak your office.

VIOLA It alone concerns your ear. I bring no overture of   200
war, no taxation of homage. I hold the olive in my
hand. My words are as full of peace as matter.

OLIVIA Yet you began rudely. What are you? What would
you?

VIOLA The rudeness that hath appeared in me have I   205
learned from my entertainment. What I am and what
I would are as secret as maidenhead: to your ears,
divinity; to any others', profanation.

OLIVIA (*to Maria and attendants*) Give us the place alone,
we will hear this divinity.   210

                    Exeunt Maria and attendants

Now sir, what is your text?

VIOLA Most sweet lady—

---

197 Tell me your mind] F; *assigned to Olivia* WARBURTON   203–4 Yet . . . would you]
verse in F, *divided after* 'are you'   209–11 Give . . . text] *verse in* F, *divided after* 'alone'
210.1 *Exeunt Maria and attendants*] CAPELL; *not in* F   212 lady—] THEOBALD (Ladie. F)

196 **Some mollification for** either (a)
please pacify or (b) I have quietened
[your giant]
giant A joke about Maria's small size:
see 3.2.62 and note. Giants also
guarded ladies in myth and romance.

197 **Tell me your mind, I am a messenger**
Warburton, followed by many editors,
gives *Tell me your mind* to Olivia, implying that she, irritated at Viola's
sharp handling of Maria, tells her to
get on with what she has to say. Viola
replies that she is only a messenger. F
may be defended: Viola modulates
from coping with Maria to Olivia herself, and asks for her opinion, which
she will then relay as a *messenger* to
Orsino. The difficulty is that she hasn't
yet had the chance to communicate
any message from Orsino for Olivia to
tell her *mind* about (unless it is assumed that Viola's having come from
Orsino in itself makes the message obvious). Moreover, Olivia's next line

clearly indicates that she expects to
hear a message from Viola, not to give
her one. Warburton's arrangement
works well in performance.
messenger i.e. from Orsino. Olivia pretends to understand her to mean
King's messenger, or messenger-at-
arms, employed on important state
affairs, including apprehending state
prisoners (*OED* 3).

199 **courtesy** preamble, preliminary meeting

200 **overture** declaration

201 **taxation of homage** demand for dues
paid to a superior lord
olive olive branch (symbol of peace)

202 **matter** substance, meaning

206 **entertainment** reception

208 **divinity** religious discourse. The
terms in which their exchange is
couched move from the theatrical to
the theological: *profanation, text, doctrine, chapter, heresy* (208–22).

211 **text** theme (as if for a sermon)

OLIVIA A comfortable doctrine, and much may be said of
  it. Where lies your text?
VIOLA In Orsino's bosom.   215
OLIVIA In his bosom? In what chapter of his bosom?
VIOLA To answer by the method, in the first of his heart.
OLIVIA O, I have read it, it is heresy. Have you no more to
  say?
VIOLA Good madam, let me see your face.   220
OLIVIA Have you any commission from your lord to nego-
  tiate with my face? You are now out of your text. But
  we will draw the curtain and show you the picture.
        She unveils
  Look you sir, such a one I was this present. Is't not well
  done?   225
VIOLA Excellently done, if God did all.
OLIVIA 'Tis in grain sir, 'twill endure wind and weather.
VIOLA
  'Tis beauty truly blent, whose red and white
  Nature's own sweet and cunning hand laid on.
  Lady, you are the cruell'st she alive   230
  If you will lead these graces to the grave

223.1 *She unveils*] ROWE (*unveiling*); *not in* F

213 **comfortable** full of religious comfort.
  Compare *Romeo* 5.3.148: 'O comfortable friar'.
216 **chapter** (as of the Bible)
217 **by the method** in the same style
222 **out of your text** straying from your
  theme
223 **curtain** i.e. her veil, which she put
  on at l. 158
223–4 **picture . . . this present** Portraits
  usually gave the year in which they
  were painted. *This present* was a formal
  phrase used to date letters: it supports
  the mock-solemnity with which Olivia
  unveils.
226 **Excellently done . . . did all** Presumably Viola, struck by her rival's
  beauty, characteristically begins by
  giving Olivia her due, but cannot resist
  adding a witty quip.
    if God did all i.e. if the beauty is natu-
  ral, not the result of make-up

227 **'Tis in grain** the dye is fast. Olivia is
  quick to answer Viola's witty mockery
  in its own vein.
228 **truly blent** genuinely blended. Presumably Viola is apologizing for her jibe
  with a candid, lyrical description of
  Olivia's beauty.
    red and white A standard description
  of female beauty. Compare *LLL* 1.2.87:
  'My love is most immaculate white
  and red.'
229 **cunning** skilful
230 **she** lady
231 **lead . . . to the grave** *Graces* means
  physical beauties. But the phrase as a
  whole seems to allude to the traditional roles of the god Mercury, who
  was the leader both of the Graces (per-
  sonifications of Beauty, Chastity, and
  Sensuality) and of dead souls to the
  underworld. Cornutus, a first-century
  Stoic philosopher, says in his *Compen-*

And leave the world no copy.

OLIVIA O sir, I will not be so hard-hearted. I will give out
divers schedules of my beauty. It shall be inventoried
and every particle and utensil labelled to my will, as,   235
item, two lips, indifferent red; *item*, two grey eyes, with
lids to them; *item*, one neck, one chin, and so forth.
Were you sent hither to praise me?

VIOLA

I see you what you are, you are too proud,
But if you were the devil, you are fair.   240
My lord and master loves you. O, such love
Could be but recompensed though you were crowned
The nonpareil of beauty.

OLIVIA   How does he love me?

VIOLA

With adorations, fertile tears,
With groans that thunder love, with sighs of fire.   245

OLIVIA

Your lord does know my mind, I cannot love him.

dium of Greek Theology, 916: 'they have
handed it down that Hermes [i.e. Mer-
cury] is [the Graces'] leader'; his contemporary Seneca (*De Beneficiis* 1.3.7)
also associates Mercury with the
Graces. See Edgar Wind, *Pagan Mys-
teries in the Renaissance* (revised edn.,
1967, p. 121). At l. 92 of this scene,
Feste invested Olivia with one of Mercury's attributes; this line may associ-
ate her with others.

232 **copy** Viola means a child; Olivia
takes her to mean a list. Lines 231–2
summarize the main preoccupation of
the first seventeen Sonnets, which
urge the youth to marry and so ensure
a *copy* of himself.

234 **divers schedules** a number of inven-
tories
inventoried listed (pronounced '*invent*
ried'—three syllables, stressed on the
first, as the scansion at *Cymbeline*
2.2.30 makes clear: 'Would testify t'
enrich mine inventory')

235 **particle ... my will** single part and
household implement appended, as a
codicil to my will (legal terms, picking
up Viola's *leave* in l. 232 as meaning

'leave in a will')

236 **item** (Latin, meaning 'likewise', used
to introduce each new article in a formal list or document)
indifferent moderately

237 **lids** eye-lids (perhaps in an inventory
involving *utensils*, with a pun on pot-
lids)

238 **praise** appraise, evaluate (referring
back to the list)

239–40 **proud ... devil** The first sin of Lu-
cifer, the devil, was pride. Marlowe's
Doctor Faustus refers to 'aspiring pride
and insolence, | For which God threw
him from the face of heaven' (A text,
Revels edn. (1993), 1.3.69–70).

240 **if** even if

242 **be but recompensed though** only be
requited even if

243 **The nonpareil of beauty** an un-
equalled beauty

244 This is a four-foot line (unless *adorations* is trisyllabic), but not metrically
defective. Compare 1.2.19, 3.1.108,
3.3.15, 3.4.10, 4.1.25, 4.3.28,
5.1.374. Perhaps Viola pauses in mid-
line so as to give Orsino's *adorations* as
much weight as possible.
fertile abundant

Yet I suppose him virtuous, know him noble,
Of great estate, of fresh and stainless youth,
In voices well divulged, free, learn'd, and valiant,
And in dimension and the shape of nature   250
A gracious person; but yet I cannot love him.
He might have took his answer long ago.

VIOLA

If I did love you in my master's flame,
With such a suff'ring, such a deadly life,
In your denial I would find no sense,   255
I would not understand it.

OLIVIA   Why, what would you?

VIOLA

Make me a willow cabin at your gate
And call upon my soul within the house,
Write loyal cantons of contemnèd love,
And sing them loud even in the dead of night;   260
Halloo your name to the reverberate hills,
And make the babbling gossip of the air
Cry out 'Olivia!' O, you should not rest
Between the elements of air and earth
But you should pity me.   265

261 Halloo] F (Hallow)

249 **In voices well divulged** praised in the general opinion
  free magnanimous, generous, well bred
250 **dimension . . . shape of nature** Both mean 'bodily form'.
251 **gracious** graceful, pleasing
253 **my master's flame** with Orsino's passion
254 **deadly** death-like
257–65 For a discussion of this speech, see Introduction, p. 32.
257 **willow** emblem of rejected love. *OED sb.* 1d and 6d gives numerous examples.
  willow cabin small shelter or arbour, formed from willow branches
258 **my soul** i.e. Olivia
259 **cantons** songs. A variant form of 'canto', verse, perhaps from a confusion of the Italian words *canto* and *canzone*, both meaning 'song'.
  contemnèd despised (*OED ppl. a.*)

261 **Halloo** shout
  reverberate echoing
262 **babbling gossip** The nymph Echo, who wasted away to a mere voice repeating whatever she heard spoken (Ovid, *Metamorphoses* 3. 359–401). Samuel Daniel makes use of the myth in the ode that concludes his sonnet-sequence *Delia* (1592), which Shakespeare also seems to have in mind at 1.1.19–21 and 2.4.37–40: 'Echo, daughter of the air, | Babbling guest of rocks and hills' (13–14).
265–7 **But you should . . . parentage** Three broken verse lines; either the first two or the last two could form a complete verse line. Perhaps Olivia, entranced by the power of Viola's speech, says *You might do much* at once, completing Viola's line; or perhaps there is a pause after *pity me*, indicating Olivia's absorption in a different way,

OLIVIA You might do much.
  What is your parentage?
VIOLA
  Above my fortunes, yet my state is well.
  I am a gentleman.
OLIVIA   Get you to your lord.
  I cannot love him. Let him send no more,   270
  Unless, perchance, you come to me again
  To tell me how he takes it. Fare you well.
  I thank you for your pains. (*Offering a purse*) Spend
    this for me.
VIOLA
  I am no fee'd post, lady, keep your purse.
  My master, not myself, lacks recompense.   275
  Love make his heart of flint that you shall love,
  And let your fervour like my master's be
  Placed in contempt. Farewell, fair cruelty.   *Exit*
OLIVIA 'What is your parentage?'
  'Above my fortunes, yet my state is well.   280
  I am a gentleman.' I'll be sworn thou art.
  Thy tongue, thy face, thy limbs, actions, and spirit
  Do give thee five-fold blazon. Not too fast. Soft, soft—
  Unless the master were the man. How now?
  Even so quickly may one catch the plague?   285

---

273 *Offering a purse*] COLLIER 1858 (*offering money*); *not in* F

with Olivia's two sentences forming one
verse line. Or maybe the three broken
lines are intentional, with a second pause
after *You might do much*, before Olivia
asks *What is your parentage?* This would
help to emphasize the significance of the
question, for Olivia is actually asking if
Viola/Cesario is of the rank to qualify
as a potential husband, and thus unmistakably expressing her interest in
'Cesario' for the first time. These broken
lines may also be what Viola refers to
later when she says that Olivia spoke
in starts, distractedly (2.2.21).

268 **fortunes** as a servant
  state social status
274 **fee'd post** hired messenger (wanting

a tip)
276 **Love** i.e. may the god of love (Cupid)
  his . . . love i.e. of the man whom you
  shall love
283 **blazon** (formal description of) armor-
  ial bearings (which only a gentleman
  could display): a heraldic term
284 **the master were the man** i.e. Orsino
  were Cesario
  man servant
285 **catch the plague** i.e. fall in love. Compare *LLL* 5.2.421: 'They have the
  plague, and caught it of your eyes.'
  But the choice of this phrase to say
  'How quickly one can fall in love'
  again introduces the sombre overtone
  of the ever-threatening plague into the
  play (see 1.1.19 and note).

Methinks I feel this youth's perfections
With an invisible and subtle stealth
To creep in at mine eyes. Well, let it be.
What ho, Malvolio.

    Enter Malvolio

MALVOLIO   Here madam, at your service.

OLIVIA

Run after that same peevish messenger   290
The County's man. He left this ring behind him,
Would I or not. Tell him I'll none of it.
Desire him not to flatter with his lord,
Nor hold him up with hopes, I am not for him.
If that the youth will come this way tomorrow,   295
I'll give him reasons for't. Hie thee, Malvolio.

MALVOLIO   Madam, I will.   *Exit at one door*

OLIVIA

I do I know not what, and fear to find
Mine eye too great a flatterer for my mind.
Fate, show thy force, ourselves we do not owe.   300
What is decreed must be; and be this so.

                    Exit at another door

2.1   *Enter Antonio and Sebastian*

ANTONIO   Will you stay no longer, nor will you not that I
go with you?

---

291 County's] CAPELL, *after* F (Countes)   297 *at one door*] OXFORD; *not in* F   301.1 *Exit at another door*] OXFORD; ROWE (*Exit*); *Finis, Actus primus.* F

---

286 **perfections** (four syllables)
291 **County** An alternative form of 'Count' (i.e. Orsino).
292 **Would I** whether I wished it
293–4 **flatter with … hold him up** encourage (synonym)
296 **Hie** hasten
297, 301.1 *at one door … at another door* The standard Elizabethan terms for separate entries (though here editorial) derived from the two doors set into the back wall on either side of the stage.
299 **too great a flatterer for** an over-praiser of Cesario to
300 **owe** own
301 **What is decreed must be** A proverbial

expression—'what must be must be' (Tilley M1331)—much used in the drama of the period. Compare *Dr Faustus*: 'What doctrine call you this, *Che serà, serà,* | What will be, shall be?' (A text, 1.1.49–50), and *Romeo* 4.1.21: 'What must be shall be. | That's a certain text.'
2.1 This scene differs markedly from the apparently parallel one between Viola and the Captain (1.2). It is in prose, not verse, and it apparently takes place some while after the shipwreck, not immediately after (see Introduction, pp. 39–42, for a fuller discussion).
1 **nor will you not that I** do you not wish

SEBASTIAN By your patience, no. My stars shine darkly
over me. The malignancy of my fate might perhaps distemper yours, therefore I shall crave of you your leave   5
that I may bear my evils alone. It were a bad recompense for your love to lay any of them on you.

ANTONIO Let me yet know of you whither you are bound.

SEBASTIAN No, sooth, sir. My determinate voyage is mere
extravagancy. But I perceive in you so excellent a touch   10
of modesty that you will not extort from me what I am
willing to keep in. Therefore it charges me in manners
the rather to express myself. You must know of me
then, Antonio, my name is Sebastian, which I called
Roderigo. My father was that Sebastian of Messaline   15
whom I know you have heard of. He left behind him
myself and a sister, both born in an hour. If the heavens
had been pleased, would we had so ended. But you, sir,
altered that, for some hour before you took me from the
breach of the sea was my sister drowned.   20

ANTONIO Alas the day!

SEBASTIAN A lady, sir, though it was said she much resembled me, was yet of many accounted beautiful. But
though I could not with such estimable wonder over-far
believe that, yet thus far I will boldly publish her: she   25

---

me to. The *nor . . . not* construction is
a typical Elizabethan double negative
(Abbott 406).

3 **darkly** forebodingly, unfavourably

4 **malignancy** evil influence. An astrological term, like *stars* in the previous
line and *distemper* in the next.

4–5 **distemper** infect

6 **evils** ills, misfortunes

9 **sooth** (in) truth
    determinate planned

9–10 **mere extravagancy** nothing but
wandering. This use of *extravagancy*
appears to be peculiar to Shakespeare,
who also uses it at *Hamlet* 1.1.135
('Th' extravagant and erring spirit')
and *Othello* 1.1.138–9: 'an extravag-
ant and wheeling stranger | Of here
and everywhere'—an expression also
used by Sebastian at 5.1.222.

11 **modesty** politeness

11–12 **am willing** wish

12 **charges me** is incumbent upon me
    in manners in good manners

13 **express** reveal

14–15 **which . . . Roderigo** See Introduction, p. 42, for a discussion of this
subterfuge.

15 **Messaline** A Shakespearian invention,
perhaps suggested by a phrase in Plautus' *Menaechmi*, the main source of *The
Comedy of Errors*, where 'Massilians'
and Illyrians are mentioned together:
'Massiliensis, Hilurios' (l. 235). See L.
G. Salingar, 'The Design of *Twelfth
Night*', *SQ* 9 (1958), 117–39, Appendix c.

17 **in an** within the same

19 **some hour** an hour or so (Abbott 21)

20 **breach** breaking waves, surf: 'hence
the nautical phrase *clean, clear breach*'
(*OED sb.* 2)

24 **estimable wonder** esteem and wonder

25 **publish** speak openly of

bore a mind that envy could not but call fair. She is
drowned already, sir, with salt water, though I seem to
drown her remembrance again with more.

ANTONIO Pardon me, sir, your bad entertainment.

SEBASTIAN O good Antonio, forgive me your trouble.   30

ANTONIO If you will not murder me for my love, let me be
your servant.

SEBASTIAN If you will not undo what you have done—
that is, kill him whom you have recovered—desire it
not. Fare ye well at once, my bosom is full of kindness,   35
and I am yet so near the manners of my mother that
upon the least occasion more mine eyes will tell tales of
me. I am bound to the Count Orsino's court, farewell.
                                                     ⌈*Exit*⌉

ANTONIO
The gentleness of all the gods go with thee!
I have many enemies in Orsino's court,   40
Else would I very shortly see thee there.
But come what may, I do adore thee so
That danger shall seem sport, and I will go.   *Exit*

2.2   *Enter Viola as Cesario, and Malvolio, at several doors*

MALVOLIO Were not you ev'n now with the Countess
Olivia?

2.2.0.1 *as Cesario*] OXFORD; *not in* F

---

26 **envy** malice (or, as now, jealousy):
even the malicious or the jealous
would give Viola her due
28 **more** more salt water, i.e. tears
29 **bad entertainment** i.e. hospitality unworthy of the son of *Sebastian of Messaline*
31 **murder me** (by insisting that we part)
34 **recovered** rescued
35 **kindness** tenderness
36 **yet** still
manners of my mother i.e. womanish
readiness to weep
37–8 **tell tales of me** betray my feelings
39 **gentleness** favour
2.2.0.1 At first sight it seems odd that
Malvolio, who has been sent to *run
after* Viola, should enter at a different

(*several*) door. It might seem too novel-
istic to suggest that Malvolio takes a
short cut and is thus able suddenly to
confront Viola, who has come on a
moderate pace from Olivia's house. But
F's direction may contain concealed
'business', suggested in Peter Hall's
stagings. If Malvolio enters, hurried
and breathless, seeing *Sebastian* depart-
ing in the distance (2.1.38), and then
Viola enters at another entry, this provides Malvolio with the opportunity for
a 'double-take' ('Am I seeing things?').
At any rate, there is a theatrical ra-
tionale for F's *several doors*.

1 **ev'n** (even) just. F's clipped form may
suggest a breathless Malvolio (contrasted with the full form in l. 3 from

VIOLA Even now, sir, on a moderate pace, I have since
arrived but hither.

MALVOLIO (*offering a ring*) She returns this ring to you, sir.   5
You might have saved me my pains to have taken it
away yourself. She adds, moreover, that you should put
your lord into a desperate assurance she will none of
him. And one thing more: that you be never so hardy to
come again in his affairs, unless it be to report your   10
lord's taking of this. Receive it so.

VIOLA

She took the ring of me, I'll none of it.

MALVOLIO Come sir, you peevishly threw it to her, and
her will is it should be so returned.

He throws the ring down

If it be worth stooping for, there it lies, in your eye; if   15
not, be it his that finds it.   *Exit*

VIOLA (*picking up the ring*)

I left no ring with her. What means this lady?
Fortune forbid my outside have not charmed her.
She made good view of me, indeed so much
That straight methought her eyes had lost her tongue,   20
For she did speak in starts, distractedly.

---

5 *offering a ring*] OXFORD; *not in* F   12 the] F; no DYCE 1866 (*conj.* Malone)   14.1 *He throws the ring down*] OXFORD; *not in* F   17 *picking up the ring*] OXFORD; *not in* F   20 straight] OXFORD (*conj.* G. R. Proudfoot); *not in* F1; sure F2

a Viola who has proceeded *on a moderate pace*) or perhaps a puritanical mannerism.

3 **on** at (Abbott 180)
4 **but hither** only this far
6 **to have taken** by taking
8 **desperate assurance** certainty of hopelessness
  will none of will have nothing to do with
9 **hardy** bold. Not otherwise used in this sense by Shakespeare, although *Richard II* 1.3.42–3 has 'no person be so bold | Or daring-hardy as to touch the lists'.
11 **taking of this** reception of this message
12 **of me** from me
14 **so** i.e. thrown
15 **eye** sight, view. Compare *Hamlet* 4.4.6:

'We shall express our duty in his eye'.
18 **outside** appearance
   charmed enchanted, captivated
19 **made good view of** looked carefully at
20 **straight** at once. Oxford's emendation makes the line regular (*Re-Editing*, pp. 50–1). F might be defended as a four-foot line with an extra initial unstressed syllable.
   lost made her lose
21 **in starts** in broken phrases, or sudden bursts (*OED sb.*² 4e). Compare modern 'in fits and starts'.
   distractedly as if she were mad. A strong expression that implies more than simply 'disjointedly', and one of a number of phrases equating love with madness: compare 3.4.14–15, 4.3.14–16, 5.1.62, and increasingly during the final scene.

She loves me sure, the cunning of her passion
Invites me in this churlish messenger.
None of my lord's ring! Why, he sent her none.
I am the man. If it be so—as 'tis—   25
Poor lady, she were better love a dream!
Disguise, I see thou art a wickedness
Wherein the pregnant enemy does much.
How easy is it for the proper false
In women's waxen hearts to set their forms!   30
Alas, our frailty is the cause, not we,
For such as we are made of, such we be.
How will this fadge? My master loves her dearly,
And I, poor monster, fond as much on him,
And she, mistaken, seems to dote on me.   35
What will become of this? As I am man,
My state is desperate for my master's love.
As I am woman, now alas the day,
What thriftless sighs shall poor Olivia breathe!
O time, thou must untangle this, not I.   40
It is too hard a knot for me t'untie.   *Exit*

31 our] F2; O F1   32 made of,] RANN (*conj.* Thirlby, Tyrwhitt *independently*); made, if
F   41 *Exit*] ROWE; *not in* F

22 **cunning** craftiness
23 **in** by means of
25 **the man** the object of her love
28 **pregnant enemy** an enemy who is re-
    sourceful, always ready (*OED, preg-
    nant, a.*² 3d) to take advantage. See
    note to 3.1.87.
29 **proper false** attractive but deceitful
    (men). The use of one part of speech
    for another (the adjective *false* for
    the noun) is characteristically Shake-
    spearian.
30 **In women's waxen hearts to set their
    forms** to impress their appearance on
    women's affections (as a seal makes its
    image in wax)
32 **such as we are made of, such we be**

i.e. being made of frail flesh, we are
frail. Compare *Hamlet* 1.2.146: 'frailty,
thy name is woman'.
33 **fadge** turn out (*OED v.* 4)
34 **monster** (since in her disguise she is
    both man and woman)
    fond dote. This verb seems to have
    been growing obsolete even in Shakes-
    peare's time; this is the last of the four
    examples given at *OED v.* 2.
36–7 **As I am man ... master's love** Since
    I am disguised as a man, my love for
    my master is hopeless.
37 **state** condition
    desperate hopeless
39 **thriftless** unprofitable

2.3   *Enter Sir Toby and Sir Andrew*

SIR TOBY Approach, Sir Andrew. Not to be abed after midnight is to be up betimes, and *diluculo surgere*, thou know'st.

SIR ANDREW Nay, by my troth, I know not; but I know to be up late is to be up late.   5

SIR TOBY A false conclusion. I hate it as an unfilled can. To be up after midnight and to go to bed then is early; so that to go to bed after midnight is to go to bed betimes. Does not our lives consist of the four elements?

SIR ANDREW Faith, so they say, but I think it rather consists of eating and drinking.   10

SIR TOBY Thou'rt a scholar; let us therefore eat and drink. Marian, I say, a stoup of wine.

Enter Feste the clown

SIR ANDREW Here comes the fool, i'faith.

FESTE How now, my hearts. Did you never see the picture   15
of 'we three'?

SIR TOBY Welcome, ass. Now let's have a catch.

2.3.9 lives] F; life ROWE 1714   13.1 *Feste the*] *not in* F

2.3 This was formerly known as 'the kitchen scene' because it was traditionally staged there. Two influential productions departed from this tradition: Harley Granville Barker at the Savoy Theatre, London, in 1912 set the scene in a small tapestried room (see fig. 4), and Peter Hall 'in a glowing Warwickshire walled garden' (Roy Walker, 'The Whirligig of Time', *SS* 12 (Cambridge, 1959), p. 128). But traditions die hard. Reviewing the following Stratford production, Hugh Leonard missed 'beamed ceilings ... with the firelight glinting on pewter' (*Plays and Players*, August 1966, p. 16); and the traditional setting resurfaced at Stratford in 1991, with Toby and Andrew clanging saucepans to add to the general racket.

2 **betimes** early
   diluculo surgere part of a Latin proverb, *Diluculo surgere saluberrimum est* ('to get up at dawn is most healthy'). Since it occurs in William Lily's *A Short Introduction of Grammar* (1567 edn., C5), which was used in Elizabethan schools, Sir Andrew's ignorance in the next line (*I know not*) is the more evident. F's spelling '*Deliculo*' may be Shakespeare's slip, or the printer's, or Sir Toby's, his speech slurred by drink.

6 **can** metal mug, tankard

9 **four elements** earth, air, fire, and water

13 **Marian** Originally a diminutive of Mary (of which *Maria* is the Latin form).
   stoup two-pint (one litre) tankard

15–16 **picture of 'we three'** A caption to a trick picture showing two fools' or asses' heads; the third was the viewer. See fig. 10. Sir Toby's reply *Welcome, ass* suggests that he is thinking of the asses version. John Barton's 1969 RSC production offered another interpretation: Feste covered his eyes, Toby his ears, Andrew his mouth, as in the traditional emblem of the three monkeys: 'See no evil, hear no evil, speak no evil.'

17 **catch** a round, a popular song sung in canon

SIR ANDREW By my troth, the fool has an excellent breast.
I had rather than forty shillings I had such a leg, and so
sweet a breath to sing, as the fool has. In sooth, thou   20
wast in very gracious fooling last night, when thou
spok'st of Pigrogromitus, of the Vapians passing the
equinoctial of Queubus. 'Twas very good, i'faith. I sent
thee sixpence for thy leman, hadst it?

FESTE I did impeticos thy gratility; for Malvolio's nose is   25
no whipstock. My lady has a white hand, and the
Myrmidons are no bottle-ale houses.

SIR ANDREW Excellent! Why, this is the best fooling, when
all is done. Now a song.

SIR TOBY *(to Feste)* Come on, there is sixpence for you.   30
Let's have a song.

---

18 **breast** singing voice, i.e. coming from
'the place where the lungs are situated' (*OED* 6, which cites other examples in 1547, 1553, and 1621, so the term was an accepted if not common one)

19 **leg** either (a) leg for dancing or (b) bow preceding his song

22–3 **Pigrogromitus ... Vapians ... Queubus** Probably examples of Feste's mock-learning. Hotson attempts to make them yield some meaning: *Pigrogromitus* 'seems to be compounded of the Italian for *lazy* and *scab* or *scurf* .... A *Va-pian* should be an Easy-goer ... from *Chi va pian piano va lontano*: "Fair and softly goes far in a day". And ... the Equinoctial or Equator of *Cubus* ... in Plato's cosmology, is the Earth' (p. 157). But perhaps the joke is simply that Sir Andrew is solemnly repeating Feste's gibberish as if it had meaning; or perhaps he is distorting, through drunkenness or ignorance, what Feste said (*Queubus* being a corruption of *Cubus*, for example).

24 **sixpence** Until the introduction of decimal currency to England in 1971, a *sixpence* was a single coin, often used as a tip (compare *Dream* 4.2.18–22). With the revaluation of a penny in 1971, the sixpenny coin disappeared, and *sixpence* has therefore lost its traditional connotation.

leman girlfriend (from Early Middle English *leofmon*, 'dear one')

25 **impeticos** A burlesque word, meaning 'impocket', also suggesting 'petticoat', a long, skirted robe worn by fools (i.e. Feste pocketed the money).
gratility for 'gratuity' (another burlesque word)

25–7 **Malvolio's nose ... houses** Feste leads his listeners to expect insult, revelation, and recondite information, and then deflates expectation by stating the obvious.

27 **Myrmidons** In Greek myth, and in *Troilus*, they are Achilles' bodyguard. Shakespeare's audience may have heard a pun on 'Mermaid Inns'. There was a Mermaid Tavern in Bread Street, London, known to Shakespeare since its landlord was involved in his purchase of the Blackfriars Gatehouse in 1613. (See S. Schoenbaum, *William Shakespeare: A Documentary Life* (Oxford, 1975), pp. 208, 223.)

27 **bottle-ale houses** low taverns, perhaps contrasted with the Mermaid Tavern—see previous note; or perhaps off-licences. *Bottle-ale* seems to have been an inferior kind of ale; it is used as a term of abuse at *2 Henry IV* 2.4.127: 'you bottle-ale rascal'.

28–9 **when all is done** Proverbial: 'when all is said and done' (Dent A211.1).

SIR ANDREW *(to Feste)* There's a testril of me too. If one
  knight give a—
FESTE Would you have a love-song, or a song of good life?
SIR TOBY A love-song, a love-song.   35
SIR ANDREW Ay, ay. I care not for good life.
FESTE *(sings)*
      O mistress mine, where are you roaming?
      O stay and hear, your true love's coming,
        That can sing both high and low.
      Trip no further, pretty sweeting.   40
      Journeys end in lovers meeting,
        Every wise man's son doth know.
SIR ANDREW Excellent good, i'faith.
SIR TOBY Good, good.
FESTE What is love? 'Tis not hereafter,   45
      Present mirth hath present laughter.
        What's to come is still unsure.
      In delay there lies no plenty,
      Then come kiss me, sweet and twenty.
        Youth's a stuff will not endure.   50

---

33 give a—] F2; giue a‿ F1   37 FESTE *(sings)*] F *(Clowne sings.)*

---

32 **testril** a sixpenny coin. The only
known instance before 1905 of this
corruption of 'teston' or 'testoon', originally a shilling of the reign of Henry
VIII which had gradually declined in
value by 1601. The reward may seem
paltry; but in 1587 the standard wage
for a linen weaver was sixpence a day
with meat and drink, or ten pence
without (Sandra K. Fischer, *Econolin-
gua, A Glossary of Coins and Economic
Language in Renaissance Drama* (Dela-
ware, 1985), p. 154).

33 **give a** In F, this comes at the end of
a justified line, so perhaps there has
been an accidental omission; or perhaps Sir Andrew lapses into inarticu-
lacy; or perhaps Feste interrupts him,
in order to get on with the song.

34, 36 **song of good life** drinking song;
Andrew understands him to mean a
moral song, or even a hymn.

37–50 The words of Feste's song, as of his
other songs, are not certainly by
Shakespeare. For a full discussion, see
Appendix.

39 **high and low** (in either volume or
pitch)

40 **Trip** i.e. go
  sweeting darling

42 **wise man's son** Wise men were
thought to have foolish sons (*ODEP* M
421, p. 900).

45 **hereafter** in the future

47 **still** always

48 **plenty** profit; perhaps related to the
proverb 'Delay in love is dangerous'
(Tilley D196)

49 **sweet and twenty** Either the whole
phrase is an endearment ('You lovely
twenty-year-old') as in *The Life and
Death of the Merry Devil of Edmonton*
(not the anonymous play but a collection of stories by Thomas Brewer,
1631): 'his little wanton wagtails, his
sweet and twenties'; or *and twenty* is

SIR ANDREW   A mellifluous voice, as I am true knight.

SIR TOBY   A contagious breath.

SIR ANDREW   Very sweet and contagious, i'faith.

SIR TOBY   To hear by the nose, it is dulcet in contagion. But
shall we make the welkin dance indeed? Shall we rouse   55
the night-owl in a catch that will draw three souls out
of one weaver? Shall we do that?

SIR ANDREW   An you love me, let's do't. I am dog at a
catch.

FESTE   By'r Lady, sir, and some dogs will catch well.   60

SIR ANDREW   Most certain. Let our catch be 'Thou knave'.

FESTE   'Hold thy peace, thou knave', knight. I shall be
constrained in't to call thee knave, knight.

SIR ANDREW   'Tis not the first time I have constrained one
to call me knave. Begin, fool. It begins 'Hold thy peace'.   65

FESTE   I shall never begin if I hold my peace.

SIR ANDREW   Good, i'faith. Come, begin.

> *They sing the catch.*
> *Enter Maria*

MARIA   What a caterwauling do you keep here! If my lady

67.1 *They sing the catch*] *Catch sung* F

---

an intensive ('twenty-times sweet') as at *Merry Wives* 2.1.185–6: 'Good even and twenty, good Master Page'.

52 **contagious** It is *contagious* because like an illness the tune is something you catch (compare modern 'catchy')— also relating to the sung *catch* which has been on Toby's mind from the start of the scene (l. 17).

54 **by the nose** by breathing infected air. Like *dulcet* (sweet) *in contagion*, this carries on the joke about catching the song like an illness.

55 **welkin** sky, heavenly bodies. See note to 3.1.57.

56–7 **draw three souls out of one weaver** Weavers were traditionally addicted to psalm-singing, so to move them with popular catches would be a great triumph. Music was thought to affect the soul in this way (compare *Much Ado* 2.3.58–9, where music is said to 'hale souls out of men's bodies'). The *three* singers would have thrice the

usual effect.

58 **dog at** good at. Proverbial: 'be old dog at it' (Tilley D506). At *Two Gentlemen* 4.4.13, Lance varies the phrase to '*a* dog at all things', in order to apply it to the real dog on stage with him; and Feste also applies it to literal dogs in his reply, where *some dogs will catch well* may mean that they will bite, or simply catch things like balls in their mouths.

60 **By'r Lady** by Our Lady, i.e. the Virgin Mary (a mild oath)

61 **'Thou knave'** The words of the catch are 'Hold thy peace, thou knave', so each singer repeatedly calls the others knaves, and tells them to stop singing.

64 **constrained** caused, compelled

67.1 *They sing* The singers start one after another, repeating the song vigorously and boisterously until Maria interrupts. For the tune, see Appendix.

68 **caterwauling** a noise like the cry of cats at mating-time

68–70 **If my lady … doors** Perhaps Olivia has done just that, so that Malvolio is

have not called up her steward Malvolio and bid him
turn you out of doors, never trust me.   70
SIR TOBY My lady's a Cathayan, we are politicians, Malvo-
lio's a Peg-o'-Ramsey, and 'Three merry men be we'.
Am not I consanguineous? Am I not of her blood? Tilly-
vally, lady! 'There dwelt a man in Babylon, lady, lady.'

71 Cathayan] F (*Catayan*)

representing, and exaggerating, her
message (see particularly ll. 89–94);
but he probably needs no prompting
to be officious.

71–2 **My lady's ... be we** Sir Toby is contrasting the revellers first with Olivia,
and then with Malvolio, but in different ways. See the following notes.

71 **Cathayan** This is usually taken to
mean 'Chinese' (inhabitant of Cathay)
and to be an insult, as at *Merry Wives*
2.1.136–7: 'I will not believe such a
Cathayan though the priest o'th' town
commended him for a true man.' Gus-
tav Ungerer, however, argues that the
Elizabethans saw Chinese as noble sav-
ages (' "My Lady's a *Catayan*", SS 32
(Cambridge, 1979), 85–104). Insult or
not, the Chinese comparison is point-
less. *Cathayan* may not in fact mean
'Chinese', but be Sir Toby's slurred
version of 'Catharan'. The word derived
from medieval Latin *Cathari*, 'the
pure', and was applied to puritans,
for example by Archbishop Whitgift,
'Puritans or Catharans' (1574), cited by
OED. This would fit Sir Toby's speech
very well: 'My lady is an extreme,
rigid moralist, whereas we are flexible
politicians' (see the next note). It also,
incidentally, fits the *Merry Wives* context equally well, the parish priest
vouching for a member of an extreme
sect as a 'true man' or true believer.
politicians devious intriguers. Compare
Hamlet 5.1.78–9: 'a politician ... that
would circumvent God'. Sir Toby implies that they can keep on the right
side of Olivia.

72 **Peg-o'-Ramsey** the title of a popular
song. Ungerer (see note to l. 71) quotes
enough of its words to make clear that
Sir Toby compares Malvolio to a lewd,
incontinent woman (for similar com-

parisons, see 2.5.38, and perhaps
2.5.109, and notes). Toby may also
imply that Malvolio's extreme beliefs
are fake, whereas Olivia's are not; but
the main contrast is between a lewd
effeminate and good chaps like us
(*Three merry men*).

72 **'Three merry men be we'** This popular refrain occurs in various contexts.
The earliest comes in Peele's *Old Wives
Tale* (published 1595), ll. 19–24,
where it is called an 'old proverb'; but
Shakespeare may be recalling a different version which contrasts *merry men*
(or in yet other versions 'boys') with
'wise men' (like Malvolio?) Both versions are given in the Appendix.

72, 74, 79 **Three merry men ... There
dwelt a man ... O' the twelfth day** This
edition assumes that the actors sing
only the quoted phrases (and therefore
supplies only the relevant music in the
Appendix) rather than taking them as
cues to reconstruct *in extenso* the popular
songs from which they come, as in John
Barton's 1969–71 production. To do the
latter unduly prolongs the scene and
alters its rhythm and balance; simply to
sing the quoted phrases demonstrates
how quickly and economically Shakespeare establishes the drinking party.

73 **consanguineous** closely related (to Olivia), as he goes on to explain in *of her
blood*. It is a word that is usefully tricky
for a drunk to pronounce.

73–4 **Tilly-vally** nonsense, 'fiddlesticks'

74 **lady** Perhaps *lady* refers to Olivia—
'You talk of "my lady"!'—or, mockingly, to Maria herself.
'There dwelt ... lady, lady' The opening and the refrain of a song about
Susannah and the Elders, also quoted
by Sir Hugh Evans in the 'bad' Quarto
of *Merry Wives* (1602), D2 verso. See
Appendix for the music.

FESTE Beshrew me, the knight's in admirable fooling. 75
SIR ANDREW Ay, he does well enough if he be disposed,
    and so do I too. He does it with a better grace, but I do it
    more natural.
SIR TOBY
    'O' the twelfth day of December'—
MARIA For the love o' God, peace. 80
      Enter Malvolio
MALVOLIO My masters, are you mad? Or what are you?
    Have you no wit, manners, nor honesty, but to gabble
    like tinkers at this time of night? Do ye make an ale-
    house of my lady's house, that ye squeak out your
    coziers' catches without any mitigation or remorse of 85
    voice? Is there no respect of place, persons, nor time in
    you?
SIR TOBY We did keep time, sir, in our catches. Sneck up!
MALVOLIO Sir Toby, I must be round with you. My lady
    bade me tell you that though she harbours you as her 90
    kinsman she's nothing allied to your disorders. If you
    can separate yourself and your misdemeanours you are
    welcome to the house. If not, an it would please you to

---

79 O'] F (O)   93 an] F (and)

---

75 **Beshrew me** curse me (another mild oath)

78 **more natural** effortlessly (with the additional ironic sense 'more like a fool, a *natural*', the same joke as at 1.3.26)

79 **'O' the twelfth day of December'** Another allusion to a song. No music survives, unless it is the carol 'The Twelve Days of Christmas', often used in performance, since the twelfth day is of course Twelfth Night. See Appendix.

80.1 ***Enter Malvolio*** For a discussion of Malvolio's entry, see Introduction, pp. 46–7.

82 **wit** intelligence
honesty decency (*OED* 2)

82–5 **gabble like tinkers … coziers' catches** These are abusive expressions. *Tinkers* were noted for drinking and cant speech: *OED sb.* 1 cites phrases like 'as drunk' or 'as quarrelsome as a tinker', adding that *tinker* was synony-

mous with 'vagrant' or 'gypsy'. Tinkers were often hanged by puritan town councils (see Hotson, p. 101), so this is an appropriate insult for the puritan Malvolio to use. *Coziers* means 'cobblers', adapted from Old French *cousere*, seamster; they sang at their work.

85 **mitigation or remorse** considerate lowering

88 **Sneck up** *OED* takes this to mean 'go hang', glossing *sneck* as a dialect word of obscure origin (*snick*, v.^{1}); but *sneck* also means to close or fasten with a latch (a *sneck*) (*OED, sneck, v.^{1}*), so maybe Sir Toby is telling Malvolio to shut up.

89 **round** plain-spoken. Compare *Hamlet* 3.4.5: 'Pray you be round with him.'

90 **harbours** lodges, provides shelter

91 **nothing allied** in no way related (Abbott 55)

take leave of her she is very willing to bid you farewell.

SIR TOBY

   'Farewell dear heart, since I must needs be gone.'   95

MARIA Nay, good Sir Toby.

FESTE

   'His eyes do show his days are almost done.'

MALVOLIO Is't even so?

SIR TOBY

   'But I will never die.'

FESTE

   'Sir Toby, there you lie.'   100

MALVOLIO This is much credit to you.

SIR TOBY

   'Shall I bid him go?'

FESTE

   'What an if you do?'

SIR TOBY

   'Shall I bid him go, and spare not?'

FESTE

   'O no, no, no, no, you dare not.'   105

SIR TOBY Out o' tune, sir, ye lie. (*To Malvolio*) Art any
   more than a steward? Dost thou think because thou art
   virtuous there shall be no more cakes and ale?

95–105 **'Farewell . . . dare not.'** Sir Toby
and Feste adapt the words of the first
two verses of a ballad first printed in
Robert Jones's *First Book of Songs or
Airs* (1600) to fit the situation. The
relevant lines of the original are:

Farewell dear love, since thou wilt
  needs be gone.
Mine eyes do show my life is almost
  done.
   Nay, I will never die,
   So long as I can spy . . .

   Shall I bid her go?
   What an if I do?
Shall I bid her go and spare not?
O no, no, no, no, I dare not.

Shakespeare conflates these two stanzas so that they can be sung as one;

for the music, see Appendix. Malvolio's
farewell (l. 94) triggers Sir Toby's burst
of song; Feste alters 'mine eyes' of the
second line to apply to Malvolio and the
fourth to Sir Toby; then they jump to
the second verse so that Sir Toby can
raise the possibility of dismissing Malvolio and Feste can dare him to do it.

106 **Out o' tune** false. Sir Toby responds
to Feste's *you dare not* by snubbing
Malvolio as a mere servant. For the
figurative usage, compare *Some Godly
Treatise* (1588): 'Your note must be . . .
justly met with. Otherwise you sing
out of tune' (cited by Dent, T598.1).

108 **cakes and ale** (associated with
church festivals, and so abhorrent to
a puritan, as would be the reference
in the next line to Saint Anne, mother
of the Virgin Mary)

FESTE Yes, by Saint Anne, and ginger shall be hot i'th'
     mouth too.   110
SIR TOBY Thou'rt i'th' right. (*To Malvolio*) Go sir, rub your
     chain with crumbs. (*To Maria*) A stoup of wine, Maria.
MALVOLIO Mistress Mary, if you prized my lady's favour at
     anything more than contempt you would not give
     means for this uncivil rule. She shall know of it, by this   115
     hand.   *Exit*
MARIA Go shake your ears.
SIR ANDREW 'Twere as good a deed as to drink when a
     man's a-hungry to challenge him the field and then to
     break promise with him, and make a fool of him.   120
SIR TOBY Do't, knight. I'll write thee a challenge, or I'll
     deliver thy indignation to him by word of mouth.
MARIA Sweet Sir Toby, be patient for tonight. Since the

---

109 **ginger** used to spice ale, and regarded
     as an aphrodisiac by, for example,
     John Gerard in his *Herbal* (1633 edi-
     tion, p. 62)
110 To give Feste an exit after this line,
     as some editors do, is unnecessary.
     Feste has no motive for leaving; and
     while he does not speak again in the
     scene, Maria's phrase *let the fool make
     a third* (ll. 161–2) does not necessarily
     imply that he is no longer present. And
     his silence may make dramatic points.
     Peter Hall's 1958 production, for in-
     stance, let Feste 'feign sleep, head on
     arm, at a table. As the others went out
     he raised his head and stared thought-
     fully after them' (Roy Walker, *SS 12*,
     p. 128): this Feste was a detached
     observer. The Feste of Hall's 1991
     version made this detachment more
     specific: after Malvolio's exit, he
     lay stretched out on a seat, and
     when Maria said *let the fool make a
     third*, he simply waved a dismissive
     hand; Fabian was clearly needed to *make
     a third* here.
111–12 **rub your chain with crumbs** i.e.
     to clean it: Sir Toby is again humilia-
     tingly reminding Malvolio of his sub-
     servient status by referring to his chain
     of office.
115 **means** i.e. drink
     uncivil rule disorderly behaviour
117 **shake your ears** i.e. like an ass. Com-

pare *Julius Caesar* 4.1.26, where
Antony proposes to unload Lepidus'
power 'Like to the empty ass, to shake
his ears'. The expression was proverbial (Tilley E16). But Stephen Dickey
('Shakespeare's Mastiff Comedy', *SQ*
42 (1991), 255–75) sees the phrase
as one of several allusions to bear-baiting in the play (2.5.7, 3.1.116–17,
3.4.283–4, perhaps 5.1.368), and
compares Robert Laneham or Langham's account of the 'Princely Pleasures' at Kenilworth Castle in 1575
(see note to 1.2.14), where a baited
bear is said to 'shake his ears twice or
thrice with the blood and the slaver
about his physiognomy' (Laneham,
p. 48).
118 **as good a deed as to drink** A proverbial expression (Dent D183.1) which
occurs twice in *1 Henry IV* (2.1.29,
2.2.22–3). Sir Andrew's amplification
when a man's a-hungry makes nonsense
of it.
119 **a-hungry** *OED a.* says that the prefix
'was probably taken as emphatic'.
     challenge him the field challenge him
to a duel. *OED v.* 8c implies that this
(and not '*to* the field') was the standard form for a challenge. The idea suits
one who is a *great quarreller* (1.3.27),
but when it materializes later, Cesario
rather than Malvolio is its victim.

youth of the Count's was today with my lady she is
much out of quiet. For Monsieur Malvolio, let me alone   125
with him. If I do not gull him into a nayword and make
him a common recreation, do not think I have wit
enough to lie straight in my bed. I know I can do it.
SIR TOBY Possess us, possess us, tell us something of him.
MARIA Marry, sir, sometimes he is a kind of puritan.   130
SIR ANDREW O, if I thought that I'd beat him like a dog.
SIR TOBY What, for being a puritan? Thy exquisite reason,
dear knight.
SIR ANDREW I have no exquisite reason for't, but I have
reason good enough.   135
MARIA The dev'l a puritan that he is, or anything constantly but a time-pleaser, an affectioned ass that cons
state without book and utters it by great swathes; the
best persuaded of himself, so crammed, as he thinks,
with excellencies, that it is his grounds of faith that all   140

---

126 a nayword] ROWE, *after* F (an ayword)

125-6 **let me alone with him** leave him
to me (*OED, let, v.*[1] 18b)
126 **gull** trick
  nayword byword—presumably for
  stupidity, gullibility. Riverside retains
  F's 'an ayword', noting that 'Shakespeare seems to have been the first
  to use the phrase and its etymo-
  logy is doubtful'. But *nayword*, unlike
  'ayword', is authenticated elsewhere;
  Shakespeare uses it twice in *Merry
  Wives* (2.2.122, 5.2.5), where it means
  'password'); and to the ear the forms
  are indistinguishable.
127 **common recreation** source of general
  amusement
129 **Possess us** put us in possession of
  your idea
132 **puritan** one who professes high
  moral scruples; specifically, a member
  of the protestant reforming party
  exquisite ingenious. Sir Toby would
  presumably find *being a puritan* a perfectly good reason for beating Malvolio, so he is probably expecting Sir
  Andrew to reveal some fatuous reason—and is disappointed in the next

speech.
134-5 **I have reason good enough** i.e. I
  have an important reason, but I'm not
  going to disclose it.
136 **dev'l** (devil). F's form may reflect one
  of the monosyllabic forms cited by *OED
  sb.* (*deul, dele, del*).
136-7 **anything constantly but** As with 'a
  kind of puritan' (l. 130), this phrase
  suggests that Malvolio is only a puritan when it suits him.
  constantly consistently
137 **time-pleaser** time-server
  affectioned affected (*OED sb.* 13). Compare *LLL* 5.1.4: 'witty without affection'.
137-8 **cons state without book** learns
  high-flown language by heart (a theatrical expression, used at *Romeo* 1.4.7:
  'without-book Prologue'); Sir Andrew
  proposes to do this at 3.1.89.
138 **utters it by great swathes** comes out
  with it in great masses (like hay falling
  under a mower's scythe)
138-9 **the best . . . himself** having the
  highest opinion of himself
140 **his grounds** the foundation of his

131

that look on him love him; and on that vice in him will
my revenge find notable cause to work.

SIR TOBY What wilt thou do?

MARIA I will drop in his way some obscure epistles of
love, wherein by the colour of his beard, the shape of his   145
leg, the manner of his gait, the expressure of his eye,
forehead, and complexion, he shall find himself most
feelingly personated. I can write very like my lady your
niece; on a forgotten matter we can hardly make distinction of our hands.   150

SIR TOBY Excellent, I smell a device.

SIR ANDREW I have't in my nose too.

SIR TOBY He shall think by the letters that thou wilt drop
that they come from my niece, and that she's in love
with him.   155

MARIA My purpose is indeed a horse of that colour.

SIR ANDREW And your horse now would make him an ass.

MARIA Ass I doubt not.

SIR ANDREW O, 'twill be admirable.

MARIA Sport royal, I warrant you. I know my physic will   160
work with him. I will plant you two—and let the fool
make a third—where he shall find the letter. Observe his
construction of it. For this night, to bed, and dream on
the event. Farewell.   *Exit*

SIR TOBY Good night, Penthesilea.   165

SIR ANDREW Before me, she's a good wench.

---

144 **epistles** letters
146 **expressure** expression; for the form,
  compare 'impressure' (2.5.89)
148 **feelingly** appropriately, in a way that
  will do him justice (*OED adv.* 2)
  personated described (or impersonated:
  OED ppl. a. 1)
149–50 **on a . . . hands** when we have
  forgotten the original topic, we cannot
  tell our handwriting apart
151 **smell a device** detect a stratagem.
  Compare *Winter's Tale* 4.4.643–4: 'I
  smell the trick on't.'
156 **horse of that colour** Proverbial (Tilley
  H665); compare *As You Like It*
  3.2.398–9: 'boys and women are for
  the most part cattle of this colour'.
158 **Ass I doubt not** Maria picks up (or

anticipates) Sir Andrew's word, turning it back on him, with a pun on 'as'.
The same pun occurs at *Hamlet*
5.2.44: 'many such like "as"es of
great charge'.
160 **physic** medicine
161–2 **let the fool make a third** See note
  to l. 110 above, and Introduction,
  p. 53.
163 **construction**   interpretation, con-
  struing (*OED* 6)
164 **event** outcome
165 **Penthesilea** Queen of the Amazons,
  warrior maidens (a joke about Maria's
  small size)
166 **Before me** 'Before God' (a mild oath;
  hence 'by my soul' (Schmidt))

SIR TOBY She's a beagle true bred, and one that adores me.
      What o' that?
SIR ANDREW I was adored once too.
SIR TOBY Let's to bed, knight. Thou hadst need send for   170
      more money.
SIR ANDREW If I cannot recover your niece, I am a foul
      way out.
SIR TOBY Send for money, knight. If thou hast her not i'th'
      end, call me cut.   175
SIR ANDREW If I do not, never trust me, take it how you
      will.
SIR TOBY Come, come, I'll go burn some sack, 'tis too late
      to go to bed now. Come knight, come knight.

                                                    Exeunt

2.4   *Enter Duke Orsino, Viola as Cesario, Curio, and*
           others

ORSINO
   Give me some music. Now good morrow, friends.
   Now good Cesario, but that piece of song,

2.4.0.1 *Orsino] not in* F   *as Cesario] not in* F

167 **beagle** a small hunting-dog, skilful in
    pursuit, and therefore an apt compari-
    son for a small pursuer of Malvolio.
    The phrase is a natural one for an
    Elizabethan country gentleman like Sir
    Toby to use.
172 **recover** win, obtain (*OED v.*[1] 6a)
172-3 **a foul way out** *OED* (*way, sb.*[1] 8c)
    says that this is an adverbial phrase
    used figuratively, meaning 'miserably
    far from success', and for the idiom
    compares *All's Well* 1.1.100, 'a great
    way fool'. But then the whole sentence
    would approach tautology, and this
    phrase is likelier to mean 'grievously
    out of pocket'. *OED* cites several uses
    of *foul* meaning 'grievously' (*adv.* 4a),
    all earlier than *Twelfth Night*, so per-
    haps Shakespeare is giving his bump-
    kin knight an old-fashioned turn of
    phrase, though *OED*'s earliest example
    of 'out' meaning 'out of pocket' is from
    1632 (*adv.* 21).
175 **cut** A proverbial term of abuse (Tilley

C940). It literally means a cart-horse,
    perhaps one that has had its tail
    cropped or been gelded. The second
    meaning may have led to its obscene
    use, as at 2.5.83: see note.
178 **burn some sack** warm and spice some
    wine. *Sack* was the general name for
    a class of white wines imported from
    Spain and the Canary Islands; it is a
    favourite drink of Falstaff's in *Henry
    IV*, and at *Henry V* 2.3.26 he is said
    to have 'cried out of sack' as he died.
2.4.0.2 *others* These must include a mu-
    sician or musicians to *play the tune* of
    Feste's song at l. 13, and probably to
    accompany him when he sings it.
1 **Give me some music . . . good morrow**
    Orsino asks for music even before
    wishing his court good morning, so
    the musician(s) should probably re-
    spond at once rather than waiting
    until l. 13.
2 **but** just (i.e. let us hear that). Pres-
    umably Orsino is inviting his favourite

That old and antic song we heard last night.
Methought it did relieve my passion much,
More than light airs and recollected terms   5
Of these most brisk and giddy-pacèd times.
Come, but one verse.

CURIO He is not here, so please your lordship, that should
sing it.

ORSINO Who was it?   10

CURIO Feste the jester, my lord, a fool that the lady Olivia's
father took much delight in. He is about the house.

ORSINO

Seek him out, and play the tune the while.   *Exit Curio*
   Music plays
(*To Viola*) Come hither, boy. If ever thou shalt love,
In the sweet pangs of it remember me;   15
For such as I am, all true lovers are,
Unstaid and skittish in all motions else
Save in the constant image of the creature
That is beloved. How dost thou like this tune?

---

13 *Exit Curio*] POPE; *not in* F

Cesario to listen to the song with him
rather than asking him to sing it. See
Introduction, p. 75.

3 **antic** quaint (the stress is on the first
syllable)
4 **passion** suffering
5 **airs** Orsino draws a contrast between
old and antic songs, i.e. folk songs, and
fashionable 'art songs' which were appearing at this time in such collections
as Dowland's *First Book of Songs or
Airs* (1597).
  recollected terms studied, artificial
phrases. For *recollect*, compare *Pericles*
Sc. 5.91–2, 'And from their wat'ry
empire recollect | All that may men
approve or men detect', where 'recollect' means 'gather and store up in
memory'. If the musicians have played
from the start of the scene, this phrase
may criticize what they are actually
playing.
6 **giddy-pacèd** whirling in confusion

(*OED a.* 2)
11–12 **a fool ... delight in** This characterizes Feste as an 'old-timer', a member of the old count's generation, and
so the right man to sing *old and antic*
songs.
17 **Unstaid** unstable
  skittish frivolous
  motions emotions (the word 'emotion'
does not occur in Shakespeare)
18–19 **in the constant image ... beloved**
in faithfully contemplating the image
of the loved one
18 **constant** From Latin *constans*, constant
basically means 'consistent, holding
firm', but when Shakespeare uses it in
contexts involving love, it also carries
the implication 'true' or 'faithful':
compare *Cymbeline* 5.6.450, where In-
nogen is celebrated as 'this most constant wife', and Sonnet 105.5–6: 'Kind
is my love today, tomorrow kind, |
Still constant in a wondrous excellence.'

VIOLA

  It gives a very echo to the seat   20

  Where love is throned.

ORSINO   Thou dost speak masterly.

  My life upon't, young though thou art thine eye

  Hath stayed upon some favour that it loves.

  Hath it not, boy?

VIOLA   A little, by your favour.

ORSINO

  What kind of woman is't?

VIOLA   Of your complexion.   25

ORSINO

  She is not worth thee then. What years, i'faith?

VIOLA About your years, my lord.

ORSINO

  Too old, by heaven. Let still the woman take

  An elder than herself, so wears she to him;

  So sways she level in her husband's heart.   30

  For boy, however we do praise ourselves,

  Our fancies are more giddy and unfirm,

  More longing, wavering, sooner lost and worn,

  Than women's are.

VIOLA   I think it well, my lord.

---

33 worn] F; won HANMER

20–1 **gives . . . throned** reflects exactly the feelings of the heart (because the heart was thought to be the seat of love; compare 1.1.34–8)

21 **masterly** expertly

23 **stayed upon some favour** fixed upon some face

24 **by your favour** by your leave (with a pun on 'a face like yours')

25 **complexion** colouring (or 'temperament')

29 **wears she to him** she adapts herself to him (as clothes do to the wearer); perhaps related to the proverb 'Win it and wear it' (Tilley W408)

30 **sways she level** she exerts a consistent influence. *Sways* is a pun: (a) 'holds sway' (b) 'swings in perfect balance'. Compare 1 *Henry IV* 3.2.12–17: 'Could such inordinate and low desires

. . . hold their level with thy princely heart?'

32 **fancies** affections (used in the sense of *giddy and unfirm* emotions which 'fancy' often implies in Shakespeare: see note to 1.1.14–15)

33 **worn** worn out. Hanmer and other editors emend to 'won', following the catch-phrase 'lost and won'. But that phrase itself is the surest evidence that *worn* is correct: Shakespeare leads the audience to expect 'won' after *lost and,* and then shocks them with the image of love wearing out and decaying. *Worn* is perfectly attuned to Orsino's particular style, as in his lingering over and relishing the *dying fall* in his opening speech.

34 **think** believe

ORSINO

  Then let thy love be younger than thyself,   35

  Or thy affection cannot hold the bent;

  For women are as roses, whose fair flower

  Being once displayed, doth fall that very hour.

VIOLA

  And so they are. Alas that they are so:

  To die even when they to perfection grow.   40

    Enter Curio and Feste the clown

ORSINO (*to Feste*)

  O fellow, come, the song we had last night.

  Mark it Cesario, it is old and plain.

  The spinsters and the knitters in the sun,

  And the free maids that weave their thread with

      bones,

  Do use to chant it. It is silly sooth,   45

  And dallies with the innocence of love,

  Like the old age.

FESTE Are you ready, sir?

40.1 *Feste the*] *not in* F

---

36 **hold the bent** remain at full stretch, remain taut and true (an image from archery)

37–40 **For women are as roses . . . perfection grow** These four lines are a poignant statement of the price of perfection—that at just (*even*) the very moment when women, like roses, are fully revealed (*displayed*) and most perfect, they begin to decline. In emphasizing that perfection is defined by its very vulnerability, Shakespeare may have been influenced by Daniel's *Delia*: 'Look, Delia, how w'esteem the half-blown rose, | The image of thy blush, and summer's honour, . . . No sooner spreads her glory in the air, | But straight her wide-blown pomp comes to decline. | She then is scorned, that late adorned the fair; | So fade the roses of those cheeks of thine' (sonnet 39, 1–2, 5–8, quoted from the revised 1601 edition, which is closer to Shakespeare's wording here than the 1592 original).

43 **spinsters** women spinning. But by 1617, according to *OED*, it was also used, as now, to denote unmarried women. Both senses are probably present in this line, where the women sit spinning and knitting in the sun; compare the Nurse suckling Juliet while 'Sitting in the sun under the dovehouse wall' (*Romeo* 1.3.29).

44 **free** carefree

  weave their thread with bones make lace with bone bobbins

45 **Do use** are accustomed (Abbott 303)

  silly sooth simple truth. *Silly* is here used in an archaic sense, from Middle English *seely*, meaning 'unsophisticated' or 'rustic' (*OED a.* 3). Compare *Cymbeline* 5.5.86: 'a fourth man, in a seely [F: silly] habit'. The general point is that the song tells older, simpler truths about love.

46 **dallies with** lingers lovingly on

47 **old age** golden age of pastoral poetry, an ideal world of positive values

ORSINO I prithee sing.
    Music
FESTE (*sings*)
    Come away, come away death,   50
        And in sad cypress let me be laid.
    Fie away, fie away breath,
        I am slain by a fair cruel maid.
    My shroud of white, stuck all with yew,
        O prepare it.   55
    My part of death no one so true
        Did share it.

    Not a flower, not a flower sweet
        On my black coffin let there be strewn.
    Not a friend, not a friend greet   60
        My poor corpse, where my bones shall be thrown.
    A thousand thousand sighs to save,
        Lay me O where
    Sad true lover never find my grave,
        To weep there.   65

---

49 I prithee sing] F; Ay, prithee sing THEOBALD 1740   50 FESTE (*sings*)] *The Song*. F
52 Fie . . . fie] F; Fly . . . fly ROWE   54–7 My shroud . . . share it] *As* POPE; *two lines in* F,
divided after 'prepare it'   62–5 A thousand . . . weep there] *As* POPE; *two lines in* F, *divided*
after 'where'

49 **I prithee sing** F's *I prethee sing* could
also be modernized, as by Theobald, to
'Ay, prithee sing'.
49.1 **Music** F's direction here implies that
the accompaniment is not played by
the singer himself. There are various
possibilities. In Peter Gill's 1974 RSC
production, for instance, the musicians
accompanied Feste on lute and violin;
but as the song proceeded, Feste imposed his own rougher tempo, beaten
out on his tabor (see 3.1.0.2), assert-
ing, as it were, what was *old and plain*
against their more formal *recollected*
terms (l. 5).
50–65 The words of this song may or may
not be by Shakespeare. No contemporary setting survives; but see the Appendix.
50 **Come away** Come here quickly. Compare Prospero's summoning of Ariel at
Tempest 1.2.188: 'Come away, servant'.

51 **cypress** This must refer to a black
coffin of cypress wood, not to the material which Olivia mentions at
3.1.119, since in l. 54 the corpse's
shroud is said to be *white*. The *cypress*,
like the *yew* of l. 54, is a tree associated with churchyards and with
mourning.
52 **Fie away** Be off! Hotson (p. 144)
points out that this expression is common in Elizabethan English, citing for
instance John Florio's glossing 'O' as
'an interjection of . . . reproving, as . . .
fie, away' (*A World of Words* (1598),
p. 242). It is therefore unnecessary to
emend to 'Fly away', as many editors
have done.
54 **yew** yew twigs, strewn over the
shrouded corpse
56–7 **My part of death . . . share it** no one
so faithful has ever received his al-
lotted portion, death

ORSINO (*giving money*) There's for thy pains.

FESTE No pains, sir, I take pleasure in singing, sir.

ORSINO I'll pay thy pleasure then.

FESTE Truly, sir, and pleasure will be paid, one time or
     another.   70

ORSINO Give me now leave to leave thee.

FESTE Now the melancholy god protect thee, and the tailor
     make thy doublet of changeable taffeta, for thy mind is
     a very opal. I would have men of such constancy put to
     sea, that their business might be everything, and their   75
     intent everywhere, for that's it that always makes a
     good voyage of nothing. Farewell.

                                                          Exit

ORSINO
     Let all the rest give place.   *Exeunt Curio and others*
                    Once more, Cesario,

---

66 *giving money*] COLLIER 1858; *not in* F   78 *Exeunt Curio and others*] CAPELL (*subs.*); *not
in* F

---

66 **There's for thy pains** The natural deduction from the line is that Orsino
gives Feste money; but in Robin Phil-
lips's production at Stratford, Ontario
in 1980, Orsino presented Feste with
the song-book from which he had been
singing, to Feste's delight.
  Orsino's phrase sets off a sequence
of word-play on *pains/pleasure* and on
paying for pleasures. First, in l. 67,
Feste's *I take pleasure in singing* perhaps
contains a professional artist's rebuke
to an employer who thinks art is something to be bought and sold—which
does not prevent Feste from taking the
money, as always. Then, when Orsino
says that he will *pay thy pleasure* (l.
68), Feste plays upon various proverbs
about *pain* (rather than payment) following pleasure (Tilley P408, 412,
413, 419, 420).

71 **to leave** to dismiss

72 **melancholy god** Saturn. Perhaps Feste
invokes him because Orsino is not in
the mood to listen to jests, or (especially in view of what follows) to ac-
cuse Orsino of moodiness in ordering
Feste to sing one moment and dismissing him the next.

73 **changeable taffeta** silk whose colour
changes with the light and the angle
of view. This seems to have been a
standard description or trade name,
since the theatrical impresario Philip
Henslowe twice refers to 'changeable
taffeta' in his diary, on 23 October
1594 and 9 December 1602 (*Henslowe's Diary*, pp. 259, 221).

74 **opal** an iridescent gemstone (hence an
image of changeability and inconstancy, and perhaps specifically of a
lover's changeability, for according to
Leslie Hotson 'the opal is Venus's stone'
(*Shakespeare's Motley* (1952), p. 120))

75 **sea** (another image of the changeable;
compare 1.1.10–14)

75–6 **their business . . . everywhere** drawing upon another proverbial expression: 'he that is everywhere is nowhere'
(Tilley E194)

76–7 **that's it . . . of nothing** that attitude
of mind that sees value in purposeless ac-
tivity. Feste's caustic irony increases
during this speech: he takes the professional fool's licence to criticize very
far, accusing Orsino of changeability
and inconstancy.

78 **give place** leave

Get thee to yon same sovereign cruelty.
Tell her my love, more noble than the world,   80
Prizes not quantity of dirty lands.
The parts that fortune hath bestowed upon her
Tell her I hold as giddily as fortune;
But 'tis that miracle and queen of gems
That nature pranks her in attracts my soul.   85
VIOLA
But if she cannot love you, sir?
ORSINO
I cannot be so answered.
VIOLA   Sooth, but you must.
Say that some lady, as perhaps there is,
Hath for your love as great a pang of heart
As you have for Olivia. You cannot love her.   90
You tell her so. Must she not then be answered?
ORSINO There is no woman's sides
Can bide the beating of so strong a passion
As love doth give my heart; no woman's heart
So big, to hold so much. They lack retention.   95
Alas, their love may be called appetite,
No motion of the liver, but the palate,
That suffer surfeit, cloyment, and revolt.

87 I] HANMER; It F   98 suffer] F; suffers ROWE

79 **sovereign cruelty** (a) supremely cruel lady (b) (Orsino's) cruel sovereign
80 **the world** society in general (which values possessions)
82 **parts** possessions and status
83 **giddily** lightly (because fortune was traditionally fickle)
84 **miracle and queen of gems** i.e. Olivia's beauty (or more generally, Olivia herself—what nature has made her—as opposed to the possessions that *fortune* has given her)
85 **pranks her in** adorns her with. Compare *Winter's Tale* 4.4.9–10: 'me, poor lowly maid, | Most goddess-like pranked up.'
87 **Sooth** in truth
93 **bide** withstand
95 **retention** the power to retain (a medical expression meaning 'the body's power to retain its contents' (*OED* 1a and b)
96 **appetite** i.e. without depth of feeling
97 **motion** impulse, or perhaps emotion in general, as at l. 17. *OED* lists these two meanings under one heading (*sb.* 9).
liver (the seat of the passions; compare 1.1.36–7)
palate (the organ of taste, easily sated)
98 **cloyment . . . revolt** Orsino criticizes women for indulging appetite to the point of *cloyment* (satiety) and *revolt* (revulsion, sickening), which is exactly what he wanted the music to do for him in the opening speech of the play. According to *OED*, *cloyment* is a Shakespearian coinage, and *revolt* is its only example of the word used in this sense (*sb.*¹ 2c); both are also the only Shakespearian usages in this sense.

But mine is all as hungry as the sea,
And can digest as much. Make no compare   100
Between that love a woman can bear me
And that I owe Olivia.
VIOLA Ay, but I know—
ORSINO What dost thou know?
VIOLA
Too well what love women to men may owe.   105
In faith, they are as true of heart as we.
My father had a daughter loved a man
As it might be, perhaps, were I a woman
I should your lordship.
ORSINO   And what's her history?
VIOLA
A blank, my lord. She never told her love,   110
But let concealment, like a worm i'th' bud,
Feed on her damask cheek. She pined in thought,
And with a green and yellow melancholy
She sat like patience on a monument,
Smiling at grief. Was not this love indeed?   115
We men may say more, swear more, but indeed
Our shows are more than will; for still we prove
Much in our vows, but little in our love.
ORSINO
But died thy sister of her love, my boy?
VIOLA
I am all the daughters of my father's house,   120

99 **as hungry as the sea** Orsino re-employs the image he used at 1.1.11.
102, 105 **owe** have for
109 **history** story
110–24 **A blank . . . no denay** For the psychological implications of these lines, and some theatrical ways of realizing them, see Introduction, pp. 37–9.
112 **damask** pink and white, like a damask rose, so called because it reputedly came originally from Damascus. Compare *As You Like It* 3.5.121–4: 'There was a pretty redness in his lip, | . . . 'Twas just the difference | Betwixt the constant red and mingled damask.'

113 **green and yellow** pale and sallow. Perhaps a reference to 'green sickness' or chlorosis, 'an anaemic sickness of young women' taken 'as a sign of a girl's love-sickness, or of vague desire, for a man' (Eric Partridge, *Shakespeare's Bawdy* (revised edn., 1968), p. 117).
114–15 **She sat . . . grief** Viola compares her imaginary sister to a figure on a memorial statue symbolizing patience and smiling.
117 **Our shows . . . will** our outward displays have more substance than our passions
still always

And all the brothers too; and yet I know not.
Sir, shall I to this lady?
ORSINO   Ay, that's the theme,
To her in haste, give her this jewel, say
My love can give no place, bide no denay.

Exeunt severally

2.5   *Enter Sir Toby, Sir Andrew, and Fabian*
SIR TOBY Come thy ways, Signor Fabian.
FABIAN Nay, I'll come. If I lose a scruple of this sport let
me be boiled to death with melancholy.
SIR TOBY Wouldst thou not be glad to have the niggardly
rascally sheep-biter come by some notable shame?   5
FABIAN I would exult, man. You know he brought me out
o' favour with my lady about a bear-baiting here.
SIR TOBY To anger him we'll have the bear again, and we
will fool him black and blue, shall we not, Sir Andrew?

1 24.1 *severally*] OXFORD; *not in* F

123 **jewel** piece of jewellery, probably a
ring
124 **can give ... denay** cannot ebb, or tol-
erate denial
2.5.1 **Come thy ways** come along (*OED*,
way, *sb.*¹ 23b)
  Signor Fabian Fabian is abruptly introduced into the action as a substitute
  for Feste (see 2.3.161–2, and Introduction, p. 53). Perhaps *Signor* (Italian for
  'Master') is more than a mere courtesy
  title, implying that he is a gentleman
  of Olivia's household rather than a
  menial. His name may have been suggested by *Fabio*, the heroine's assumed
  name in *Gl'Ingannati*, one of the play's
  probable sources, or it may mean a
  reveller or roisterer: *OED* cites John
  Florio's glossing *Bravazzo* in his Ita-
  lian/English dictionary *A World of
  Words* (1598) as 'a flaunting fabian'
  (p. 48). But everything about Fabian
  seems uncertain.
2 **Nay** not a negative, but an intensifier
  lose a scruple miss a scrap. For *scruple*,
  see note to 3.4.75–6.
3 **boiled to death with melancholy** A
  joke, because melancholy was supposed to be a cold humour; but it

also refers to the situation: Olivia's
mourning and Malvolio's behaviour
are turning the house into a *melancholy* one.
4 **niggardly** grudging
5 **sheep-biter** Literally, a dog that attacks
sheep. Figuratively, it had several abusive meanings. Through the pun on
'sheep' and 'mutton' (whose slang
meaning was 'whore'), it could mean
'a woman-hunter, whoremonger'
(*OED* 4); but it is also associated with
puritans by Nashe, for example in *The
Unfortunate Traveller*, where a pander
is said to 'leer like a sheep-biter. If he
be half a puritan, with scripture
continually in his mouth, he speeds
the better' (Nashe, *Works*, 2. 260). A
hypocritical puritan might aptly be
called a *sheep-biter* precisely because it
implied whore-monger, just as Malvolio is elsewhere called both a lewd
'Peg-o'-Ramsey' and 'a kind of puritan' (2.3.72, 130).
7 **bear-baiting** (condemned particularly
by puritans)
9 **fool him black and blue** i.e. make a
thorough fool of Malvolio

SIR ANDREW An we do not, it is pity of our lives.   10
    Enter Maria with a letter
SIR TOBY Here comes the little villain. How now, my metal
    of India?
MARIA Get ye all three into the box-tree. Malvolio's com-
    ing down this walk. He has been yonder i' the sun pract-
    ising behaviour to his own shadow this half-hour.   15
    Observe him, for the love of mockery, for I know this
    letter will make a contemplative idiot of him. Close, in
    the name of jesting!
    The men hide. Maria places the letter
    Lie thou there, for here comes the trout that must be
    caught with tickling.   *Exit*   20
    Enter Malvolio
MALVOLIO 'Tis but fortune, all is fortune. Maria once told
    me she did affect me, and I have heard herself come
    thus near, that should she fancy it should be one of my

2.5.10.1 *with a letter*] OXFORD; *not in* F
18.1 *The men hide.*] CAPELL (*subs.*); *not in* F   *Maria places the letter*] THEOBALD (*Throws down
a letter* (*after* 'tickling')); *not in* F

---

10 **pity of our lives** a shame that we
should live (a common construction;
see Dent P368.1, and compare *Dream*
3.1.38–9: 'If you think I come hither
as a lion, it were pity of my life.')
11–12 **metal of India** i.e. piece of gold,
treasure. India was 'proverbially rich'
(Schmidt).
12 **of** from (Abbott 166)
13 **box-tree** a hedge of boxwood. Box is
an evergreen whose thick growth is
ideal for clipping into topiary shapes in
formal gardens. The *box-tree* in performance has taken many forms: a
hedge, a large tree, shrubs in wooden
tubs (see fig. 8). Property trees were
certainly used on the Elizabethan
stage, as the list of properties compiled
by Philip Henslowe on 10 March 1598
makes clear (*Henslowe's Diary*, pp.
319–20).
15 **behaviour** courtly gestures
17 **contemplative** i.e. vacantly staring (a
parody of someone who follows the
'contemplative' rather than the 'active' life, a major Renaissance preoccupation)

Close i.e. keep close, hide
20 **tickling** i.e. flattery. Proverbial—'to
catch one like a trout with tickling'
(Tilley T537)—but based on fact: trout
can be caught by stroking them under
the gills in shallow water, as described
by T. R. Henn in *The Living Image*,
pp. 61–2, with all the immediacy of
personal experience. This book illumi-
nates the numerous hunting expressions in this scene: see notes to ll. 43,
79, 109, 117–18, 121.
21 **'Tis but ... fortune** Everything is at
the mercy of fickle fortune. Here Malvolio picks up Orsino's reference to the
giddiness of fortune in the previous
scene (2.4.82–3). It was a commonplace, also used at *Tempest* 5.1.260.
22 **she did affect** Olivia was fond of. The
structure of the sentence misleadingly
suggests that it is Maria who *affects*
Malvolio; *herself* in the next line helps
to clarify matters.
23 **fancy** fall in love (with the implication—unconscious   on   Malvolio's
part—of deluded love: see note to
1.1.14–15)

complexion. Besides, she uses me with a more exalted
respect than anyone else that follows her. What should   25
I think on't?

SIR TOBY Here's an overweening rogue.

FABIAN O, peace. Contemplation makes a rare turkeycock
of him—how he jets under his advanced plumes!

SIR ANDREW 'Slight, I could so beat the rogue.   30

SIR TOBY Peace, I say.

MALVOLIO To be Count Malvolio!

SIR TOBY Ah, rogue.

SIR ANDREW Pistol him, pistol him.

SIR TOBY Peace, peace.   35

MALVOLIO There is example for't: the Lady of the Strachey
married the yeoman of the wardrobe.

SIR ANDREW Fie on him, Jezebel.

31, 35 SIR TOBY] F (*To.*); *Fabian* WILSON

---

24 **complexion** colouring (or 'temperament'), as at 2.4.25

25 **follows her** (as her servant, perhaps
with secondary meaning 'as a suitor')

26 **on't** of it. 'Of' and 'on' could be used
interchangeably in Elizabethan English
(Abbott 175).

28 **turkeycock** Proverbially proud—'He
swells like a turkey cock' (Tilley
T612)—they display their tail-feathers
like peacocks (*advanced plumes*, l. 29).

29 **jets** struts. Since one of the senses of
jet is 'of a bird: To move the tail up
and down' (*OED*, *v.*² 6), this extends
the image of the *turkeycock* in l. 28,
and is another image of pride: it is used
specifically of an uppish steward in the
anonymous *Arden of Faversham* (published 1592) Sc. 1.29–30, who 'bravely jets it in his silken gown'.
advanced displayed (developing the
image of the preening *turkeycock*)

30 **'Slight** an oath (by God's light)

34 **Pistol him** shoot him

36 **example** precedent

36–7 **the Lady of the Strachey . . . yeoman
of the wardrobe** This probably alludes
to an actual lady who married a social
inferior (a *yeoman of the wardrobe* is the
keeper of clothes and linen in a noble
household). C. J. Sisson unearthed a

William Strachey, in 1606 a 'sharer'
or part-owner of the Blackfriars
Theatre, and a David Yeomans, who
was 'tireman' or wardrobe-master of
the company. As Sisson points out,
'Yeomans was a tailor, and illiterate,
obviously an inferior to "William Strachey, gentleman" and to his lady. And
[Malvolio's] *married* might well be a
euphemism' (*New Readings in Shakespeare*, 2 vols. (Cambridge, 1956), I.
188–91)—just as the phrase '*the* Strachey' might be mock-heroic: compare
'The Douglas and the Hotspur' (*1
Henry IV* 5.1.116). The combination of
names seems beyond coincidence; if
Yeomans was involved with Strachey's
lady, this allusion is a glance at Shakespeare's rivals like that to their boy-
actors at *Hamlet* 2.2.340–63. But of
course the line is perfectly comprehens-
ible as it stands: Malvolio appeals to a
precedent of a lady marrying an inferior, and in the process reveals his
interest in salacious gossip.

38 **Jezebel** A biblical example of a
'painted' *woman* of deceiving appearance (2 Kings 9: 30–7); Malvolio is
also likened to a lascivious woman at
2.3.72, and perhaps at l. 109 of this
scene.

FABIAN O, peace, now he's deeply in. Look how imagin-
   ation blows him.   40
MALVOLIO Having been three months married to her, sit-
   ting in my state—
SIR TOBY O for a stone-bow to hit him in the eye!
MALVOLIO Calling my officers about me, in my branched
   velvet gown, having come from a day-bed where I have   45
   left Olivia sleeping—
SIR TOBY Fire and brimstone!
FABIAN O, peace, peace.
MALVOLIO And then to have the humour of state and—
   after a demure travel of regard, telling them I know my   50
   place, as I would they should do theirs—to ask for my
   kinsman Toby.
SIR TOBY Bolts and shackles!
FABIAN O, peace, peace, peace, now, now.
MALVOLIO Seven of my people with an obedient start   55
   make out for him. I frown the while, and perchance
   wind up my watch, or play with my—some rich jewel.
   Toby approaches; curtsies there to me.

---

42 state—] F (state.)   46 sleeping—] F (sleeping.)   57 my—some] COLLIER; my some F

39 **deeply in** absorbed (in his fantasies)
40 **blows him** puffs him up, swells him out
42 **state** chair of state with a canopy over
   it
43 **stone-bow** modification of crossbow to
   fire stones for killing birds (see T. R.
   Henn, p. 78)
44 **officers** attendants, household officials
   branched embroidered with branch-
   patterns. This may have been a standard contemporary description of a
   particular patterned or embossed material, comparable as a phrase to
   'changeable taffeta' in the previous
   scene (see note to 2.4.73). Philip Henslowe uses both phrases together in his
   diary entry for 23 October 1594.
45 **gown** expensive, elaborate garment for
   men of dignity, or perhaps specifically
   dressing-gown, in view of what follows
   day-bed a bed or couch to recline on
   in the daytime—with an obviously lascivious significance (compare *Richard
   III* 3.7.72, 'a lewd day-bed') that pro-
   vokes Sir Toby's outrage in the next

speech
47 **Fire and brimstone** Toby consigns Malvolio to hell.
49 **humour of state** temperament of the
   great, 'grand manner'
50 **demure travel of regard** i.e. casting my
   eyes gravely around the room
   telling indicating to
52 **Toby** (not 'Sir Toby'—provoking the
   next outburst)
53 **Bolts and shackles** fetters (of a prisoner)
55 **start** sudden movement (jumping to
   attention?)
56 **make out** go out
57 **watch** (new to England at this date,
   and therefore expensive)
   play . . . jewel F's 'play with my some
   rich jewel' is usually explained as Malvolio fingering his steward's chain of
   office which he then realizes he will no
   longer be wearing. But the phrase may
   be less specific, Malvolio lost in fantasies of greatness, searching for something appropriately grand.
58 **curtsies** bows

SIR TOBY Shall this fellow live?

FABIAN Though our silence be drawn from us with cars,   60
yet peace.

MALVOLIO I extend my hand to him thus, quenching my
familiar smile with an austere regard of control—

SIR TOBY And does not Toby take you a blow o' the lips,
then?   65

MALVOLIO Saying 'Cousin Toby, my fortunes, having cast
me on your niece, give me this prerogative of speech'—

SIR TOBY What, what!

MALVOLIO 'You must amend your drunkenness.'

SIR TOBY Out, scab.   70

FABIAN Nay, patience, or we break the sinews of our plot.

MALVOLIO 'Besides, you waste the treasure of your time
with a foolish knight'—

SIR ANDREW That's me, I warrant you.

MALVOLIO 'One Sir Andrew.'   75

SIR ANDREW I knew 'twas I, for many do call me fool.

MALVOLIO (*seeing the letter*) What employment have we
here?

FABIAN Now is the woodcock near the gin.

SIR TOBY O peace, and the spirit of humours intimate   80
reading aloud to him.

---

77 *seeing the letter*] WILSON (*subs., after* l. 75); *not in* F   79 FABIAN] F (*Fa.*); DONNO (*conj.*
Wilson) *reads* SIR TOBY   80 SIR TOBY] F (*To.*); DONNO (*conj.* Wilson) *reads* FABIAN

---

60 **with cars** A prisoner might be tied to
two carts or chariots (*cars*) pulled by
horses in different directions, to extort
information. Compare *Two Gentlemen*
3.1.263–4: 'a team of horse shall not
pluck that from me'.

62 **extend my hand** (probably to be kissed,
not shaken, implying that Toby should
kneel)

63 **familiar** friendly
regard of control gaze of authority

64 **take** give, 'fetch'

77 **employment** business (i.e. the letter)

79–121 **Now is the woodcock . . . at faults**
In this section of the scene, the eaves-
droppers see Malvolio in hunting
terms: first as a bird approaching a
trap (*woodcock, staniel,* l. 109), then as

a hound following a scent (*Sowter, cur,*
ll. 117–120). Such references take us
very far from the geographical Illyria
to an English country estate.

79 **woodcock near the gin** The *woodcock*
was a proverbially foolish bird (Tilley
S788). Compare Polonius describing
Hamlet's vows as 'springes to catch
woodcocks' (*Hamlet* 1.3.115). *Gin,* an
aphetic form of 'engine', means 'trap'.
T. R. Henn describes how gins or springes work in *The Living Image,* p. 2.

80 **the spirit of humours intimate** may
the god of odd behaviour suggest. It
was believed that if any one of the
four *humours* or bodily fluids (blood,
phlegm, choler, melancholy) dominated,
this affected a person's disposition, and

MALVOLIO (*taking up the letter*) By my life, this is my lady's hand. These be her very c's, her u's, and her t's, and thus makes she her great P's. It is in contempt of question her hand.   85

SIR ANDREW Her c's, her u's, and her t's? Why that?

MALVOLIO (*reads*) 'To the unknown belov'd, this, and my good wishes.' Her very phrases! By your leave, wax— soft, and the impressure her Lucrece, with which she uses to seal—'tis my lady. To whom should this be?   90

He opens the letter

FABIAN This wins him, liver and all.

MALVOLIO   'Jove knows I love,
                But who?
                Lips do not move,
                No man must know.'   95

'No man must know.' What follows? The numbers altered. 'No man must know.' If this should be thee, Malvolio?

SIR TOBY Marry, hang thee, brock.

---

82 *taking up the letter*] ROWE (*subs., after l. 78*); *not in* F   87 *reads*] CAPELL; *not in* F   90.1 *He opens the letter*] WILSON; *not in* F   92–5 'Jove knows . . . must know.'] *as* CAPELL; *prose in* F   96–8 The numbers . . . Malvolio] *verse in* F, *divided after* 'know'

consequently *humour* came to describe the extreme disposition itself. Shakespeare usually associates the word with eccentrics like Nim in *Merry Wives*, who keeps using it to the irritation of Master Page: 'The humour of it, quoth a? Here's a fellow frights English out of his wits' (2.1.130–1).

81 **reading aloud** (so that they can hear the contents of Maria's letter)

83–4 **c's . . . u's . . . t's . . . great P's** In fact the words Malvolio reads from the outside of the letter do not include 'c' or capital P. They are there for an obscene joke. 'Cut' was slang for the female genitals; compare the bawdy pun in Webster's Induction (1603–4) to Marston's *The Malcontent*, ll. 25–6: 'the longest cut still to draw an apricock'. And *makes her great 'P's'* suggests 'urinates copiously'. Presumably this word-play is unconscious on Malvolio's part.

84 **in contempt of** beyond (i.e. it is absurd to raise the question)

88 **By your leave, wax** (an affected expression, as he goes to break the seal)

89 **soft** not so fast—or just possibly, as in some productions, an indication that the *wax* is still *soft* from sealing
impressure impression, image (of the seal on the wax)
Lucrece figure of Lucrece, the Roman model of chastity, on her seal-ring

90 **uses to seal** habitually seals

91 **liver** the seat of passion, as at 1.1.36–7 and 2.4.97

96–7 **numbers altered** metre changed

99 **brock** badger. Perhaps because it smells; but Malvolio is usually dressed in puritan black and white, which may suggest the comparison.

MALVOLIO

    'I may command where I adore,   100
        But silence like a Lucrece knife
    With bloodless stroke my heart doth gore.
    M.O.A.I. doth sway my life.'

FABIAN A fustian riddle.

SIR TOBY Excellent wench, say I.   105

MALVOLIO 'M.O.A.I. doth sway my life.' Nay, but first let
me see, let me see, let me see.

FABIAN What dish o' poison has she dressed him!

SIR TOBY And with what wing the staniel checks at it!

MALVOLIO 'I may command where I adore.' Why, she   110
may command me. I serve her, she is my lady. Why,
this is evident to any formal capacity. There is no
obstruction in this. And the end—what should that

100–3 'I may command . . . my life.'] *as* HANMER; *two lines in* F, *divided after* 'knife'
109 staniel] HANMER; stallion F

---

101 **Lucrece knife** (i.e. the knife with which Lucrece—see note to l. 89—committed suicide)

102 **bloodless** (because, while the knife that stabbed Lucrece was real and drew blood, this one is metaphorical)

103 **sway** rule

104 **fustian** high-sounding but meaningless (literally, cheap imitation silk). Presumably Fabian means that this is the right kind of riddle to lure Malvolio.

108 **dressed** prepared for

109 **wing** flight
    staniel kestrel. The context of *wing* and *checks* justifies Hanmer's emendation of F's *stallion*. Following the *woodcock* of l. 79, it sustains the image of Malvolio as a bird approaching a lure. But if, as *OED* claims, *stallion* is a corrupt or dialect form of *staniel*, perhaps it is used here for its additional slang sense 'prostitute'. This would match the comparisons of Malvolio to Jezebel (l. 38) and Peg-o'-Ramsey (2.3.72). But 'kestrel' is the primary meaning, so *staniel* is the lesser of two evil readings—for if modern audiences are bewildered by *staniel*, they will be positively misled by *stallion*.
    checks at It is hard to be sure of the precise sense. *Checks at* means 'shies

away from' (see note to 3.1.63), yet Malvolio seems to be poring over the letter, swallowing the *poison* of l. 108. Perhaps the image is of the kestrel attracted by the poisoned bait, but excitedly fluttering its wings as it nervously hovers over it.

112 **formal capacity** normal intelligence. Compare *Errors* 5.1. 106, where the Abbess proposes to make Antipholus 'a formal man again'—i.e. properly formed, normal, no longer mad (*OED a.* 4a). Hotson thinks that Shakespeare chooses the word *formal* for its additional Elizabethan sense of 'affected', as in 'this formal ape' (Middleton and Dekker, *The Roaring Girl* (*c.*1611) 1.1.30), so that Malvolio unconsciously demonstrates his own affectation (p. 111). *Formal* certainly sounds mannered, like *obstruction* (see next note).

113 **obstruction** difficulty, obstacle. Shakespeare uses this word three times in *Twelfth Night* and only twice elsewhere. It seems to be a Malvolio mannerism; he uses it again at 3.4.20, and Feste turns it against him when exorcizing his 'madness' as Sir Topaz (4.2.39–40). It may be an analogous case to 'element' (see 1.1.25, 3.1.58, 3.4.119, and notes).

alphabetical position portend? If I could make that
resemble something in me. Softly—'M.O.A.I.'   115

SIR TOBY O ay, make up that, he is now at a cold scent.

FABIAN Sowter will cry upon't for all this, though it be as
rank as a fox.

MALVOLIO 'M.' Malvolio. 'M'—why, that begins my name.

FABIAN Did not I say he would work it out? The cur is   120
excellent at faults.

MALVOLIO 'M.' But then there is no consonancy in the
sequel. That suffers under probation: 'A' should follow,
but 'O' does.

FABIAN And 'O' shall end, I hope.   125

SIR TOBY Ay, or I'll cudgel him, and make him cry 'O!'

MALVOLIO And then 'I' comes behind.

FABIAN Ay, an you had any eye behind you you might
see more detraction at your heels than fortunes before
you.   130

MALVOLIO 'M.O.A.I.' This simulation is not as the former;

---

123 sequel. That] ROWE; sequell that F

---

114 **position** arrangement
116 **O ay** (punning on 'O. I.')
   cold scent (where the scent of a
   hound's quarry is lost)
117 **Sowter** the name of a hound. T. R.
   Henn, who points out that hounds'
   names often survive the centuries, has
   not come across this one; 'souter'
   means 'cobbler', and *OED* gives examples of its depreciatory use in the sixteenth and seventeenth centuries. But
   see the next note.
117–18 **cry ... rank as a fox** This is sometimes interpreted 'bay as if it were as
   stinkingly obvious as a fox's scent'—
   i.e. *Sowter*, the 'cobbler', is a clumsy
   dog who makes a fuss about the obvious. But this assumes that *though*
   means 'as if', and T. R. Henn offers
   an explanation that makes much better sense: 'Sowter, a notable hound, is
   able to pick up the cold scent [of l.
   116], even though the trail has been
   crossed by a fox, the beast of "stinking
   flight" ' (p. 47).
121 **excellent at faults** clever at finding
   the scent again after the trail has been
   lost. Compare *Shrew* Induction 1.17–18:

'Silver made it good | At the hedge
corner, in the coldest fault'.
122–3 **there is no consonancy ... probation** 'There is no consistency in what
   follows. That weakens on being put to
   the test.' The Folio punctuation runs
   the two phrases together, and the use
   of *consonancy*, a rare word, and *probation*, rare in this sense (*OED sb.* 1), is
   probably intended to reinforce Malvolio's affected, mannered delivery suggested by *formal capacity* and
   obstruction (ll. 112–13). Shakespeare
   only uses *consonancy* elsewhere at
   Hamlet 2.2.285–7, where the tone
   may also be mannered, as Hamlet, in
   the suspicious, ironical exchange with
   Rosencrantz and Guildenstern, 'con-
   jure[s]' them 'by the consonancy of
   our youth, by the obligation of our
   ever-preserved love'. F's lack of punctuation implies that it is the *sequel*
   which will not bear examination,
   Rowe's (followed here) that the failure
   in consistency *suffers under probation*.
129 **detraction** defamation
131 **simulation** disguise, puzzle
   former (i.e. *I may command where I adore*)

and yet to crush this a little, it would bow to me, for
every one of these letters are in my name. Soft, here follows prose: 'If this fall into thy hand, revolve. In my stars
I am above thee, but be not afraid of greatness. Some   135
are born great, some achieve greatness, and some have
greatness thrust upon 'em. Thy fates open their hands,
let thy blood and spirit embrace them, and to inure thyself to what thou art like to be, cast thy humble slough,
and appear fresh. Be opposite with a kinsman, surly with   140
servants. Let thy tongue tang arguments of state; put
thyself into the trick of singularity. She thus advises
thee that sighs for thee. Remember who commended
thy yellow stockings, and wished to see thee ever cross-

136 born] ROWE; become F   achieve] F2; atcheeues FI

132 **crush** squeeze out of natural shape,
force
  bow to (a) yield its meaning to (b)
  indicate, point to
133 **every one ... are** Singular nouns
  with plural verbs, and vice versa, are
  common in Elizabethan usage (Abbott
  333, 336, 412).
134 **revolve** consider, reflect. This is the
  earliest example of this usage given at
  OED v. 10, suggesting that it may be
  intended to sound like an affected
  novelty. The word is a great temptation for actors to gain an easy laugh
  by slowly revolving; but it is funnier if
  instead of this gag the actor points
  what the line means. In Peter Hall's
  1991 version, for instance, Eric Porter
  glanced up after *revolve* as if to say
  'What an odd way of putting it' (thus
  neatly reflecting *OED's* evidence),
  shrugged, and continued reading at
  once.
134 **stars** fortune and rank (as determined
  by the *stars*). For the use of the stars
  as a way of expressing the difference
  in rank between lover and beloved,
  compare *All's Well* 1.1.84–6: ' 'Twere
  all one | That I should love a bright
  particular star | And think to wed it,
  he is so above me.'
137 **fates** Maria skilfully incorporates into
  the letter thoughts characteristic of
  Olivia. Compare 1.5.300: 'Fate, show
  thy force'.

  open their hands (to give)
138 **blood and spirit** i.e. whole being
  ('body and soul'). Compare *Hamlet*
  3.2.66–7: 'blest are those | Whose
  blood and judgement are ... well com-
  mingled'.
  embrace them fully accept your fortunes
  inure accustom. *OED v.*[1] 2 only cites
  one example of this usage, from Elizabeth I's translation of Plutarch (1598)—
  more stylistic difficulty for Malvolio
  here, perhaps.
139 **cast thy humble slough** abandon
  your lowly behaviour (as a snake casts
  off its old skin). *OED sb.*[2] records a
  dialect form 'sluff' which indicates the
  pronunciation.
140 **opposite with** openly hostile to
141 **tang** ring out, like a bell (*OED v.*[2])
  arguments of state political matters,
  important topics
141–2 **put ... singularity** cultivate ori-
  ginality
142 **trick** habit (*OED sb.* 7)
144 **yellow stockings** Probably a garish
  fashion associated with bachelors. In
  the ballad 'Peg-o'-Ramsey', which Sir
  Toby mentions at 2.3.72, a married
  man laments the loss of his bachelor
  state: 'Give me my yellow hose again'
  (quoted by Hotson, p. 106). 'To wear
  yellow stockings and cross garters' became proverbial (Tilley S868).

gartered. I say remember, go to, thou art made if thou   145
desir'st to be so; if not, let me see thee a steward still, the
fellow of servants, and not worthy to touch Fortune's
fingers. Farewell. She that would alter services with
thee,

                    The Fortunate Unhappy.'   150
Daylight and champaign discovers not more. This is
open. I will be proud, I will read politic authors, I will
baffle Sir Toby, I will wash off gross acquaintance, I will
be point-device the very man. I do not now fool myself,
to let imagination jade me; for every reason excites to   155
this, that my lady loves me. She did commend my
yellow stockings of late, she did praise my leg being
cross-gartered, and in this she manifests herself to my
love, and with a kind of injunction drives me to these
habits of her liking. I thank my stars, I am happy. I will   160

150–1 The Fortunate Unhappy.' Daylight] CAPELL (*subs.*); tht fortunate vnhappy daylight F

144–5 **cross-gartered** A way of tying a garter, going round once below the knee, crossing behind it, and knotting above the knee at the side. It is not clear from contemporary accounts whether cross-gartering was in or out of fashion in 1601, and the point may be not so much fashionable or unfashionable as gartered or ungartered. In *As You Like It*, Rosalind contrasts the unrequited lover whose 'hose should be ungartered' with one who is 'point-device in [his] accoutrements, as loving [himself] than seeming the lover of any other' (3.2.366–71). So perhaps the gartered man is an image of self-love (compare 1.5.85); and Malvolio also resolves to be 'point-device': see l. 154 and note.

145 **go to** A catch-phrase, often of impatience—'come on!'—but here of encouragement: 'go on'.
    thou art made i.e. thy fortune is made. Compare *Dream* 4.2.17: 'made men'.

147 **fellow** companion, equal

147–8 **touch Fortune's fingers** (in receiving her gifts)

148 **alter services** change places (of servant and mistress or master)

150 **Fortunate Unhappy** i.e. prosperous but unhappy in love

151 **champaign** open countryside (which, like daylight, reveals everything), from Old French *champaigne* (*OED sb.* 1)
    discovers reveals

152 **open** absolutely clear
    politic authors writers on political science (from whom he can learn *arguments of state* (l. 141))

153 **baffle** disgrace. The word is repeated, and intensified, at Malvolio's own disgrace (see 5.1.360 and note).

154 **point-device the very man** meticulously the identical man (described in the letter). *OED adv.* derives *point-device* from the Middle English phrase *at point devis*, 'to the point of perfection', 'precisely'.

155 **jade** trick (like a wily old horse, a jade)
    excites to urges

156–7 **She did commend . . . stockings** Malvolio must be making this up, since Maria says that yellow is a colour Olivia *abhors* (l. 189).

158 **manifests herself to** reveals herself as

160 **habits** conflates two senses (*OED sb.* 1 and 4): (a) dress (b) behaviour. See note to 3.4.71.
    happy fortunate (in love)

be strange, stout, in yellow stockings, and cross-gartered,
even with the swiftness of putting on. Jove and my stars
be praised. Here is yet a postscript. 'Thou canst not
choose but know who I am. If thou entertain'st my love,
let it appear in thy smiling, thy smiles become thee well.   165
Therefore in my presence still smile, dear my sweet, I
prithee.' Jove, I thank thee. I will smile, I will do everything that thou wilt have me.   *Exit*

> *Sir Toby, Sir Andrew, and Fabian come from hiding*

FABIAN I will not give my part of this sport for a pension
of thousands to be paid from the Sophy.   170
SIR TOBY I could marry this wench for this device.
SIR ANDREW So could I too.
SIR TOBY And ask no other dowry with her but such an-
other jest.

> *Enter Maria*

SIR ANDREW Nor I neither.   175
FABIAN Here comes my noble gull-catcher.
SIR TOBY (*to Maria*) Wilt thou set thy foot o' my neck?
SIR ANDREW (*to Maria*) Or o' mine either?
SIR TOBY (*to Maria*) Shall I play my freedom at tray-trip,
and become thy bondslave?   180
SIR ANDREW (*to Maria*) I'faith, or I either?

---

166 dear] F2; *deero* F1 (*interpreted by* DANIEL *as* 'dear, O')   168.1 *Sir Toby . . . from hiding*]
OXFORD; *not in* F

---

161 **strange** remote, aloof. Compare *Errors* 2.2.113, 'look strange and frown',
and *Romeo* 2.1.144: 'I should have
been more strange, I must confess'.
stout proud. Compare *Contention*
1.1.185: 'As stout and proud as he
were lord of all'.
162, 167 **Jove** To suggest, as editors have
done, that *Jove* here merely replaces
'God' to conform with the prohibition
in 1606 of the use of God's name in
stage plays, completely misses the
point: the amorous ruler of the classical gods is the perfect deity for Malvolio in his amorous triumph (and again
at 3.4.72, 79).
164 **entertain'st** accept

166 **still** always
170 **thousands** (of pounds, or ducats)
Sophy Shah of Persia. In 1599 Sir
Robert Shirley returned from an embassy to the Shah and boasted of the
rewards (compare *pension* at l. 169) he
had received. An account of his adven-
tures and those of his two brothers was
published in 1600, and a play, *The
Travels of the Three English Brothers*, by
John Day, William Rowley, and George
Wilkins, in 1607.
176 **gull-catcher** fool-tricker
179 **play** wager
tray-trip a dice-game in which winning
depended on throwing a three (*tray*,
from Old French *treis* or Italian *tre*)

151

SIR TOBY (*to Maria*) Why, thou hast put him in such a
   dream that when the image of it leaves him, he must
   run mad.

MARIA Nay, but say true, does it work upon him?   185

SIR TOBY Like aqua vitae with a midwife.

MARIA If you will then see the fruits of the sport, mark his
   first approach before my lady. He will come to her in
   yellow stockings, and 'tis a colour she abhors, and cross-
   gartered, a fashion she detests; and he will smile upon   190
   her, which will now be so unsuitable to her disposition,
   being addicted to a melancholy as she is, that it cannot
   but turn him into a notable contempt. If you will see it,
   follow me.

SIR TOBY To the gates of Tartar, thou most excellent devil   195
   of wit.

SIR ANDREW I'll make one too.   *Exeunt*

3.1   *Enter Viola as Cesario and Feste the clown, with*
        ⌈*pipe and*⌉ *tabor*

VIOLA Save thee, friend, and thy music. Dost thou live by
   thy tabor?

---

197 Exeunt] *Exeunt. Finis Actus secundus* F
  3.1.0.1–2 *Enter Viola . . . tabor*] OXFORD; *Enter Viola and Clowne.* F

183–4 **dream . . . run mad** The association of dreaming and madness recurs
   later in the play, for example in Sebastian's 'Or I am mad, or else this is a
   dream' (4.1.59).
186 **aqua vitae** brandy or other spirits
   with a midwife Shakespeare seems to
   have associated *aqua vitae* with mid-
   wives and nurses: Juliet's nurse twice
   asks for it at moments of stress (*Romeo*
   3.2.88, 4.4.43).
189 **a colour she abhors** At this point in
   Clifford Williams's 1966 RSC staging,
   'everyone looked sorrowfully at Aguecheek, who at that moment realized
   that he had been fruitlessly wooing
   Olivia while dressed from head to foot
   in vilest yellow' (Hugh Leonard, *Plays
   and Players*, August 1966, p. 17). Subsequent productions have borrowed
   the idea, often modifying it to a single
   item (hat, or plumes, or gloves) to
   avoid the risk of blunting the impact

of Malvolio's yellow stockings later.
193 **notable contempt** notorious object of
   contempt
195 **Tartar** the hell of classical mythology
3.1.0.1 *Enter Viola . . . and Feste* Beneath
   the wit of their exchange runs an
   undercurrent of wry, wary tension:
   both are paid servants who are more
   than they seem and are therefore to
   some extent rivals. For a fuller discussion, see Introduction, pp. 56–7.
0.2 ⌈*pipe and*⌉ *tabor* Jesters commonly
   played a pipe with one hand while
   tapping out a *tabor* (small drum, hanging
   from the neck or belt) with the other.
   The dialogue specifies only the *tabor*,
   and it is possible, if Feste is simply
   tapping out a rhythm, that Viola's *thy
   music* in her first line is an ironic over-
   statement, so that it is she who establishes the tone of witty banter.
1 **Save** God save
   live by make your living with

FESTE No sir, I live by the church.

VIOLA Art thou a churchman?

FESTE No such matter, sir. I do live by the church for I do   5
live at my house, and my house doth stand by the
church.

VIOLA So thou mayst say the king lies by a beggar if a
beggar dwell near him, or the church stands by thy
tabor if thy tabor stand by the church.   10

FESTE You have said, sir. To see this age! A sentence is but
a chev'rel glove to a good wit, how quickly the wrong
side may be turned outward.

VIOLA Nay, that's certain. They that dally nicely with
words may quickly make them wanton.   15

FESTE I would therefore my sister had had no name, sir.

VIOLA Why, man?

FESTE Why sir, her name's a word, and to dally with that
word might make my sister wanton. But indeed, words
are very rascals since bonds disgraced them.   20

VIOLA Thy reason, man?

FESTE Troth sir, I can yield you none without words, and

8 king] F2; Kings F1

3 **by** next to

4 **Art thou a churchman** Since Feste is
presumably wearing jester's motley
(see 1.5.52), Viola is either playing the
stooge or 'straight man' to the professional fool, or else her question is
ironical or incredulous.

8 **lies by** lives near (punning on 'goes to
bed with')

9 **stands** is maintained

11 **You have said, sir** Feste ruefully (and
perhaps ironically) acknowledges
Viola's word-play, as he does Maria's
at 1.5.24. The tone is carried through
into *To see this age* (i.e. 'just listen to
them!'), the professional commenting
on amateurs and potential rivals.
A **sentence** any saying (from Latin *sen-
tentia*, opinion, maxim)

12 **chev'rel** literally kid (from Middle English *chevrelle*), a very soft, pliable
leather (*OED sb.*[1]) easily turned inside
out, and so an apt expression for the

way in which a phrase can be man-
ipulated for witty purposes. Compare
Romeo 2.3.77–8: 'here's a wit of
cheveril, that stretches from an inch
narrow to an ell broad.'

12–13 **how   quickly ... outward** Proverbial ('To turn the wrong side out'
(Dent S431.1)), it may also serve as
a comment on those (like Feste himself
and Viola) who are not what they
seem.

14 **dally nicely** play subtly. Viola may
here be thinking ruefully of Orsino's
verbal elaboration and/or Olivia's declarations of love (with which she has
now to deal).

15, 19 **wanton** Viola means 'equivocal',
Feste 'unchaste'.

20 **bonds disgraced them** i.e. legal con-
tracts replaced a man's word of honour, thus *disgracing* him by implying
that his *word* was not to be trusted

words are grown so false I am loath to prove reason
with them.

VIOLA I warrant thou art a merry fellow, and car'st for   25
nothing.

FESTE Not so, sir, I do care for something; but in my conscience, sir, I do not care for you. If that be to care for
nothing, sir, I would it would make you invisible.

VIOLA Art not thou the Lady Olivia's fool?   30

FESTE No indeed sir, the Lady Olivia has no folly, she will
keep no fool, sir, till she be married, and fools are as like
husbands as pilchards are to herrings—the husband's
the bigger. I am indeed not her fool, but her corrupter of
words.   35

VIOLA I saw thee late at the Count Orsino's.

FESTE Foolery, sir, does walk about the orb like the sun, it
shines everywhere. I would be sorry, sir, but the fool
should be as oft with your master as with my mistress. I
think I saw your wisdom there.   40

VIOLA Nay, an thou pass upon me, I'll no more with thee.
Hold, *(giving money)* there's expenses for thee.

42 *giving money*] HANMER (*subs.*); *not in* F

28 **I do not care for you** The first overt
statement of the animosity underly-
ing the scene: Feste sees Viola as a
rival in the service of Orsino and
Olivia.

33 **pilchards** small fish similar to herrings.
Feste makes a double joke: he first
suggests that, since pilchards and herrings are alike, husbands are fools;
then, when the audience thinks the
joke is over, adds that husbands are in
fact bigger fools.

34–5 **corrupter of words** one who plays
with language

36 **late** lately

37 **Foolery . . . like the sun** The Elizabethans still believed that the sun cir-
cled the earth (*orb*).

37–8 **it shines everywhere** Proverbial:
'The sun shines upon all alike' (Tilley
S985).

38–40 **I would . . . wisdom there** Feste
appears to be saying that he would

be sorry if he were not allowed to
visit Orsino as much as Olivia; but
he is also responding to Viola's implied
criticism that he, Olivia's professional
fool, works for Orsino as well by
hinting that Viola does the same in
reverse: *I think I saw your wisdom*,
who also visits Olivia, *there* (with
Orsino). *Wisdom* is an ironic courtesy
title, implying that Viola, like Feste,
is a hired fool. Viola's next speech
makes it clear that she takes the
point.

38 **but** if it were not that

41 **pass upon** (a) express an opinion of,
or joke about (from the fencing term
meaning 'thrust', as at *Hamlet*
5.2.252–3: 'I pray you pass with your
best violence. | I am afeard you
make a wanton of me') (b) pass judgement upon (compare *Measure* 2.1.19:
'The jury passing on the prisoner's
life')

FESTE Now Jove in his next commodity of hair send thee a
beard.

VIOLA By my troth I'll tell thee, I am almost sick for one,   45
though I would not have it grow on *my* chin. Is thy lady
within?

FESTE Would not a pair of these have bred, sir?

VIOLA Yes, being kept together and put to use.

FESTE I would play Lord Pandarus of Phrygia, sir, to bring   50
a Cressida to this Troilus.

VIOLA (*giving money*) I understand you, sir, 'tis well
begged.

FESTE The matter I hope is not great, sir, begging but a
beggar: Cressida was a beggar. My lady is within, sir. I   55
will conster to them whence you come. Who you are
and what you would are out of my welkin—I might say
'element', but the word is over-worn.   *Exit*

46 *my*] F (my)   52 *giving money*] COLLIER 1858 (*subs.*); *not in* F

43 **commodity** consignment, supply. Compare 1 *Henry IV* 1.2.82–3: 'a commodity of good names'.

43–4 **send thee a beard** Actors sometimes
hint that Feste sees through Viola's
disguise, thus adding to the tension
between them, though she saves the
situation with her witty next line, and
quickly changes the subject. Perhaps,
too, Feste delicately puts pressure on
her in order to wring more money out
of her.

48–55 **Would not a pair . . . a beggar** Feste
as usual (see especially 5.1.22–43) is
quick to beg money (or more money).
By contrast Viola had indignantly rejected the idea that she was a *fee'd post*
at 1.5.274, when Olivia offered to pay
her. Whatever their similarities in
other respects, Viola's generosity contrasts sharply with Feste's mercenari-
ness.

48 **these** i.e. coins such as these
have bred have produced offspring
(with a possible pun on '(be enough
to) buy bread')

49 **put to use** (a) set to make (b) invested
to produce interest, as in 'usury'

50 **Pandarus** The archetypal go-between
or 'pander'; Shakespeare dramatized

him in *Troilus and Cressida*, probably
written soon after *Twelfth Night*.
Phrygia A country in Asia Minor; Troy
was reputedly on its western coast.

54 **matter** amount begged

54–5 **begging but a beggar** Guardianship
of rich orphans was 'begged' from the
sovereign.

55 **Cressida was a beggar** In some versions
of the story earlier than Shakespeare's,
she became a leprous beggar.

56 **conster to them** construe, explain to
those in the house. From Middle English *constru-en*. This phrase is *OED*'s
sole example of *conster* meaning 'explain'. Feste presumably chooses it to
give an air of mock-learning, as in
welkin and *element*, which follow.

57 **welkin** A word as affected as *element*,
for which Feste substitutes it. Shakespeare normally uses it in verbally extravagant contexts, especially at *LLL*
4.2.5, where Holofernes employs it as
part of a dictionary definition: 'the sky,
the welkin, the heaven'. Feste uses it
figuratively to mean 'beyond me', as
he uses *element* in the next line.

58 **element** This could mean 'sky, heaven'
(like *welkin* in the previous line), or 'of
the air' (one of the four 'elements'); so

VIOLA

This fellow is wise enough to play the fool,
And to do that well craves a kind of wit.   60
He must observe their mood on whom he jests,
The quality of persons, and the time,
And like the haggard, check at every feather
That comes before his eye. This is a practice
As full of labour as a wise man's art,   65
For folly that he wisely shows is fit,
But wise men, folly-fall'n, quite taint their wit.
        Enter Sir Toby and Sir Andrew
SIR TOBY Save you, gentleman.
VIOLA And you, sir.

---

63 And] F; Not RANN (*conj.* Johnson)   67 wise men] CAPELL; wisemens F   67.1 *Sir Andrew*] *Andrew* F

out of my . . . element means 'beyond my capacity, none of my business'. As *the word is over-worn* suggests, it had become an affectation, also mocked twice in Dekker's *Satiromastix* of 1601 (1.2.187–8 and 5.1.119–20).

59 **wise . . . fool** A complimentary version of the proverbial 'no man can play the fool so well as the wise man' (Tilley M321).

60 **wit** intelligence

61 **their mood** the mood of those

62 **quality** nature. Compare *Antony* 1.1.56: 'The qualities of people'.

63 **haggard** a wild hawk caught as an adult and then tamed
check at every feather start at, respond sensitively to, the slightest thing. Most editors take this to mean 'fly indiscriminately at every bird', sometimes referring to *OED, check, v.*[1] 6b, which cites Simon Latham's *Falconry* (1615), where *check* means when the hawk 'forsaketh her natural flight' to fly at other birds which distract her. But Maurice Pope demonstrates an important difference between *check* and *check at*: in the second book of Latham's *Falconry* (1618), a well-trained hawk is said 'never to understand what it is to check at the fist' but will prove 'a certain and bold comer' (Latham, 2.11, p. 37), and he compares *Hamlet*

4.7.61, 'As checking at his voyage', i.e. shying away from it (*OED, check, v.*[1] 6a). And *feather* never means 'bird' in Shakespeare, but 'its most frequent association . . . is lightness' (as at *Venus* l. 302: 'Anon he starts at stirring of a feather'), and Latham advises trainers to touch the *haggard* with a feather rather than the hand until she is 'willing to be touched without starting'. Pope concludes that, as the haggard is 'wild, unaccustomed to humans, and thoroughly nervous', the fool 'has not been bred in . . . educated society' and 'has to find out for himself the dangers and the opportunities it offers' ('Shakespeare's Falconry', *SS 44* (1992), 131–43; pp. 139–42).

64 **practice** skill

66 **wisely shows is fit** consciously adopts is to the point

67 **wise men, folly-fall'n** wise men who have fallen into folly (like Malvolio in the previous scene). Compare *As You Like It* 2.7.56–7: 'The wise man's folly is anatomized | Even by the squandering glances of the fool.' In her distinction between the fool's wisdom and the wise man's folly, Viola echoes Olivia's view at 1.5.88–91.
taint discredit (or stronger, 'disease', as at 3.4.13, where Malvolio is said to be *tainted in's wits*, i.e. mad)

SIR ANDREW *Dieu vous garde, monsieur.*   70

VIOLA *Et vous aussi, votre serviteur.*

SIR ANDREW I hope, sir, you are, and I am yours.

SIR TOBY Will you encounter the house? My niece is desirous you should enter if your trade be to her.

VIOLA I am bound to your niece, sir: I mean she is the list   75
of my voyage.

SIR TOBY Taste your legs, sir, put them to motion.

VIOLA My legs do better understand me, sir, than I understand what you mean by bidding me taste my legs.

SIR TOBY I mean to go, sir, to enter.   80

VIOLA I will answer you with gait and entrance.

    Enter Olivia, and Maria, her gentlewoman

But we are prevented. (*To Olivia*) Most excellent accomplished lady, the heavens rain odours on you.

SIR ANDREW (*to Sir Toby*) That youth's a rare courtier;
'rain odours'—well.   85

VIOLA My matter hath no voice, lady, but to your own
most pregnant and vouchsafed ear.

81.1 *Enter Olivia . . . gentlewoman*] *after* 'preuented' *in* F   *Maria, her*] CAMBRIDGE (*subs.*);
not in F

70–2 **Dieu . . . yours** *Dieu vous garde* ('God save you') is the first line of John Eliot's *Ortho-epia Gallica* (1593), a series of dialogues in French with English on the facing page, which Shakespeare is believed to have drawn on for *Henry V* (J. W. Lever, 'Shakespeare's French Fruits', *SS* 6 (Cambridge, 1953), 79–90). It gives the reader the chance to pick up French phrases without learning French, which Sir Andrew has presumably done. So when Viola replies *Et vous aussi, votre serviteur* ('And you, too; (I am) your servant'), he thinks it expedient to switch back into English straight-away.

73 **encounter** go to meet (as if the house were a person), i.e. enter. Sir Toby mocks Viola's courtly *votre serviteur*.

75 **bound to** bound for (a nautical phrase, continuing Toby's metaphor of *trade*) **list** boundary, furthest point (*OED sb.*[3] 8)—hence 'destination'. Compare *1 Henry IV* 4.1.51–2: 'The very list, the

very utmost bound | Of all our fortunes.'

77 **Taste** try (from Old French *taster*, to touch or feel; *OED v.* 1). Compare 3.4.236: 'to taste their valour'.

78–9 **understand . . . understand** stand under . . . comprehend. Compare *Two Gentlemen* 2.5.26–8: 'I'll but lean, and my staff under-stands me. | It stands under thee indeed.'

81 **gait and entrance** (replying to Toby's *to go* and *to enter*, with a quibble on 'gate', the spelling in F)

82 **prevented** anticipated, forestalled

83 **the heavens rain** i.e. may the heavens rain

85 **well** i.e. that sounds good

86 **hath no voice** must not be spoken

87 **pregnant** receptive. This sense of *pregnant* (*OED a.*[2] 3d) seems to have been introduced into English by Shakespeare. Compare *Hamlet* 3.2.59: 'crook the pregnant hinges of the knee'.
vouchsafed attentive (literally, 'bestowed', 'granted')

SIR ANDREW (*to Sir Toby*) 'Odours', 'pregnant', and
  'vouchsafed'—I'll get 'em all three all ready.
OLIVIA Let the garden door be shut, and leave me to my   90
  hearing.   *Exeunt Sir Toby, Sir Andrew, and Maria*
  Give me your hand, sir.
VIOLA
  My duty, madam, and most humble service.
OLIVIA What is your name?
VIOLA
  Cesario is your servant's name, fair princess.   95
OLIVIA
  My servant, sir? 'Twas never merry world
  Since lowly feigning was called compliment.
  You're servant to the Count Orsino, youth.
VIOLA
  And he is yours, and his must needs be yours.
  Your servant's servant is *your* servant, madam.   100
OLIVIA
  For him, I think not on him. For his thoughts,
  Would they were blanks rather than filled with me.
VIOLA
  Madam, I come to whet your gentle thoughts
  On his behalf.
OLIVIA   O by your leave, I pray you.
  I bade you never speak again of him;   105

---

91 *Exeunt Sir Toby . . . and Maria*] ROWE; *not in* F   100 *your*] F (your)

89 **all ready** fully prepared, 'on the tip of
  my tongue'
90 **garden door** A door set into a garden
  wall; a walled garden provides a suitably enclosed location for intimate
  exchanges, and Olivia's next phrase
  seeks to capitalize on their privacy at
  once.
92 **Give me your hand** In their previous
  scene together (1.5), Viola made the
  emotional running by eloquently advocating Orsino's cause and thus arous-
  ing Olivia's interest in herself; in this
  scene, the initiative passes to Olivia,
  putting Viola on the defensive.
93 **My duty** Viola keeps her distance: this

implies a bow, and perhaps a formal
kissing of Olivia's hand.
94 **What is your name** Again Olivia tries
  to steer the conversation to personal
  topics. Viola's *your servant* (l. 95) is
  another attempt to back off.
95 **princess** (a flattering exaggeration, but
  also part of the attempt to be courtly
  rather than intimate, by exaggerating
  the difference in rank between them)
96 **'Twas never merry world** A proverbial
  phrase (Dent W878.1), meaning
  'Things have never been the same'.
97 **lowly feigning** pretended humility
102 **blanks** unused sheets of paper

But would you undertake another suit,
I had rather hear you to solicit that
Than music from the spheres.
VIOLA   Dear lady—
OLIVIA
Give me leave, beseech you. I did send,
After the last enchantment you did here,   110
A ring in chase of you. So did I abuse
Myself, my servant, and I fear me you.
Under your hard construction must I sit,
To force that on you in a shameful cunning
Which you knew none of yours. What might you   115
    think?
Have you not set mine honour at the stake
And baited it with all th'unmuzzled thoughts
That tyrannous heart can think? To one of your
    receiving
Enough is shown. A cypress, not a bosom,
Hides my heart. So let me hear you speak.   120
VIOLA
I pity you.
OLIVIA   That's a degree to love.

110 here] F (heare)

108 **music from the spheres** heavenly
  music thought to be made by the heavens as they moved (a belief attributed
  to Pythagoras)
111 **abuse** wrong
113 **hard construction** unfavourable interpretation (of my behaviour)
114 **To force** for having forced
116–17 **at the stake ... baited ... unmuzzled** as bears were tied up and baited
  with dogs. The ferocity of this image
  echoes that of Orsino at 1.1.21–2: 'my
  desires, like fell and cruel hounds, |
  E'er since pursue me.' Both indicate
  intensity of feeling.
118–20 **To one ... my heart** To someone
  of your perception, nothing more
  needs to be said, because my heart is
  covered not even by flesh, but merely
  by a transparent film (presumably
  figurative, since the metaphor of ex-

posing her heart is weakened if she is
actually wearing dark gauze; the implication is that she has changed out
of her mourning clothes, reflecting the
new interest in life given by her dawn-
ing love for Cesario).
118 **receiving** perception
119 **cypress** veil of transparent silken
  gauze (with the additional sombre
  overtone of the tree of the churchyard;
  compare 2.4.51)
121 **degree** step. The word often had a
  specifically theatrical connotation,
  meaning 'stepped tiers of seats', as in
  the Lord Chamberlain's memoranda
  about arrangements for Elizabeth I's
  entertainment of Duke Virginio Orsino
  in 1601, cited by Hotson, p. 15:
  Whitehall 'was richly hanged and de-
  grees placed round about it'.

VIOLA

No, not a grece, for 'tis a vulgar proof
That very oft we pity enemies.

OLIVIA

Why then, methinks 'tis time to smile again.
O world, how apt the poor are to be proud!   125
If one should be a prey, how much the better
To fall before the lion than the wolf!
    Clock strikes
The clock upbraids me with the waste of time.
Be not afraid, good youth, I will not have you;
And yet when wit and youth is come to harvest   130
Your wife is like to reap a proper man.
There lies your way, due west.

VIOLA   Then westward ho!

---

122 grece] F (grize)

---

122 **grece** step. Editors either retain F's
spelling 'grize' or alter it to 'grise'.
OED lists the word as 'grece', and
derives it from the plural form of Old
French *gré*, taken as a collective singular meaning 'flight of steps', from
which, in the fifteenth century, the
singular form *grece* developed. But it
seems to have been unfamiliar even in
Shakespeare's day, for when he uses it
again, at *Othello* 1.3.199, he explains
what it means: 'a grece or step'. Its
use there may reflect the Duke's embarrassed attempt to win Brabanzio
round to the marriage of Othello and
Desdemona; it is hard to see why it is
used here. It is probably the most
difficult word in the play to make com-
prehensible to a modern audience, or
even to pronounce (*OED* proposes
'grīs'). Since it means the same as
degree in the previous line, the effect of
the exchange is: 'That's a step towards
love. | No, not one!'
    vulgar proof common experience.
124-7 It is hard to be sure of Olivia's
exact meaning in these lines; but perhaps their incoherence dramatizes the
confusion of Olivia's emotions.
124 **to smile again** perhaps 'to discard
melancholy'; or perhaps Olivia is
trying to put a brave face on her re-

jection by Cesario
125 **O world ... proud** Either Olivia is
commenting on Cesario, proudly rejecting what is offered, or on herself,
being proud of falling in love with such
a *proper man* (l. 131).
127 **the lion than the wolf** This probably
means: a *proud* creature (Cesario), not
an ignoble one; or (less likely) Orsino—a king of men as the *lion* is among
beasts—rather than Cesario (Olivia
consoling herself for her failure).
127.1-28 *Clock ... time* Perhaps Shakespeare introduces the striking clock to
check, temporarily, the mounting tension of the scene; and Olivia's *waste of
time* may allude to her convoluted attempt to make the best of things in her
previous four lines.
130 **when wit ... to harvest** when wit ri-
pens into wisdom, and youth grows up
131 **proper** handsome
132 **due west** Perhaps Olivia uses *west*
metaphorically, to express sadly the end
of their relationship; compare Sonnet
73.5-6: 'In me thou seest the twilight
of such day | As after sunset fadeth in
the west'. If so, Viola's next phrase
vigorously dispels any such implication.
    westward ho! Thames watermen's cry
to attract passengers for the court at
Westminster from the City of London.

Grace and good disposition attend your ladyship.
You'll nothing, madam, to my lord by me?
OLIVIA
Stay: 135
I prithee tell me what thou think'st of me.
VIOLA
That you do think you are not what you are.
OLIVIA
If I think so, I think the same of you.
VIOLA
Then think you right, I am not what I am.
OLIVIA
I would you were as I would have you be.   140
VIOLA
Would it be better, madam, than I am?
I wish it might, for now I am your fool.
OLIVIA (*aside*)
O what a deal of scorn looks beautiful
In the contempt and anger of his lip!
A murd'rous guilt shows not itself more soon   145

135-6 Stay: | ... of me] *as* CAPELL; *one line in* F

133 **good disposition** peace of mind
135-6 **Stay ... of me** This is printed as a
single line in F, perhaps a hexameter
with an omitted first syllable, or a
pause after *Stay*; but to follow Capell
and to print *Stay* as a separate line
focuses an important dramatic point.
Up to now, Olivia has tried in vain to
draw some positive response from
Viola/Cesario; now she is forced to
come out into the open and ask, hu-
miliatingly, for Viola's opinion of her.
For Olivia to cry *Stay!* (i.e. 'don't go!'),
but then to have a long pause, emphasizes that this is an emotional crisis
for her, and the turning-point of their
exchange.
136 **thou** Olivia changes from 'you' to the
familiar form.
137 **think you are not what you are** either
in loving a woman, or in loving beneath your rank, or more generally:
you do not know yourself (first in at-

tempting to shut yourself away for
seven years, now in rushing to the
opposite extreme and falling for a page
who is not even that)
138 **the same of you** Perhaps Olivia implies that she thinks Cesario to be of
noble birth in spite of serving Orsino.
Or she may not mean that much; she
may simply be answering Viola back:
the five one-liners of ll. 136-40 indicate that the scene is speeding up and
hotting up.
139 **what I am** what I seem
142 **might** might be better
  I am your fool you have put me in a
foolish position
143-4 **O what a deal ... his lip** Viola's
anger only intensifies Olivia's passion,
as the similarly disguised Rosalind's
does Phoebe's at *As You Like It* 3.5.65-
6: 'Sweet youth, I pray you chide a
year together. | I had rather hear you
chide than this man woo.'

Than love that would seem hid. Love's night is noon.
(*To Viola*) Cesario, by the roses of the spring,
By maidhood, honour, truth, and everything,
I love thee so that maugre all thy pride,
Nor wit nor reason can my passion hide.   150
Do not extort thy reasons from this clause:
For that I woo, thou therefore hast no cause.
But rather reason thus with reason fetter:
Love sought is good, but given unsought is better.

VIOLA
By innocence I swear, and by my youth,   155
I have one heart, one bosom, and one truth,
And that no woman has, nor never none
Shall mistress be of it save I alone.
And so adieu, good madam, never more
Will I my master's tears to you deplore.   160

OLIVIA
Yet come again, for thou perhaps mayst move
That heart which now abhors, to like his love.

                                        Exeunt severally

3.2   *Enter Sir Toby, Sir Andrew, and Fabian*
SIR ANDREW No, faith, I'll not stay a jot longer.
SIR TOBY Thy reason, dear venom, give thy reason.
FABIAN You must needs yield your reason, Sir Andrew.

162.1 *severally*] OXFORD; *not in* F

146 **love that would seem hid** Olivia seems
   to be indulging in wishful thinking,
   suggesting that Viola's anger indicates
   concealed passion. Perhaps this embol-
   dens her to make her first overt declaration of love in the next lines.
   Love's night is noon i.e. love shines out
   even while attempting concealment
149 **maugre** despite (Old French *maugré,
   malgré*)
151 **extort thy reasons . . . clause** draw a
   forced conclusion . . . premiss
152 **For that . . . cause** Because I woo, you
   do not need to do so (or to love in return)
153 **reason thus . . . fetter** overcome one
   argument with another thus
156 **bosom** 'that part of the body which
   contains the heart' (Schmidt)

160 **master's tears to you deplore** try to
   make you feel sorry for Orsino's suffering
161 **thou** i.e. you if anyone
3.2 This is the half-way point in playing
   time. So far, the structure of the play
   alternates two principal actions:
   Viola's wooing of Olivia on Orsino's
   behalf, and the plot against Malvolio.
   The next section is based upon two
   stratagems: the further gulling and
   maddening of Malvolio, and the mock-
   duel between Viola and Sir Andrew,
   which is vigorously launched in this
   scene with Sir Andrew's furious entry
   (Sir Toby refers to his *venom* in l. 2).
2–3 **Thy . . . You** Toby uses the familiar
   thy, Fabian the polite *you*.

SIR ANDREW Marry, I saw your niece do more favours to
  the Count's servingman than ever she bestowed upon   5
  me. I saw't i'th' orchard.
SIR TOBY Did she see thee the while, old boy? Tell me that.
SIR ANDREW As plain as I see you now.
FABIAN This was a great argument of love in her toward
  you.   10
SIR ANDREW 'Slight, will you make an ass o' me?
FABIAN I will prove it legitimate, sir, upon the oaths of
  judgement and reason.
SIR TOBY And they have been grand-jurymen since before
  Noah was a sailor.   15
FABIAN She did show favour to the youth in your sight
  only to exasperate you, to awake your dormouse valour, to put fire in your heart and brimstone in your
  liver. You should then have accosted her, and with
  some excellent jests, fire-new from the mint, you should   20
  have banged the youth into dumbness. This was looked
  for at your hand, and this was balked. The double gilt of
  this opportunity you let time wash off, and you are now
  sailed into the north of my lady's opinion, where you
  will hang like an icicle on a Dutchman's beard unless   25

3.2.7 thee the] F3; the F1

4 **favours** Sir Andrew saw Olivia give
  Viola her hand as he left the stage at
  3.1.91–2.
6 **orchard** An *orchard* is not distinguished from a garden in Shakespeare's
  works; but the modern sense of 'an
  area of fruit-trees' existed during Shakespeare's life-time, and in 1616 his
  will distinguished between orchards
  and gardens (see S. Schoenbaum, *William Shakespeare: A Documentary Life*
  (Oxford, 1975), p. 248). So perhaps Sir
  Andrew means that *he* was in the orchard or less formal area beyond the
  door of the walled garden in which
  Olivia received Cesario (3.1.91).
7 **the while** at the time
9 **argument** proof
11 **'Slight** (by) God's light (a favourite
  oath of Sir Andrew's: compare 2.5.30)
  will you make an ass of me Proverbial
  (Dent A379.1).

12 **prove it legitimate** give authority for
  my case
14 **grand-jurymen** A grand jury decided if
  the evidence was strong enough for a
  case to go to full trial.
17 **dormouse** i.e. sleeping (also 'timid')
18 **brimstone** sulphur (associated with
  hell-fire)
20 **fire-new from the mint** brand-new,
  straight from the melting-pot, like a
  newly-forged coin
22 **balked** shirked
22–3 **double gilt of this opportunity**
  double-gilding (maintaining the image
  of the *mint*; compare modern 'golden
  opportunity')
24 **into the north ... opinion** i.e. into Olivia's cold disfavour
25 **Dutchman** Probably William Barentz,
  who led an expedition to the Arctic in
  1596–7.

you do redeem it by some laudable attempt either of
valour or policy.

SIR ANDREW   An't be any way, it must be with valour, for
policy I hate. I had as lief be a Brownist as a politician.

SIR TOBY   Why then, build me thy fortunes upon the basis   30
of valour. Challenge me the Count's youth to fight with
him, hurt him in eleven places. My niece shall take note
of it; and assure thyself, there is no love-broker in the
world can more prevail in man's commendation with
woman than report of valour.   35

FABIAN   There is no way but this, Sir Andrew.

SIR ANDREW   Will either of you bear me a challenge to
him?

SIR TOBY   Go, write it in a martial hand, be curst and brief.
It is no matter how witty so it be eloquent and full of   40
invention. Taunt him with the licence of ink. If thou
'thou'st' him some thrice, it shall not be amiss, and as
many lies as will lie in thy sheet of paper, although the
sheet were big enough for the bed of Ware in England,

27 **policy** political strategy
29 **Brownist** member of an extreme puritan sect founded in 1581 by Robert
Browne (*c*.1550–1633) who advocated
the separation of church and state
politician intriguer, strategist
30, 31 **me ... me** Examples of the so-
called 'ethic dative' in which *me* originally meant 'for me'. By Shakespeare's
time, however, it had become little
more than an intensifier, by which the
speaker drew attention to himself. It is
not surprising that it is used collo-
quially by self-assertive characters like
Sir Toby and Falstaff (e.g. at *1 Henry
IV* 2.5.204: 'I made me no more ado').
Sir Andrew picks it up at l. 37.
39 **martial hand** military style (or perhaps, if it refers to the handwriting,
aggressive flourishes)
39–45 **be curst ... down** Sir Toby's advice
follows contemporary duelling manuals in advocating brevity but not in
urging eloquence and multiple giving
of the lie. In his *Book of Honour and
Arms* (1590), Sir William Segar recom-
mends 'all plainness of words and
phrases, leaving aside eloquence and

ambiguity of speech; for it sufficeth . . .
[to] say "Thou liest", without adding
any word thereunto' (p. 17). Presumably Sir Toby looks forward to the
verbal fatuity which Sir Andrew duly
provides (3.4.144–64).
39 **curst and brief** sharp and terse
40 **so** provided that
41 **invention** matter
licence of ink freedom encouraged by
writing rather than speaking
42 **thou'st** call him 'thou' (an insult to a
stranger: *you* is the polite form, *thou* is
used to inferiors. A striking contemporary example of the insulting use of
thou occurred at the trial of Sir Walter
Raleigh in 1603: 'All that he did was
by thy instigation, thou viper; for I
"thou" thee, thou traitor!' (first cited
by Theobald).)
43 **lies** accusations of lying. 'Giving the
lie' was the deadliest insult, which
could only be answered by a duel.
44 **bed of Ware** Famous Elizabethan bed-
stead, eleven feet (3.35 metres) square,
now in the Victoria and Albert Mu-
seum, London.

set 'em down, go about it. Let there be gall enough in   45
thy ink; though thou write with a goose-pen, no matter.
About it.

SIR ANDREW Where shall I find you?

SIR TOBY We'll call thee at the cubiculo. Go.

Exit Sir Andrew

FABIAN This is a dear manikin to you, Sir Toby.   50

SIR TOBY I have been dear to him, lad, some two thousand
strong or so.

FABIAN We shall have a rare letter from him; but you'll
not deliver't.

SIR TOBY Never trust me then; and by all means stir on the   55
youth to an answer. I think oxen and wain-ropes cannot hale them together. For Andrew, if he were opened
and you find so much blood in his liver as will clog the
foot of a flea, I'll eat the rest of th'anatomy.

FABIAN And his opposite, the youth, bears in his visage   60
no great presage of cruelty.

Enter Maria

SIR TOBY Look where the youngest wren of nine comes.

MARIA If you desire the spleen, and will laugh yourselves
into stitches, follow me. Yon gull Malvolio is turned
heathen, a very renegado, for there is no Christian that   65

---

45 down, go about it] F; down. Go, about it CAPELL   49 the] F; thy HANMER *(conj.* Thirlby)
62 nine] THEOBALD; mine F

---

45 **gall** (a) oak-gall, an ingredient of ink
   (b) bitterness
46 **goose-pen** quill made of goose-feather
   (the goose is proverbially cowardly: 'to
   say "bo" to a goose' is cited from a
   pamphlet of 1588 by *OED (Bo, int.* b))
49 **cubiculo** bedroom (a humorous or
   affected usage, from the Italian word
   for bedchamber)
50 **manikin** puppet (literally 'little man')
51 **dear** costly
   two thousand (pounds, or ducats; see
   note to 1.3.20)
56 **oxen and wain-ropes** i.e. waggon-ropes
   pulled by oxen
57 **hale** drag
58 **liver** (supposed to be the source of
   blood, which engendered courage)
58 **clog** weigh down

59 **anatomy** skeleton (implying that he is
   merely skin and bone: compare Dr
   Pinch in *Errors* 5.1.238–9: 'a hungry
   lean-faced villain, | A mere anatomy')
60 **opposite** opponent
61 **presage** anticipation
62 **youngest wren of nine** i.e. the youngest hatched, and so supposedly the
   smallest, of the brood of the smallest
   bird (another joke about Maria's size);
   but F's *wren of mine* may be correct,
   Sir Toby playing on the phrase to
   claim possession of Maria
63 **the spleen** a fit of laughter (the spleen
   was believed to be the seat of laughter)
64 **gull** fool, dupe
65 **renegado** Spanish form of 'renegade',
   Christian converted to Islam

means to be saved by believing rightly can ever believe
such impossible passages of grossness. He's in yellow
stockings.

SIR TOBY And cross-gartered?

MARIA Most villainously, like a pedant that keeps a school   70
i'th' church. I have dogged him like his murderer. He
does obey every point of the letter that I dropped to betray him. He does smile his face into more lines than is
in the new map with the augmentation of the Indies.
You have not seen such a thing as 'tis. I can hardly for-   75
bear hurling things at him. I know my lady will strike
him. If she do, he'll smile, and take't for a great favour.

SIR TOBY Come bring us, bring us where he is.   *Exeunt*

3.3   *Enter Sebastian and Antonio*

SEBASTIAN

I would not by my will have troubled you,
But since you make your pleasure of your pains
I will no further chide you.

ANTONIO

I could not stay behind you. My desire,
More sharp than filèd steel, did spur me forth,   5
And not all love to see you—though so much
As might have drawn one to a longer voyage—
But jealousy what might befall your travel,
Being skilless in these parts, which to a stranger,
Unguided and unfriended, often prove   10
Rough and unhospitable. My willing love
The rather by these arguments of fear

---

78 *Exeunt*] F (*Exeunt Omnes.*)

---

66 **rightly** orthodoxly
    can (who) can
67 **passages of grossness** grossly improb-
    able statements (in the letter)
70 **villainously** abominably (compare *1
    Henry IV* 2.5.407–8: 'a villainous trick
    of thine eye')
    pedant teacher
70–1 **keeps a school i'th' church** (because
    no schoolroom is available, for
    example in a small rural community)
73–4 **more lines . . . Indies** This probably

refers to a map published in 1599
showing the East Indies more fully than
in earlier maps (i.e. in *augmentation*),
and criss-crossed by many rhumb-lines.

3.3.5 **filèd steel** (as in a sword?)
6 **all** only
8 **jealousy** fear, concern
9 **skilless in** unacquainted with
    stranger foreigner
12 **rather** more speedily (the comparative
    of the obsolete adverb 'rathe', *OED
    adv.* 1)

Set forth in your pursuit.

SEBASTIAN   My kind Antonio,
I can no other answer make but thanks,
And thanks; and ever oft good turns   15
Are shuffled off with such uncurrent pay.
But were my worth as is my conscience firm,
You should find better dealing. What's to do?
Shall we go see the relics of this town?

ANTONIO
Tomorrow sir, best first go see your lodging.   20

SEBASTIAN
I am not weary, and 'tis long to night.
I pray you let us satisfy our eyes
With the memorials and the things of fame
That do renown this city.

ANTONIO   Would you'd pardon me.
I do not without danger walk these streets.   25
Once in a sea-fight 'gainst the Count his galleys
I did some service, of such note indeed
That were I ta'en here it would scarce be answered.

SEBASTIAN
Belike you slew great number of his people.

ANTONIO
Th'offence is not of such a bloody nature,   30
Albeit the quality of the time and quarrel
Might well have given us bloody argument.

3.3.15 ever oft] F; ever thanks; and oft THEOBALD; ever. Oft STEEVENS

15 **ever oft** very often, a variant of the idiomatic 'ever and oft'. For discussion of the short line, see Introduction, p. 40.
16 **shuffled off** shrugged aside
uncurrent worthless, not legal tender. This is *OED*'s earliest example of the word.
17 **worth** wealth. Compare *Romeo* 2.5.32–4: 'They are but beggars that can count their worth, | But my true love is grown to such excess | I cannot sum up some of half my wealth.'
conscience sense of indebtedness
firm substantial
19 **relics** antiquities. Compare *Errors* 1.2.12–13, where Antipholus of Syracuse arrives in Ephesus eager to 'view

the manners of the town, | Peruse the traders, gaze upon the buildings'.
26 **Count his** Count's (a common Elizabethan form of the possessive (Abbott 217))
28 **ta'en** captured
scarce be answered be difficult for me to make reparation (i.e. his life would be in danger)
29 **Belike** perhaps, I suppose
31 **quality** circumstances
32 **bloody argument** reason for bloodshed. According to the First Officer and Orsino at 5.1.45–66, there was *bloody argument*. See Introduction p. 41 for a discussion of this discrepancy.

It might have since been answered in repaying
What we took from them, which for traffic's sake
Most of our city did. Only myself stood out,   35
For which if I be latchèd in this place
I shall pay dear.

SEBASTIAN   Do not then walk too open.

ANTONIO
It doth not fit me. Hold sir, here's my purse.
In the south suburbs at the Elephant
Is best to lodge. I will bespeak our diet   40
Whiles you beguile the time and feed your knowledge
With viewing of the town. There shall you have me.

SEBASTIAN Why I your purse?

ANTONIO
Haply your eye shall light upon some toy
You have desire to purchase; and your store   45
I think is not for idle markets, sir.

SEBASTIAN
I'll be your purse-bearer, and leave you
For an hour.

ANTONIO   To th' Elephant.

SEBASTIAN   I do remember.

                                  Exeunt severally

---

36 latchèd] KEIGHTLEY (*conj.* Hunter); lapsed F   48.1 *severally*] OXFORD; *not in* F

---

34 **traffic** trade
36 **latchèd** caught. *OED*, *lapse*, *v.* 8, ten-
    tatively suggests that F's 'lapsed' may
    be related to the noun *laps* or *lap* ('in
    the power of ') and so mean 'to pounce
    upon, apprehend'. This, *OED*'s only
    example of *lapse* in this sense, is
    strained, and *latchèd* is supported by
    Shakespearian usage elsewhere, for in-
    stance Sonnet 113.5–6, where the eye
    'no form delivers to the heart | Of bird,
    of flower, or shape which it doth latch'.
37 **pay dear** A grim pun: he will pay with
    his life.
38 **fit** suit

39 **Elephant** A common Elizabethan name
    for an inn. There was an Elephant inn
    in the south suburbs on Bankside near
    the Globe theatre, so this sounds like
    a local joke, especially since, according
    to Gustav Ungerer (see note to 2.3.71),
    the Elephant was 'an inn-cum-brothel'
    (p. 103).
40 **bespeak our diet** order our meal
42 **have me** meet me, find me (Schmidt)
44 **Haply** perhaps
    toy trifle
45 **your store** the money that you have
46 **not for idle markets** i.e. not large
    enough to spend on luxuries

3.4   *Enter Olivia and Maria*

OLIVIA *(aside)*

I have sent after him, he says he'll come.
How shall I feast him? What bestow of him?
For youth is bought more oft than begged or borrowed.
I speak too loud.
(To Maria) Where's Malvolio? He is sad and civil,   5
And suits well for a servant with my fortunes.
Where is Malvolio?

MARIA He's coming, madam, but in very strange manner.
He is sure possessed, madam.

OLIVIA

Why, what's the matter, does he rave?   10

MARIA No, madam, he does nothing but smile. Your
ladyship were best to have some guard about you if he
come, for sure the man is tainted in's wits.

OLIVIA

Go call him hither.
      As Maria goes to call him, enter Malvolio, cross-
      gartered and wearing yellow stockings
                                       I am as mad as he,

3.4.4–5 I speak . . . civil] *as* POPE; *one line in* F   8–9 He's coming . . . possessed, madam]
as POPE; *verse in* F, *divided after* 'coming, madam'   14 *As Maria goes . . . stockings*] This
edition; *Enter Maluolio.* F

3.4 This huge scene (only the final scene is as long) covers a great deal of ground. For a discussion of some problems in sustaining it during performance, see Introduction, pp. 52–5.

1 **him** i.e. Cesario
  he says he'll come (theatrical sleight-of-hand, since Olivia is not actually told of this till ll. 54–6)

2 **of** on. See note to 2.5.26.

3 **youth . . . borrowed** The usual proverb was 'Better to buy than borrow (or beg, or beg or borrow)' (Tilley B783). Olivia is trying to be worldly-wise in order to bolster her confidence, or, as John Russell Brown suggests, 'repeating old saws with a new understanding of their truth' (*Shakespeare's Plays in Performance* (1966), p. 209).

5 **sad . . . civil** serious . . . respectful

9 **possessed** (by devils, mad)

13 **tainted** diseased

14 *As Maria goes . . . stockings* Some editors, including Wells in Oxford, give Maria an exit after *call him hither*, and delay Malvolio's entry, accompanied by Maria, until after Olivia's *equal be* (l. 15), so that Olivia speaks her couplet alone on a bare stage. Warren argues that the positioning of F's direction may imply that as Maria moves upstage to obey Olivia's order, Malvolio appears and thus makes an exit for her superfluous. This version has the advantage that Olivia and Malvolio vividly illustrate her point about *sad and merry madness*, the disadvantage that laughter at his appearance might drown her line.

If sad and merry madness equal be.   15
How now, Malvolio!
MALVOLIO Sweet lady, ho, ho!
OLIVIA
Smil'st thou? I sent for thee upon a sad occasion.
MALVOLIO Sad, lady? I could be sad. This does make some
   obstruction in the blood, this cross-gartering, but what   20
   of that? If it please the eye of one, it is with me as the
   very true sonnet is, 'Please one, and please all'.
⌈OLIVIA⌉
Why, how dost thou, man? What is the matter with
   thee?
MALVOLIO Not black in my mind, though yellow in my

19–22 Sad, lady . . . all'] *as* POPE; *verse in* F, *divided after* 'sad', 'blood', 'that', 'true'
23 OLIVIA] F2; *Mal.* F1; *Mar.* COLLIER 1858 *conj.*   Why, how . . . with thee?] *as* POPE; *two
verse lines in* F, *divided after* 'man'

17 **ho, ho** This presumably indicates that
Malvolio laughs as well as smiles (see
next line). John Russell Brown suggests that Laurence Olivier's Malvolio,
a 'petty, ambitious vulgarian', focused
an aspect of the character which comes
to the fore in this scene as he 'addresses his mistress with "Sweet lady,
ho, ho!" and with tags from popular
ballads' (*Shakespeare's Plays in Performance* (1966), p. 208). See notes to ll.
22, 24, and 28–9.
18 **upon a sad occasion** about a serious
matter
19 **Sad** The joke depends upon the two
meanings of *sad*: Olivia means 'serious', Malvolio 'melancholy', thought
to be caused by sluggish circulation,
which leads naturally into his reference to *obstruction in the blood* in the
next line.
21 **the eye of one** i.e. of Olivia—but by
using an allusive rather than a direct
style, Malvolio increases Olivia's bewil-
derment.
22 **sonnet** Not restricted, as now, to a
fourteen-line poem but used of any
lyric poem, as in Slender's 'book of
songs and sonnets' (*Merry Wives*
1.1.181–2).
   'Please one, and please all' A bawdy

ballad, published in 1592, implying
that all women want their own will,
in the sense of sexual desire. Malvolio
uses this bawdy familiarity in response
to what he thinks is Olivia's will, as
expressed in the letter, thus offending
and alarming her the more.
23 **OLIVIA** This is F2's correction of F's
Mal. It is surely correct (and not an
error for *Mar.*) since Malvolio's familiarity in the previous speech must
draw some reaction from Olivia herself; moreover, it is Olivia who uses the
'thou' form, from a lady to a servant
(though Malvolio presumably takes it
as affectionate familiarity), whereas
Maria always addresses him as 'you'.
F's *Mal*. could as easily be a misread-
ing of *Ol.* as of *Mar.*
24 **black in my mind** i.e. melancholy
(thought to be caused by black bile)
   black . . . yellow The association of the
two colours probably alludes to a
popular song. 'In 1567 (?) appeared
"A Doleful Ditty or Sorrowful sonet of
the Lord Darnley . . . to be sung to the
tune of Black and Yellow" ' (M. C.
Linthicum, *Costume in the Drama of
Shakespeare and his Contemporaries* (Oxford, 1936), p. 50).

legs. It did come to his hands, and commands shall be   25
executed. I think we do know the sweet roman hand.

OLIVIA
Wilt thou go to bed, Malvolio?

MALVOLIO 'To bed? Ay, sweetheart, and I'll come to
thee.'

He kisses his hand

OLIVIA God comfort thee. Why dost thou smile so, and   30
kiss thy hand so oft?

MARIA How do you, Malvolio?

MALVOLIO At your request? Yes, nightingales answer
daws.

MARIA Why appear you with this ridiculous boldness   35
before my lady?

MALVOLIO 'Be not afraid of greatness'—'twas well writ.

OLIVIA What mean'st thou by that, Malvolio?

MALVOLIO 'Some are born great'—

OLIVIA Ha?   40

MALVOLIO 'Some achieve greatness'—

OLIVIA What sayst thou?

MALVOLIO 'And some have greatness thrust upon them.'

OLIVIA Heaven restore thee.

MALVOLIO 'Remember who commended thy yellow   45
stockings'—

29.1 *He kisses his hand*] OXFORD (*subs., after speech prefix*); *not in* F   33–4 At your . . .
daws] *as* CAPELL; *two lines in* F, *divided after* 'request'

25 **It** i.e. the letter—another knowing allusion from Malvolio, more bewilder-
ment for Olivia.

26 **roman hand** fashionable Italian style,
rather than the native English 'secret-
ary' hand

27 **to bed** i.e. to cure his madness with
sleep. Malvolio mistakes her solicitous
concern for an amorous invitation.

28–9 **'To bed . . . to thee'** Morton Luce in
the original Arden edition (1906)
shows that this is another quotation
from a bawdy ballad, of which slightly
more is quoted in Richard Brome's *The
English Moor* (1659) 1.3.68–9: 'Go to
bed, sweetheart, I'll come to thee, |
Make thy bed fine and soft, I'll lie with
thee.'

31 **kiss thy hand** i.e. blowing a kiss with
his fingers, which Malvolio takes to be
the courtly manners of a *sir of note*
(l. 71). Compare *Othello* 2.1.175–7: 'it
had been better you had not kissed
your three fingers so oft, which now
again you are most apt to play the sir
in'.

33–4 **At your request . . . daws** i.e. 'Shall
I deign to reply to *you*? Yes, since even
the nightingale sings in response to the
crowing of a jackdaw' (thought to be
both noisy and stupid, and so an apt
way for Malvolio to describe Maria;
compare *1 Henry VI* 2.4.17–18: 'in
these nice sharp quillets of the law, |
Good faith, I am no wiser than a daw')

OLIVIA 'Thy yellow stockings'?

MALVOLIO 'And wished to see thee cross-gartered.'

OLIVIA 'Cross-gartered'?

MALVOLIO 'Go to, thou art made, if thou desir'st to be so.'   50

OLIVIA Am I made?

MALVOLIO 'If not, let me see thee a servant still.'

OLIVIA Why, this is very midsummer madness.

    Enter a Servant

SERVANT Madam, the young gentleman of the Count
    Orsino's is returned. I could hardly entreat him back.   55
    He attends your ladyship's pleasure.

OLIVIA I'll come to him.   *Exit Servant*
    Good Maria, let this fellow be looked to. Where's my
    cousin Toby? Let some of my people have a special care
    of him, I would not have him miscarry for the half of my   60
    dowry.   *Exeunt Olivia and Maria, severally*

MALVOLIO O ho, do you come near me now? No worse
    man than Sir Toby to look to me. This concurs directly
    with the letter, she sends him on purpose, that I may
    appear stubborn to him, for she incites me to that in the   65
    letter. 'Cast thy humble slough', says she, 'be opposite
    with a kinsman, surly with servants, let thy tongue
    tang arguments of state, put thyself into the trick of sin-
    gularity', and consequently sets down the manner how,

53.1 *a*] *not in* F   57 *Exit Servant*] CAPELL; *not in* F   61 *Exeunt . . . severally*] CAPELL (*subs.*);
exit F   68 tang] CAPELL; langer with F; tang with F2

---

53 **midsummer madness** the height of in-
   sanity. A proverbial remark—'It is
   midsummer moon with you' (Tilley
   M1117)—rather than an indication of
   the season in which the play is taking
   place: compare 'More matter for a May
   morning' (l. 137).

55 **hardly** with difficulty

60–1 **I would not . . . my dowry** Beneath
   all the extravagant humour of the
   scene, this statement (though of course
   Malvolio mistakes its import) reminds
   us that Olivia does value Malvolio, and
   that he is reliable and dependable as a
   steward when not side-tracked into
   playing the lover.

60 **miscarry** come to harm

62 **come near me** begin to understand me,
   i.e. to value me properly. Dent (N56.1)
   dates the expression from *c.* 1585.

65 **stubborn** harsh, rude

68 **tang** F reads 'langer with'; F2 corrects
   this to 'tang with'; Capell in turn
   emends to *tang*, omitting 'with' to
   bring it in line with the original letter
   (2.5.141). This is not absolutely essential, since not all quotations from the
   letter in the play are accurate. *Tang* is
   a rare word, apparently first used in
   this sense by Shakespeare (*OED v.*[2] 2),
   who himself uses it nowhere else as a
   verb.

69 **consequently** subsequently (the older
   use of the word (*OED adv.* 1))

as a sad face, a reverend carriage, a slow tongue, in the   70
habit of some sir of note, and so forth. I have limed her,
but it is Jove's doing, and Jove make me thankful. And
when she went away now, 'let this fellow be looked to'.
Fellow!—not 'Malvolio', nor after my degree, but 'fellow'. Why, everything adheres together that no dram of   75
a scruple, no scruple of a scruple, no obstacle, no incredulous or unsafe circumstance—what can be said?—
nothing that can be can come between me and the full
prospect of my hopes. Well, Jove, not I, is the doer of
this, and he is to be thanked.   80
  Enter Sir Toby, Fabian, and Maria
SIR TOBY Which way is he, in the name of sanctity? If all
the devils of hell be drawn in little, and Legion himself
possessed him, yet I'll speak to him.

80.1 *Sir*] CAPELL; *not in* F

70 **slow** deliberate (appropriate to one de-
livering *arguments of state*)
71 **habit** If each of the items in this list
refers to a different aspect of Malvolio's
appearance and behaviour, this may
mean 'way of dressing', as at *Hamlet*
3.4.126: 'My father, in his habit as he
lived.' Otherwise, it may refer to the
preceding *slow tongue*, i.e. the manner appropriate to a *sir of note*, as at
As You Like It 3.2.289–90: 'I will
speak to him like a saucy lackey, and
under that habit play the knave with
him.'
 sir of note distinguished gentleman
 limed Birds were caught by smearing
birdlime (a white sticky paste that dries
very slowly) on branches. Shakespeare
frequently uses this metaphorically, as
at *Hamlet* 3.3.68–9: 'O limèd soul that,
struggling to be free, | Art more en-
gaged!'
72 **Jove** See note to 2.5.162.
73 **fellow** The word originally meant
'companion' but became a condescending usage to inferiors (compare
5.1.9). Malvolio assumes that Olivia
uses it affectionately.
74 **after my degree** according to my rank
(as a steward)

75 **adheres together that** conspires to ensure that
75–6 **dram of a scruple . . . scruple of a
scruple** Both phrases mean 'scrap of
doubt', 'minute obstacle'. A *dram* is a
tiny weight. *Scruple* also means a tiny
weight and, figuratively, a doubt or
obstacle. This speech brilliantly brings
out the logic of Malvolio's thinking, his
steward's precision underpinning his
fantasies—and perhaps, too, his puritan precision, for another contemporary name for puritan was 'precisian',
'one who is rigidly precise or puncti-
lious in the observance of rules or
forms' (*OED, precisian*).
76–7 **incredulous or unsafe** incredible or
untrustworthy
82 **drawn in little** contracted into a small
space (punning on 'painted in miniature')
 Legion Sir Toby wrongly supposes this
to be a devil's name, misinterpreting
Mark 5:9, where the unclean spirit
says 'my name is legion [= innumer-
able], for we are many'. As there
seems to be no evidence that this was
a common error, it is presumably
Shakespeare's joke.

FABIAN Here he is, here he is. (*To Malvolio*) How is't with
  you, sir? How is't with you, man?   85

MALVOLIO Go off, I discard you. Let me enjoy my private.
  Go off.

MARIA Lo, how hollow the fiend speaks within him. Did
  not I tell you? Sir Toby, my lady prays you to have a
  care of him.   90

MALVOLIO Aha, does she so?

SIR TOBY Go to, go to. Peace, peace, we must deal gently
  with him. Let me alone. How do you, Malvolio? How is't
  with you? What, man, defy the devil. Consider, he's an
  enemy to mankind.   95

MALVOLIO Do you know what you say?

MARIA La you, an you speak ill of the devil, how he takes
  it at heart. Pray God he be not bewitched.

FABIAN Carry his water to th' wise woman.

MARIA Marry, and it shall be done tomorrow morning, if   100
  I live. My lady would not lose him for more than I'll say.

MALVOLIO How now, mistress?

MARIA O Lord!

SIR TOBY Prithee hold thy peace, this is not the way. Do
  you not see you move him? Let me alone with him.   105

FABIAN No way but gentleness, gently, gently. The fiend
  is rough, and will not be roughly used.

SIR TOBY Why how now, my bawcock? How dost thou,
  chuck?

MALVOLIO Sir!   110

SIR TOBY Ay, biddy, come with me. What man, 'tis not for

---

85 How is't with you, man?] F; *spoken by Sir Toby* WILSON

86 **private** privacy (*OED*'s earliest citation
  in this sense (*sb.* B. 6))
88 **hollow** reverberantly (adverbial use,
  presumably commenting on a loud delivery of *Go off* in the previous line)
93 **Let me alone** leave him to me
96 **Do you . . . say** A puritan's indignation
  at being told to *defy the devil* by a
  drunk.
97 **La you** look you
99 **water** urine (to be analysed for signs

of disease)
100 **tomorrow morning** (because the
  chamber-pot will have been filled during the night)
105 **move** anger
107 **rough** violent
108–9 **bawcock . . . chuck** terms of endearment: 'fine bird' (i.e. good fellow)
  . . . 'chicken' (also found together at
  Henry V 3.2.25–6)
111 **biddy** hen (perhaps Sir Toby imitates

gravity to play at cherry-pit with Satan. Hang him, foul
collier.

MARIA Get him to say his prayers, good Sir Toby, get him
to pray.   115

MALVOLIO My prayers, minx?

MARIA No, I warrant you, he will not hear of godliness.

MALVOLIO Go hang yourselves all. You are idle shallow
things, I am not of your element. You shall know more
hereafter.   *Exit* 120

SIR TOBY Is't possible?

FABIAN If this were played upon a stage now, I could con-
demn it as an improbable fiction.

SIR TOBY His very genius hath taken the infection of the
device, man.   125

MARIA Nay, pursue him now, lest the device take air and
taint.

FABIAN Why, we shall make him mad indeed.

MARIA The house will be the quieter.

SIR TOBY Come, we'll have him in a dark room and bound.   130
My niece is already in the belief that he's mad. We may
carry it thus for our pleasure and his penance till our
very pastime, tired out of breath, prompt us to have
mercy on him, at which time we will bring the device to

---

the clucking noise used to call in
chickens)

112 **gravity** a man of dignity. Compare *1
Henry IV* 2.5.297: 'What doth gravity
out of his bed at midnight?'
cherry-pit a children's game in which
cherry stones are thrown into a
hole

112–13 **foul collier** dirty coalman (because
of the Devil's blackness)

116 **minx** impertinent girl

117 **he will . . . godliness** (the ultimate insult to a puritan)

118 **idle** worthless

119 **of your element** at your (low, earthy)
level. For the fashionable phrase, see
note to 3.1.58.

122 **now** either (a) at this moment, or
(b) the phrase 'used to introduce an
important or noteworthy point'

(*OED adv.* 10)

124 **genius** soul (literally 'attendant
spirit')

126–7 **take air and taint** spoil (like left-
over food) by exposure to air. This
and the next three lines mark a major
turning-point in the action. Malvolio's exit marks the end of the
first section of the scene, and the
success of the plot against him;
but now it is given a darker twist
as they resolve to *make him mad indeed.*

130 **in . . . bound** The customary treatment of madness, as in Dr Pinch's
'exorcism' of Antipholus and Dromio
of Ephesus at *Errors* 4.4.95.

132 **carry it thus** continue the pretence

134–5 **to the bar** into the open (literally,
open court)

the bar and crown thee for a finder of madmen. But see,   135
but see.

Enter Sir Andrew with a paper

FABIAN More matter for a May morning.

SIR ANDREW Here's the challenge, read it. I warrant
there's vinegar and pepper in't.

FABIAN Is't so saucy?   140

SIR ANDREW Ay—is't? I warrant him. Do but read.

SIR TOBY Give me.
(*Reads*) 'Youth, whatsoever thou art, thou art but a
scurvy fellow.'

FABIAN Good, and valiant.   145

SIR TOBY 'Wonder not, nor admire not in thy mind why I
do call thee so, for I will show thee no reason for't.'

FABIAN A good note, that keeps you from the blow of
the law.

SIR TOBY 'Thou com'st to the Lady Olivia, and in my sight   150
she uses thee kindly; but thou liest in thy throat, that is
not the matter I challenge thee for.'

FABIAN Very brief, and to exceeding good sense (*aside*)
-less.

SIR TOBY 'I will waylay thee going home, where if it be thy   155
chance to kill me'—

FABIAN Good.

136.1 *with a paper*] OXFORD; *not in* F   143 *Reads*] ROWE; *not in* F, *which however prints the text of Sir Andrew's challenge in italic*   153–4 sense (*aside*) -less] WILSON (*subs.*) sence-lesse F   156 me'—] F (*me.*)

135 **finder of madmen** one of a jury declaring a man to be mad

137 **matter** i.e. sport fit
  May morning The reference is to May Day festivals, not necessarily to the time of year in which the action is taking place.

140 **saucy** (a) spicy (b) insolent

141 **I warrant him** I guarantee it. In Old English, *him* was the dative of the neuter 'hit', 'it', as well as of 'he', and was used as an alternative to 'it' into the seventeenth century (*OED* 2a). The usage recurs at ll. 178–9.

143 **thou . . . thou** Sir Andrew has taken

Sir Toby's advice (3.2.41–2) to heart.

146 **admire** marvel

148 **note** remark

148–9 **keeps you . . . the law** i.e. protects you from a charge of breach of the peace

151 **thou liest in thy throat** you lie deeply, utterly. Sir Andrew thus gives Cesario the lie, the deadliest insult, only to withdraw it instantly—*that is not the matter I challenge thee for*—provoking Fabian's comment in the next line.

153–4 **sense** (*aside*) **-less** F's 'sence-lesse' appears to use the hyphen to signal the aside.

SIR TOBY 'Thou kill'st me like a rogue and a villain.'

FABIAN Still you keep o'th' windy side of the law—good.

SIR TOBY 'Fare thee well, and God have mercy upon one of   160
our souls. He may have mercy upon mine, but my hope
is better, and so look to thyself.

Thy friend as thou usest him, and thy sworn enemy,
                                        Andrew Aguecheek.'

If this letter move him not, his legs cannot. I'll give't   165
him.

MARIA You may have very fit occasion for't. He is now
in some commerce with my lady, and will by and by
depart.

SIR TOBY Go, Sir Andrew. Scout me for him at the corner   170
of the orchard like a bum-baily. So soon as ever thou
seest him, draw, and as thou draw'st, swear horrible,
for it comes to pass oft that a terrible oath, with a swaggering accent sharply twanged off, gives manhood more
approbation than ever proof itself would have earned   175
him. Away.

SIR ANDREW Nay, let me alone for swearing.   *Exit*

SIR TOBY Now will not I deliver his letter, for the behaviour of the young gentleman gives him out to be of
good capacity and breeding. His employment between   180
his lord and my niece confirms no less. Therefore this
letter, being so excellently ignorant, will breed no terror
in the youth. He will find it comes from a clodpoll. But
sir, I will deliver his challenge by word of mouth, set
upon Aguecheek a notable report of valour, and drive   185

165 If] *To⟨by⟩*. If F   167 You] F2; Yon F1

159 **o'th' windy side** to windward (a nautical phrase: something to windward
would have difficulty approaching;
also proverbial (Dent WW20))
161–2 **my hope is better** Andrew means
that he expects to survive.
163 **as thou usest him** in so far as you
treat me like one
168 **commerce** transaction, conversation
170 **Scout me for him** look out for him
171 **bum-baily** A contemptuous collo-
quialism for a bailiff who crept up from

behind to arrest a debtor. This line is
OED's earliest citation under *bumbailiff*.
According to Onions, the -*baily* form
was still found in Midlands usage in
the twentieth century.
172 **horrible** horribly
174 **twanged** (suggesting nasal accent)
175 **approbation** credit
proof trial
179–80 **of good capacity and breeding** in-
telligent and well-bred
183 **clodpoll** blockhead

the gentleman—as I know his youth will aptly receive
it—into a most hideous opinion of his rage, skill, fury,
and impetuosity. This will so fright them both that they
will kill one another by the look, like cockatrices.

    Enter Olivia, and Viola as Cesario

FABIAN Here he comes with your niece. Give them way   190
till he take leave, and presently after him.

SIR TOBY I will meditate the while upon some horrid message for a challenge.

    Exeunt Sir Toby, Fabian, and Maria

OLIVIA

I have said too much unto a heart of stone,
And laid mine honour too unchary out.   195
There's something in me that reproves my fault,
But such a headstrong potent fault it is
That it but mocks reproof.

VIOLA

With the same 'haviour that your passion bears
Goes on my master's griefs.   200

OLIVIA *(giving a jewel)*

Here, wear this jewel for me, 'tis my picture—
Refuse it not, it hath no tongue to vex you—
And I beseech you come again tomorrow.
What shall you ask of me that I'll deny,

189.1 *as Cesario*] OXFORD; *not in* F   193.1 *Exeunt . . . Maria*] CAPELL; *not in* F1; *Exeunt* F2
195 out] THEOBALD; on't F   200 Goes] F; Go MALONE   griefs] F; grief ROWE   201 *(giving a jewel)*] OXFORD; *not in* F

186 **youth will aptly receive it** inexperi-
ence will readily believe the report

189 **cockatrices** mythical monsters which
killed with a glance (also called basi-
lisks). 'The cockatrice slays by sight
only' was proverbial (Tilley C495). The
joke here is that these cockatrices kill
one another.

190 **Give them way** stand aside

191 **presently** immediately

192 **horrid** terrifying

194 **heart of stone** Proverbial (Tilley
H311).

195 **laid . . . unchary out** exposed my
honour too unwarily. Most editors follow Theobald in emending F's *on't* to

out, citing what is assumed to be an
identical error at *Winter's Tale*
4.4.159–60: 'He tells her something |
That makes her blood look out' (for F's
'on't'); and F's Compositor B has a
tendency to introduce redundant apost-
rophes. But F's line makes sense—'I
have staked my honour too rashly on
what *I have said*'—so this is a knife-
edge choice. Theobald's version perhaps sounds minimally more natural.

199 **'haviour that your passion bears** behaviour that characterizes your love-
sickness

201 **jewel** a miniature painting set in
jewels

That honour saved, may upon asking give?   205
VIOLA
Nothing but this: your true love for my master.
OLIVIA
How with mine honour may I give him that
Which I have given to you?
VIOLA   I will acquit you.
OLIVIA
Well, come again tomorrow. Fare thee well,
A fiend like thee might bear my soul to hell.   *Exit* 210
    Enter Sir Toby and Fabian
SIR TOBY Gentleman, God save thee.
VIOLA And you, sir.
SIR TOBY That defence thou hast, betake thee to't. Of what
nature the wrongs are thou hast done him, I know not,
but thy intercepter, full of despite, bloody as the hunter,   215
attends thee at the orchard end. Dismount thy tuck, be
yare in thy preparation, for thy assailant is quick, skil-
ful, and deadly.

---

210 *Exit*] F2; *not in* F1   210.1 *Sir*] CAPELL; *not in* F

---

205 **That honour . . . give** that I may grant
  you, apart from yielding my *honour*
  (i.e. my virginity)
208 **acquit you** set you free from your
  vows of love
211–12 **thee . . . you** Sir Toby uses the
  disparaging form, Viola the courteous
  one.
213 **That defence . . . to't** prepare to use
  the means of defence in your possession
215 **intercepter** one who lies in wait. This
  extravagant expression is the first of
  many used by Sir Toby to inflate Sir
  Andrew's prowess in order to terrify
  Viola; many of these are duelling terms
  drawn from Italian originals and
  glossed in John Florio's Italian/English
  dictionary *A World of Words* (1598),
  from which *OED*'s earliest example of
  intercepter comes, glossing Italian *inter-*
  cettore (Florio, p. 187). *OED*'s citation
  occurs under the variant spelling *inter-*
  ceptor, which might give the actor of
  Sir Toby a hint for (mannered) pronunciation.

despite defiance and contempt
bloody as the hunter Alluding to the
  custom of smearing the victorious
  huntsman with the blood of his victim.
216 **attends** awaits
  orchard end Probably *end* means
  'boundary' (*OED sb.* 1c—its last citation is 1570) and *orchard* 'garden' (see
  note to 3.2.6)—i.e. Sir Andrew awaits
  Viola just outside the garden (*the cor-*
  ner of the orchard, ll. 170–1) so that,
  with Viola's exit and Sir Andrew's sim-
  ultaneous entry at l. 263, the audience
  may imagine that the scene changes
  to the street outside, where it is natural for Antonio to come across them.
  But see note to l. 263.
216 **Dismount thy tuck** draw your rapier.
  Dismount is another exaggerated term
  to emphasize the ferocity of the im-
  pending duel: it was used of guns and
  cannon (*OED v.* 6). *Tuck* is from Italian
  stocco, 'rapier' (*OED sb.*[3]).
217 **yare** prompt (from Anglo-Saxon
  gearo, 'ready')

VIOLA You mistake, sir, I am sure no man hath any quarrel to me. My remembrance is very free and clear from   220
any image of offence done to any man.

SIR TOBY You'll find it otherwise, I assure you. Therefore,
if you hold your life at any price, betake you to your
guard, for your opposite hath in him what youth,
strength, skill, and wrath can furnish man withal.   225

VIOLA I pray you, sir, what is he?

SIR TOBY He is knight, dubbed with unhatched rapier and
on carpet consideration, but he is a devil in private
brawl. Souls and bodies hath he divorced three, and
his incensement at this moment is so implacable that   230
satisfaction can be none but by pangs of death and
sepulchre. 'Hob nob' is his word, give't or take't.

VIOLA I will return again into the house and desire some
conduct of the lady. I am no fighter. I have heard of
some kind of men that put quarrels purposely on others,   235
to taste their valour. Belike this is a man of that quirk.

---

219 sir, . . . sure₍ₐ₎] THEOBALD (*subs.*); sir₍ₐ₎ . . . sure, F

220 **remembrance** recollection, memory

223 **hold your life at any price** value your life. Compare *Hamlet* 1.4.46: 'I do not set my life at a pin's fee'.

223–4 **betake you to your guard** take up a position of defence (a fencing term, used again in *Hamlet*: see note to l. 267)

224 **opposite** opponent

225 **withal** an emphatic form of 'with', used at the end of a sentence (Abbott 196)

227 **unhatched** unhacked (*OED ppl. a.²*, from French *hacher*, to cut), i.e. worn for ornament rather than use

228 **on carpet consideration** for courtly rather than military reasons. *OED, carpet, sb.* 2c cites a heraldic work of 1586: 'A knight . . . may be dubbed . . . in the time of peace upon the carpet . . . he is called a knight of the carpet'. A possible pun on *consideration*—'financial reward' as well as 'reason'—may suggest a purchased knighthood.

230 **incensement** wrath

232 **'Hob nob'** have or have not: Shake-
speare appears to gloss this in the following phrase *give't or take't*, i.e. either kill or be killed. *OED, Hab, adv.* (*sb.*) says that the phrase *hab nab* is known from 1550, and probably derives from Middle English *habbe he, nabbe he* ('have he, or have he not'). In this duelling context, it may have the force of the Italian *hai* ('you have it', i.e. you are stabbed), a duelling term mocked by Mercutio at *Romeo* 2.3.24, and even as he dies: 'I have it, and soundly, too' (3.1.108). **word** motto

233–4 **some conduct of** an escort from

236 **taste** test
Belike perhaps
quirk peculiarity. This is *OED*'s earliest example of *quirk* in this sense (*sb.* 4). Compare the Bawd's comment in *Pericles* about Marina's reluctance to become a prostitute: 'When she should . . . do me the kindness of our profession, she has me her quirks, her reasons, her master reasons . . .' (Sc. 19.14–17).

SIR TOBY Sir, no. His indignation derives itself out of a very competent injury, therefore get you on, and give him his desire. Back you shall not to the house, unless you undertake that with me which with as much safety you   240 might answer him. Therefore on, or strip your sword stark naked, for meddle you must, that's certain, or forswear to wear iron about you.

VIOLA This is as uncivil as strange. I beseech you do me this courteous office, as to know of the knight what my   245 offence to him is. It is something of my negligence, nothing of my purpose.

SIR TOBY I will do so. Signor Fabian, stay you by this gentleman till my return.   *Exit*

VIOLA Pray you, sir, do you know of this matter?   250

FABIAN I know the knight is incensed against you even to a mortal arbitrement, but nothing of the circumstance more.

VIOLA I beseech you, what manner of man is he?

FABIAN Nothing of that wonderful promise to read him by   255 his form as you are like to find him in the proof of his valour. He is indeed, sir, the most skilful, bloody, and fatal opposite that you could possibly have found in any part of Illyria. Will you walk towards him, I will make your peace with him if I can.   260

238 competent] F (computent)   249 *Exit*] F (*Exit Toby.*)

238 **competent** sufficient (in law), so requiring to be repaid. Hilda M. Hulme, *Explorations in Shakespeare's Language* (2nd edn. (1977), p. 165), argues that F's spelling 'computent' represents an independent word, but *OED* records 'computent' as a spelling of *competent*, and the sense seems adequate.

240 **undertake that** i.e. fight a duel. (Toby asserts that he is as dangerous as Andrew.)

242 **meddle** engage in a duel

242–3 **forswear to wear iron about you** give up wearing a sword (an admission of cowardice); compare 1.3.58

245 **as to** to (common Elizabethan usage; Abbott 280)

know of learn from

252 **mortal arbitrement** trial by combat to the death

255–6 **Nothing . . . form** from his outward appearance you cannot perceive him to be remarkable

259 **Will you walk towards him** F's punctuation, followed here, implies a conditional clause: 'If you will . . .' But another possibility is that Fabian builds up a fearsome picture of a *skilful, bloody, and fatal opposite,* and then asks casually *Will you walk towards him?* This is often the version adopted in performance.

VIOLA I shall be much bound to you for't. I am one that
had rather go with Sir Priest than Sir Knight—I care
not who knows so much of my mettle.   ⌈*Exeunt*⌉
    Enter Sir Toby and Sir Andrew

SIR TOBY Why, man, he's a very devil, I have not seen
such a virago. I had a pass with him, rapier, scabbard,   265
and all, and he gives me the stuck-in with such a mortal
motion that it is inevitable; and on the answer, he pays
you as surely as your feet hits the ground they step on.
They say he has been fencer to the Sophy.

SIR ANDREW Pox on't, I'll not meddle with him.   270

SIR TOBY Ay, but he will not now be pacified, Fabian can
scarce hold him yonder.

SIR ANDREW Plague on't, an I thought he had been valiant and so cunning in fence I'd have seen him damned

---

263 ⌈*Exeunt*⌉] F (*Exeunt.*)   263.1 *Sir Toby and Sir*] CAPELL; *Toby and* F   265 virago] F
(firago)   271–2 Ay, but . . . him yonder] *as* CAPELL; *two verse lines in* F, *divided after*
'pacified'

---

262 **Sir Priest** Priests were called *Sir*,
translating Latin *dominus*, because
they were usually graduates.

263 **mettle** temperament, quality. Originally the same word as 'metal', the two
senses were not entirely separated in
Shakespeare's day.
Exeunt The Folio direction clears the
stage, but the action is continuous.
Fabian and Viola are visible to Sir Toby
(ll. 271–2), and directors often make
comic capital out of keeping both reluctant duellists on stage.

265 **virago** woman warrior (suggesting
great ferocity at odds with an unmanly
appearance)
pass fencing bout, from Italian *passado*,
thrust. Compare *Romeo* 2.3.24: 'the
immortal *passado*'.
scabbard (implying a descent from a
duel to a brawl)

266 **stuck-in** thrust, from Italian *stoccata*,
which Shakespeare uses at *Romeo*
3.1.73. But Sir Toby's phrase has the
vivid ferocity of stabbing about it as
well; compare *Hamlet* 4.7.133, 'your
venomed stuck'; and, for *in*, '*Tybalt*
under Romeo's arm thrusts Mercutio in',

i.e. kills him (*Romeo* 3.1.88.2; the direction is from the 'bad' Quarto).

266 **mortal** fatal

267 **motion** 'A practised and regulated
movement of the body; a step, gesture,
or other movement acquired by drill
and training, e.g. in *Fencing*' (*OED sb.*
3c). Shakespeare also uses *motion*
in this sense, again in a fencing context, at *Hamlet* 4.7.129, 'When in
your motion you are hot and dry', and
Additional Passage L.2–3 (4.7.85 ff.):
'neither motion, guard, nor eye | If
you opposed them.'
inevitable unavoidable, not to be par-
ried
the answer your return attack
pays kills (puts paid to). Compare *1
Henry IV* 2.5.193: 'Two I am sure I
have paid'.

269 **Sophy** Shah of Persia (see note to
2.5.170)

271–2 **Fabian can scarce hold him** Sir
Toby means 'hold him back from attacking you'; what the audience
usually sees is Fabian trying to prevent
Viola from escaping.

274 **cunning** skilful

ere I'd have challenged him. Let him let the matter slip   275
and I'll give him my horse, grey Capilet.

SIR TOBY I'll make the motion. Stand here, make a good
show on't, this shall end without the perdition of souls.
(*Aside*) Marry, I'll ride your horse as well as I ride you.
      Enter Fabian, and Viola as Cesario
⌈*Aside to Fabian*⌉ I have his horse to take up the quarrel,   280
I have persuaded him the youth's a devil.

FABIAN (*aside to Sir Toby*) He is as horribly conceited of
him, and pants and looks pale as if a bear were at his
heels.

SIR TOBY (*to Viola*) There's no remedy, sir, he will fight   285
with you for's oath' sake. Marry, he hath better be-
thought him of his quarrel, and he finds that now scarce
to be worth talking of. Therefore draw for the support-
ance of his vow, he protests he will not hurt you.

VIOLA (*aside*) Pray God defend me. A little thing would   290
make me tell them how much I lack of a man.

FABIAN (*to Sir Andrew*) Give ground if you see him furious.

SIR TOBY Come Sir Andrew, there's no remedy, the gentleman will for his honour's sake have one bout with you,   295
he cannot by the duello avoid it, but he has promised

279.1 *as Cesario*] OXFORD; *not in* F

276 **Capilet** F's spelling here and at *All's
  Well* 5.3.149; in *Romeo*, it is 'Capulet'.
  OED lists both *capil* and *capul* as indifferent variants of an obsolete word
  'caple', meaning 'horse'.
277 **motion** offer
278 **perdition of souls** loss of life
279 **ride** The second *ride* means 'make a
  fool of'.
280 **take up** settle
282 **is as horribly conceited** has as terrifying an idea
286 **for's oath'** for his oath's (colloquial)
287 **quarrel** reason for the challenge
287–9 **and he finds . . . vow** The rules of
  the *duello* (see note to l. 296) became
  so codified that duels were often fought
  for technical rather than substantial
  reasons. This is mocked by Mercutio at

Romeo 3.1.102, 'fights by the book of
  arithmetic', and by Touchstone at *As
  You Like It* 5.4.88: 'we quarrel in
  print'; and Middleton makes it the
  turning-point of a play about duelling,
  A Fair Quarrel (*c*.1614): 'Oh, heaven
  has pitied my excessive patience, |
  And sent me a cause!' (3.1.112–13).
290–1 **A little thing . . . of a man** it would
  not take much to tell them how far I
  am from being a man (with sexual
  quibble on *a little thing*)
292–3 **furious** i.e. lose his temper
296 **duello** code of duelling, as set out for
  instance in the duelling manuals of Sir
  William Segar (*The Book of Honour and
  Arms*, 1590) and Vincentio Saviolo
  (*His Practice . . . of the Rapier and Dagger*, 1595)

me, as he is a gentleman and a soldier, he will not hurt
you. Come on, to't.

SIR ANDREW   Pray God he keep his oath.

Enter Antonio

VIOLA   (*aside to Sir Andrew*)
    I do assure you 'tis against my will.   300

Sir Andrew and Viola draw their swords

ANTONIO   (*drawing his sword, to Sir Andrew*)
    Put up your sword. If this young gentleman
    Have done offence, I take the fault on me.
    If you offend him, I for him defy you.

SIR TOBY   You, sir? Why, what are you?

ANTONIO
    One, sir, that for his love dares yet do more   305
    Than you have heard him brag to you he will.

SIR TOBY   (*drawing his sword*) Nay, if you be an undertaker, I am for you.

Enter Officers

FABIAN   O good Sir Toby, hold. Here come the officers.

SIR TOBY   (*to Antonio*) I'll be with you anon.   310

VIOLA   (*to Sir Andrew*) Pray, sir, put your sword up if you
please.

SIR ANDREW   Marry will I, sir, and for that I promised you
I'll be as good as my word. He will bear you easily, and
reins well.   315

300.1 *Sir Andrew . . . swords*] *They draw* ROWE (*after* 'to't'); *not in* F   301 *drawing his sword*] ROWE (*drawing* (*after* 'defy you')); *not in* F   307 *drawing his sword*] *Draws* ROWE; *not in* F

300–1 Often much elaborate business intervenes in performance between these
two lines, as Sir Toby and Fabian try
to bring the duellists together.

301 **Put up** sheathe

305 **his** Cesario's (or, as Antonio believes,
Sebastian's)

307–8 **undertaker** one who takes up, en-
gages himself to, a challenge; compare
l. 240

308.1 **Officers** A distinct hierarchy seems
to be operating here. The First Officer
instructs the Second to make the arrest
(in *Errors* one Officer has to do all the
work himself) and seems the senior (a
'commanding officer'?): he is familiar

with Antonio from the sea-fight, and
even addresses Orsino as an equal at
5.1.54.

309–11 **hold . . . sword up** The hasty attempt of all concerned to conceal that
a duel is taking place reflects the official disapproval of private duelling at
this period.

313 **that I promised you** i.e. his horse, of
which Viola has been told nothing: a
moment of almost surreal comedy as
the two are at complete cross-purposes
in the middle of a duel that is becoming increasingly dangerous.

315 **reins well** responds to the rider's control, through the use of the reins

Sir Andrew and Viola sheathe their swords

FIRST OFFICER This is the man, do thy office.

SECOND OFFICER Antonio, I arrest thee at the suit of
Count Orsino.

ANTONIO You do mistake me, sir.

FIRST OFFICER

No sir, no jot. I know your favour well,   320
Though now you have no seacap on your head.
(*To Second Officer*) Take him away, he knows I know
him well.

ANTONIO

I must obey. (*To Viola*) This comes with seeking you.
But there's no remedy, I shall answer it.
What will you do now my necessity   325
Makes me to ask you for my purse? It grieves me
Much more for what I cannot do for you
Than what befalls myself. You stand amazed,
But be of comfort.

SECOND OFFICER   Come, sir, away.

ANTONIO (*to Viola*)

I must entreat of you some of that money.   330

VIOLA What money, sir?

For the fair kindness you have showed me here,
And part being prompted by your present trouble,
Out of my lean and low ability
I'll lend you something. My having is not much.   335
I'll make division of my present with you.
Hold, (*offering money*) there's half my coffer.

ANTONIO   Will you deny me now?

315.1 *Sir Andrew . . . their swords*] OXFORD (*subs.*); *not in* F   337 *offering money*] *she proffers
coin* WILSON; *not in* F

---

320 **favour** face
324 **answer it** i.e. defend myself, face the
situation
328 **amazed** shocked. A stronger term in
Shakespeare's day than now; compare
Benvolio's words when Romeo stands
in shock after killing Tybalt: 'Stand
not amazed. The Prince will doom thee
death | If thou art taken' (*Romeo*
3.1.134–5).

333 **part** in part
336 **present** ready money
337 **Hold . . . deny me now** F's two short
lines make up a hexameter; but the
broken lines may be deliberate, with
an astounded pause before Antonio
asks *Will you deny me now?*
coffer money-chest (i.e. her purse—
ruefully bombastic)

Is't possible that my deserts to you
Can lack persuasion? Do not tempt my misery,
Lest that it make me so unsound a man   340
As to upbraid you with those kindnesses
That I have done for you.

VIOLA   I know of none,
Nor know I you by voice, or any feature.
I hate ingratitude more in a man
Than lying, vainness, babbling drunkenness,   345
Or any taint of vice whose strong corruption
Inhabits our frail blood.

ANTONIO O heavens themselves!

SECOND OFFICER Come sir, I pray you go.

ANTONIO

Let me speak a little. This youth that you see here   350
I snatched one half out of the jaws of death,
Relieved him with such sanctity of love,
And to his image, which methought did promise
Most venerable worth, did I devotion.

FIRST OFFICER

What's that to us? The time goes by, away.   355

ANTONIO

But O, how vile an idol proves this god!
Thou hast, Sebastian, done good feature shame.
In nature there's no blemish but the mind.
None can be called deformed but the unkind.
Virtue is beauty, but the beauteous evil   360

---

338 **deserts** services that deserve recompense

339 **persuasion** persuasive power

340 **unsound** morally defective (as kindness should expect no recompense)

351 **one half out of the jaws** i.e. out of the jaws which had half-swallowed him

352–6 **sanctity ... image ... venerable ... devotion ... idol ... god** Antonio uses the language of religion to express the intensity of his sense of betrayal (and so of his love). Shakespeare also uses such language in the Sonnets (see Introduction, p. 40), and in Helen's speeches in *All's Well*, for example:

'Indian-like, | Religious in mine error, I adore | The sun that looks upon his worshipper | But knows of him no more' (1.3.200–3).

352 **sanctity** great devotion

353 **image** appearance (with a play on 'religious image')

354 **venerable** worthy of veneration

357 **Sebastian** This must give Viola an intense shock, since it indicates that her brother is alive.

358 **the mind** i.e. in the mind, in character

359 **unkind** (a) cruel (b) unnatural (i.e. those who are *deformed* by nature)

360 **beauteous evil** Compare 1.2.45–6.

Are empty trunks o'er-flourished by the devil.

FIRST OFFICER

The man grows mad, away with him. Come, come, sir.

ANTONIO Lead me on.   *Exit with Officers*

VIOLA (*aside*)

Methinks his words do from such passion fly

That he believes himself. So do not I.   365

Prove true, imagination, O prove true,

That I, dear brother, be now ta'en for you!

SIR TOBY Come hither knight, come hither Fabian. We'll

whisper o'er a couplet or two of most sage saws.

They stand aside

VIOLA

He named Sebastian. I my brother know   370

Yet living in my glass. Even such and so

In favour was my brother, and he went

Still in this fashion, colour, ornament,

For him I imitate. O if it prove,

Tempests are kind, and salt waves fresh in love!   *Exit*   375

SIR TOBY (*to Sir Andrew*) A very dishonest, paltry boy, and

more a coward than a hare. His dishonesty appears in

leaving his friend here in necessity, and denying him;

and for his cowardship, ask Fabian.

FABIAN A coward, a most devout coward, religious in it.   380

SIR ANDREW 'Slid, I'll after him again, and beat him.

---

362 The man . . . sir] *as* DYCE; *two lines in* F, *divided after* 'him'   363 with Officers]
THEOBALD; *not in* F   369.1 They stand aside] OXFORD; *not in* F   375 Exit] F2; *not in* F1

361 **trunks o'er-flourished** (a) chests dec-
orated with visual flourishes (b) bodies
prettified. This rather bizarre phrase
perhaps suggests that Antonio's emotional shock makes him incoherent, as
the First Officer implies in his next
phrase, and as Viola too becomes in
her next speech.

365 **That he . . . not I** He believes what he
says; I believe him to be mistaken. But
So do not I may also carry the implication 'I hardly dare to believe that my
brother is alive'.

369 **saws** sayings (referring to Antonio's
couplets rather than to Viola's, which

are spoken directly to the audience,
out of Toby's hearing)

370–1 **I my brother . . . glass** I know that
my brother is still alive, looking like
me (in her disguise, she presents a
mirror-image of Sebastian)

372 **favour** appearance

372–3 **went | Still** always went about

375 **fresh** i.e. are like fresh, not salt,
water

376 **dishonest** dishonourable

377 **more . . . hare** (even) more cowardly
than a hare. Proverbial: 'as fearful as
a hare' (Tilley H147).

381 **'Slid** by God's eyelid (a mild oath)

SIR TOBY Do, cuff him soundly, but never draw thy
   sword.

SIR ANDREW An I do not—   *Exit*

FABIAN Come, let's see the event.   385

SIR TOBY I dare lay any money 'twill be nothing yet.

                                                           Exeunt

4.1   *Enter Sebastian and Feste the clown*

FESTE Will you make me believe that I am not sent for
   you?

SEBASTIAN
   Go to, go to, thou art a foolish fellow,
   Let me be clear of thee.

FESTE Well held out, i'faith! No, I do not know you nor I   5
   am not sent to you by my lady to bid you come speak
   with her, nor your name is not Master Cesario, nor this
   is not my nose neither. Nothing that is so, is so.

SEBASTIAN
   I prithee vent thy folly somewhere else,
   Thou know'st not me.   10

FESTE Vent my folly! He has heard that word of some
   great man, and now applies it to a fool. Vent my folly! I
   am afraid this great lubber the world will prove a cock-

---

384 *Exit*] THEOBALD; *not in* F   386.1 *Exeunt*] ROWE; *Exit* F
   4.1.0.1 *Feste the*] *not in* F   9–10 I prithee ... not me] *as* CAPELL; *prose in* F

---

385 **event** outcome
386 **yet** after all
4.1.1–8 The opening speeches make it
   clear that Feste and Sebastian are en-
   tering in mid-conversation.
1 **Will you** are you trying to
4 **clear of** free from
5 **held out** kept up
7–8 **nor this ... nose neither** A proverbial
   expression for a statement of the obvious: 'As plain as the nose on a man's
   face' (Tilley N215).
9 **vent** utter, give vent to (literally, let
   out breath, from Latin *ventus*, wind).
   Shakespeare uses it in a variety of
   ways. In *The Tempest*, for example, it
   is used both in the straightforward
   sense 'utter', as here—'thou didst vent
   thy groans | As fast as mill-wheels

strike' (1.2.281–2)—and also figuratively to mean 'excrete', as when
   Trinculo asks Stefano 'How cam'st
   thou to be the siege of this moon-calf?
   Can he vent Trinculos?' (2.2.104–5);
   Feste is presumably thinking of such
   mannered usage when he parodies the
   word at length in his next speech.
13–14 **this great lubber ... a cockney** i.e.
   the whole world will become affected,
   mannered
13 **lubber** lout. *OED* suggests that this
   derives ultimately from Old French *lo-
   beor*, 'swindler', modified by association with *lob*, a word of Teutonic
   origin meaning 'clown' or 'lout' which
   Shakespeare uses at *Dream* 2.1.16,
   where Robin Goodfellow is called 'thou
   lob of spirits'.

ney. I prithee now ungird thy strangeness, and tell me
what I shall 'vent' to my lady. Shall I 'vent' to her that   15
thou art coming?

SEBASTIAN

I prithee, foolish Greek, depart from me.
There's money for thee. If you tarry longer
I shall give worse payment.

FESTE By my troth, thou hast an open hand. These wise   20
men that give fools money get themselves a good report,
after fourteen years' purchase.

Enter Sir Andrew, Sir Toby, and Fabian

SIR ANDREW (*to Sebastian*) Now sir, have I met you again.
(*Striking him*) There's for you.

SEBASTIAN ⌈*striking Sir Andrew with his dagger*⌉
Why, there's for thee, and there, and there.   25
Are all the people mad?

SIR TOBY (*to Sebastian, holding him back*) Hold sir, or I'll
throw your dagger o'er the house.

FESTE This will I tell my lady straight, I would not be in
some of your coats for twopence.   *Exit*   30

17–19 I prithee . . . worse payment] *as* CAPELL; *prose in* F   22.1 *Sir . . . Sir*] ROWE; *not in*
F   24 *Striking him*] ROWE; *not in* F   25 *striking Sir Andrew with his dagger*] MAHOOD (*subs.*);
not in F   and there, and there] F; and there, and there, and there CAPELL   27 *holding
him back*] ROWE (*subs.*), *after l.* 31; *not in* F   30 *Exit*] ROWE; *not in* F

13–14 **cockney** pampered child, or fop
using affected language (*OED sb.* 2),
and so virtually the opposite of the
associations (of down-to-earth know-
ingness) that the word *cockney* has for
a modern audience

14 **ungird thy strangeness** relax your for-
mality (literally, 'unbelt your remote-
ness'), stop pretending not to know
me. Feste parodies what he takes to be
Sebastian's formal style. The phrase is a
characteristically Shakespearian ming-
ling of the concrete and the abstract.
strangeness distant behaviour, reserve
(Schmidt); *OED* 2a records 'coldness,
aloofness' as an absolete sense.

17 **foolish Greek** buffoon. 'Merry Greek'
was a standard expression, upon
which Shakespeare plays when he says
of Helen at *Troilus* 1.2.105 that 'she's
a merry Greek indeed'.

19 **worse payment** blows—and perhaps
he raises his hand warningly, prompting Feste's reply.

20 **thou hast an open hand** you are generous (with, perhaps, a pun on Sebastian's raised hand). Sebastian shows
both the generosity and the impulsive-
ness that characterize his sister: as the
first meeting of Sebastian and Olivia
approaches, Shakespeare takes care to
suggest that the twins are tem-
peramentally as well as physically
alike, so that the marriage is not *simply* a matter of mistaken identity.

21 **report** reputation

22 **after fourteen years'** purchase i.e. at a
high price (the purchase price of land
being normally twelve times its annual
rent)

29 **straight** straightaway

30 **twopence** Feste appears to regard *twopence* as worth having (unless he is

SIR TOBY Come on, sir, hold.

SIR ANDREW Nay, let him alone, I'll go another way to
work with him. I'll have an action of battery against
him if there be any law in Illyria. Though I struck him
first, yet it's no matter for that.   35

SEBASTIAN Let go thy hand.

SIR TOBY Come sir, I will not let you go. Come, my young
soldier, put up your iron. You are well fleshed. Come on.

SEBASTIAN (*freeing himself*)
I will be free from thee. What wouldst thou now?
If thou dar'st tempt me further, draw thy sword.   40

SIR TOBY What, what? Nay then, I must have an ounce or
two of this malapert blood from you.
            Sir Toby and Sebastian draw their swords.
            Enter Olivia

OLIVIA
Hold, Toby, on thy life I charge thee hold.

SIR TOBY Madam.

OLIVIA
Will it be ever thus? Ungracious wretch,   45
Fit for the mountains and the barbarous caves,
Where manners ne'er were preached—out of my sight!

---

39 *freeing himself*] CAPELL (*wrenches from him*); *not in* F   42.1 *Sir Toby . . . their swords*]
ROWE (*subs.*); *not in* F

31 **hold** hold back, restrain yourself
32–3 **I'll go . . . work** Proverbial: Tilley
W150.
33 **action of battery** lawsuit for assault—
though even Sir Andrew realizes that
he doesn't have a legal leg to stand on
since he *struck him first.*
38 **iron** This presumably refers to Sebastian's *dagger* (l. 28). The stage directions here are based on the assumption
that Sebastian strikes Sir Andrew with
his dagger and only draws his sword
after l. 42. But since *iron* is a collo-
quialism for 'sword' (but not 'dagger')
in Shakespeare, and since Sir Toby
uses it in this sense at 3.4.242–3 (*forswear to wear iron about you*), it is

possible that Toby's reference to *dagger*
in l. 28 is a facetious diminutive, and
that Sebastian has struck Sir Andrew
with the hilt or flat of his sword, so
that only Sir Toby needs to draw at
l. 42.
fleshed blooded, initiated into combat
(by striking Sir Andrew and perhaps
drawing blood), i.e. 'you've done
enough'. Compare *1 Henry IV*
5.4.128–9: 'Full bravely hast thou
fleshed | Thy maiden sword.' The ex-
pression probably derives from the
practice of rewarding hawks or hounds
with the flesh of their quarry.
42 **malapert** impudent
44 **Madam**. Sir Toby's reaction is open to
a wide range of interpretation from
total submission to open defiance.

Be not offended, dear Cesario.
(*To Sir Toby*) Rudesby, be gone.
                    Exeunt Sir Toby, Sir Andrew, and Fabian
                              I prithee, gentle friend,
Let thy fair wisdom, not thy passion sway   50
In this uncivil and unjust extent
Against thy peace. Go with me to my house,
And hear thou there how many fruitless pranks
This ruffian hath botched up, that thou thereby
Mayst smile at this. Thou shalt not choose but go.   55
Do not deny. Beshrew his soul for me,
He started one poor heart of mine in thee.

SEBASTIAN
What relish is in this? How runs the stream?
Or I am mad, or else this is a dream.
Let fancy still my sense in Lethe steep.   60
If it be thus to dream, still let me sleep.

OLIVIA
Nay, come, I prithee, would thou'dst be ruled by me.

SEBASTIAN
Madam, I will.

OLIVIA   O, say so, and so be.

                                        Exeunt

---

49 *Exeunt . . . and Fabian*] CAPELL; *not in* F

49 **Rudesby** ruffian (used by Shakespeare only here and at *Shrew* 3.2.10: 'a madbrain rudesby full of spleen')
50 **wisdom . . . passion** Alluding to that contrast between intelligence and passion already referred to at 1.5.29.
51 **uncivil** barbarous
   extent assault (a legal term, used in its literal meaning of 'seize goods for the king' at *As You Like It* 3.1.17, 'Make an extent upon his house and lands', but here used more generally (*OED sb.* 2b, c))
54 **botched up** patched together (like old clothes), clumsily contrived
56 **Beshrew his soul for me** my curse upon him
57 **started one . . . in thee** i.e. by attacking Sebastian, Sir Toby frightened Olivia, who has exchanged hearts with Sebas-

tian/'Cesario'; *start* is a hunting term (to rouse the game), thus establishing the pun *heart/hart* (deer) already used by Orsino at 1.1.16–22.
58 **relish** taste, i.e. meaning
59 **Or I am mad . . . dream** This recalls an earlier Shakespearian twin who is made love to by a strange woman, Antipholus of Syracuse in *Errors* 2.2.215–16: 'Am I in earth, in heaven, or in hell? | Sleeping or waking? Mad or well advised?'
   Or . . . or either . . . or
60 **fancy** imagination
   sense (could be either singular or plural)
   Lethe the mythical river of oblivion
62 **would thou'dst** if only you would
63 **say so, and so be** be true to what you have spoken.

4.2 *Enter Maria carrying a gown and false beard, and*
Feste the clown

MARIA Nay, I prithee put on this gown and this beard,
make him believe thou art Sir Topaz the curate. Do it
quickly. I'll call Sir Toby the whilst.   *Exit*

FESTE Well, I'll put it on, and I will dissemble myself in't,
and I would I were the first that ever dissembled in such   5
a gown.

He disguises himself

I am not tall enough to become the function well, nor
lean enough to be thought a good student, but to be
said 'an honest man and a good housekeeper' goes as
fairly as to say 'a careful man and a great scholar'. The   10
competitors enter.

Enter Sir Toby and Maria

SIR TOBY Jove bless thee, Master Parson.

FESTE *Bonos dies*, Sir Toby, for as the old hermit of Prague,

---

4.2.0.1–2 *Enter Maria . . . the clown*] OXFORD; *Enter Maria and Clowne.* F   2 Topaz] This
edition; F ('Topas' *throughout*)   3 *Exit*] THEOBALD (*subs.*); *not in* F   5 such] F1 (*catchword*),
F2; in such F1 (*text*). Text repeats 'in' *from previous page.*   6.1 He disguises himself] WILSON
(*subs.*); *not in* F   11.1 *Enter . . . and Maria*] THEOBALD; *Enter Toby.* F

4.2.2 **Sir Topaz** This name occurs in
Chaucer's *Canterbury Tales* and Lyly's
Endimion, but in both cases the character is not a priest but a knight, and
more relevant to his function in this
scene is the fact that the topaz, a
precious stone, is claimed to cure madness by Reginald Scot (*Discovery of
Witchcraft* (1584), 13.6), by Robert
Burton (*Anatomy of Melancholy* (1621),
2.4.1.4), and, according to Leslie Hotson, by Bede, Aristotle, and other
authorities (*Shakespeare's Motley*
(1952), pp. 120–1).
   Sir See note to 3.4.262.
   curate parish priest (not, as often now,
his assistant)
3 **the whilst** in the meantime
4 **dissemble** disguise
5 **dissembled** acted hypocritically
5–6 **in such a gown** This may be a gibe
at puritan clergymen who wore the
white surplice required by law over the
Calvinist's black Geneva gown, or at
religious hypocrisy in general.
7 **become the function well** grace the

office (of priest)
8 **student** scholar (of divinity)
9 **said** reputed
   an honest . . . housekeeper i.e. a good
sort and a generous host
9–10 **goes as fairly as to say** sounds as
well as
10 **careful** conscientious (or perhaps
'careworn with study')
11 **competitors** confederates, partners-in-
crime (*OED* 2). This sense occurs more
often in Shakespeare than the modern
one 'rivals'. Compare *LLL* 2.1.82:
'competitors in oath'.
12 **Jove** The leader of the classical gods
was often used interchangeably with
'God' in Renaissance literature, but
may here replace 'God' to conform
with the prohibition in 1606 of the use
of God's name in stage plays. See Introduction, p. 76.
13 *Bonos dies* With this speech Feste begins to assume his mock-clerical voice
as Sir Topaz. *Bonos dies* may be false
Latin for 'good day', but J. W. Binns
argues that '*Bonus dies* is not used even

that never saw pen and ink, very wittily said to a niece
of King Gorboduc, 'That that is, is.' So I, being Master   15
Parson, am Master Parson; for what is 'that' but 'that',
and 'is' but 'is'?

SIR TOBY To him, Sir Topaz.

FESTE What ho, I say, peace in this prison.

SIR TOBY The knave counterfeits well—a good knave.   20
   Malvolio within

MALVOLIO Who calls there?

FESTE Sir Topaz the curate, who comes to visit Malvolio
the lunatic.

MALVOLIO Sir Topaz, Sir Topaz, good Sir Topaz, go to my
lady.   25

FESTE Out, hyperbolical fiend, how vexest thou this man!
Talkest thou nothing but of ladies?

SIR TOBY Well said, Master Parson.

MALVOLIO Sir Topaz, never was man thus wronged. Good
Sir Topaz, do not think I am mad. They have laid me   30
here in hideous darkness.

FESTE Fie, thou dishonest Satan—I call thee by the most

15–16 Master.... Master] F (M.... M.)

in colloquial Latin as a greeting. What
we have here, surely, is a corrupt
form of the Spanish *buenos días*
('Shakespeare's Latin Citations', *SS*
35 (Cambridge, 1982) 119–28; p.
127).

13 **old hermit of Prague** Feste parodies the
scholarly habit of quoting 'authorities'
by inventing one, as he does at 1.5.32.

14 **never saw pen and ink** i.e. was illiterate
wittily intelligently, profoundly

15 **King Gorboduc** A legendary British
king, subject of the earliest English
blank-verse tragedy (1561), by Sack-
ville and Norton.

19 **peace in this prison** 'Peace be in this
house' is the standard opening phrase
for a priest visiting the sick in *The Book
of Common Prayer* (1559).

20.1 *Malvolio within* This, the Folio stage
direction, provides an important key to

staging the scene. *Within* makes it
clear that Malvolio is heard but not
seen. See Introduction, pp. 58–9, for
further discussion.

26 **hyperbolical fiend** raging evil spirit
(by whom Feste pretends that Malvolio is possessed). 'Hyperbole' is a
rhetorical figure that George Puttenham in his *Art of English Poesy* (1589),
3.18, calls 'the over-reacher...
or loud liar'; for the sense of *hyperbolical* here, compare modern 'raving
mad'.

26, 39, 43 **vexest ... complainest ... er-
.rest** Elsewhere, the Folio text (repro-
ducing Shakespeare's own usage?)
prints contracted forms of the endings
of second person singular of verbs
(e.g., even in this scene, 'Sayst' (l. 34),
'think'st' (l. 54)), so perhaps the full
('-est') form in these examples implies
an intoned delivery to suggest the
priest or the exorcist.

    modest terms, for I am one of those gentle ones that will
use the devil himself with courtesy. Sayst thou that
house is dark?   35

MALVOLIO As hell, Sir Topaz.

FESTE Why, it hath bay windows transparent as barricadoes, and the clerestories toward the south-north are as
lustrous as ebony, and yet complainest thou of obstruc-
tion?   40

MALVOLIO I am not mad, Sir Topaz, I say to you this
house is dark.

FESTE Madman, thou errest. I say there is no darkness but
ignorance, in which thou art more puzzled than the
Egyptians in their fog.   45

MALVOLIO I say this house is as dark as ignorance, though
ignorance were as dark as hell; and I say there was
never man thus abused. I am no more mad than you
are. Make the trial of it in any constant question.

FESTE What is the opinion of Pythagoras concerning wild-   50
fowl?

MALVOLIO That the soul of our grandam might haply inhabit a bird.

FESTE What think'st thou of his opinion?

33 **modest terms** moderate, mild expressions (referring back to *dishonest* in the
previous line)

35 **house** i.e. room. A *dark house* was a
place of confinement for a madman;
compare *As You Like It* 3.2.386–8:
'Love is merely a madness, and . . .
deserves as well a dark house and a
whip as madmen do'.

37–8 **barricadoes** barricades. The form
draws upon French *barricade* or Spanish *barricada* or both. To say that the
windows are as transparent as barricades is like calling them 'clear as
mud'.

38 **clerestories** upper windows (usually in
a church or great hall)

39 **lustrous as ebony** clear as a dense and
naturally dull black wood; again,
'clear as mud'

39–41 **thou . . . you** Malvolio uses the
courteous *you* to a priest, Feste a
condescending or abusive *thou* to a

madman.

39–40 **obstruction** shutting out of light.
This is possibly one of Malvolio's mannerisms (see 2.5.113 and 3.4.20), so
perhaps Feste is using his own language against him.

44 **puzzled** bewildered, led astray

45 **Egyptians in their fog** One of the biblical plagues of Egypt was a 'thick darkness' lasting three days (Exodus 10:
21–3).

48 **abused** ill-used, wronged

49 **constant question** consistent, logical
discussion

50 **Pythagoras** An ancient Greek philosopher who held that the same soul
could successively inhabit different
kinds of bodies. Rosalind playfully alludes to this doctrine at *As You Like It*
3.2.172–3: 'I was never so berhymed
since Pythagoras' time that I was an
Irish rat'.

52 **haply** perhaps

MALVOLIO I think nobly of the soul, and no way approve   55
his opinion.

FESTE Fare thee well. Remain thou still in darkness. Thou
shalt hold th'opinion of Pythagoras ere I will allow of
thy wits, and fear to kill a woodcock lest thou dispossess
the soul of thy grandam. Fare thee well.   60

MALVOLIO Sir Topaz, Sir Topaz!

SIR TOBY My most exquisite Sir Topaz.

FESTE Nay, I am for all waters.

MARIA Thou mightst have done this without thy beard
and gown, he sees thee not.   65

SIR TOBY (*to Feste*) To him in thine own voice, and bring
me word how thou find'st him. I would we were well rid
of this knavery. If he may be conveniently delivered, I
would he were, for I am now so far in offence with my
niece that I cannot pursue with any safety this sport   70
to the upshot. Come by and by to my chamber.

Exit with Maria

FESTE (*sings*) 'Hey Robin, jolly Robin,
Tell me how thy lady does.'

71 to the] ROWE; the F; t' the RIVERSIDE   71.1 with *Maria*] THEOBALD; *not in* F   72 *sings*]
ROWE (*subs.*); *not in* F   72–3 'Hey Robin . . . does.'] *as* CAPELL; *one line in* F

58–9 **allow of thy wits** agree that you are
sane
62 **exquisite** perfect, exact (in his port-
rayal of Sir Topaz)
63 **Nay** Not a denial, but something like
'Oh'.
　　for all waters able to turn my hand to
anything. It literally means 'prepared
for all weathers', as in the proverb 'to
have a cloak for all waters (I am for
any weather)' (Tilley C421). There is
also a pun on *water* in the sense of the
brilliance or lustre of a precious
stone—i.e. 'I am all lustre, being a
Topaz'.
68 **delivered** set free
71 **to the upshot** to its natural conclusion.
Upshot is the winning shot in an archery contest. *OED sb.* 5b gives no examples of *the upshot* carrying this sense
on its own, so that Rowe's emendation
to the upshot seems required.

71 **Come . . . chamber** This is surely addressed to Feste, like the rest of the
speech: he is to report back to Sir Toby
in his room. It has been conjectured
that the words are spoken to Maria,
either because they are already married, or because they are to be married
there; and this strained interpretation
has been given currency through John
Barton's long-running and influential
1969–71 RSC staging, in which an
ageing Maria, after hanging around
during the play hoping for attention
from a boorish Sir Toby, was at last
given the invitation she had been waiting for.
72–9 **Hey Robin** Feste lets Malvolio know
of his presence by singing lines attributed to Sir Thomas Wyatt, though
they may be traditional: 'Ah Robin |
Jolly Robin | Tell me how thy leman
doth | And thou shalt know of mine.

MALVOLIO Fool!

FESTE   'My lady is unkind, pardie.'   75

MALVOLIO Fool!

FESTE   'Alas, why is she so?'

MALVOLIO Fool, I say!

FESTE   'She loves another.'

  Who calls, ha?   80

MALVOLIO Good fool, as ever thou wilt deserve well at my
  hand, help me to a candle and pen, ink, and paper. As I
  am a gentleman, I will live to be thankful to thee for't.

FESTE Master Malvolio?

MALVOLIO Ay, good fool.   85

FESTE Alas sir, how fell you besides your five wits?

MALVOLIO Fool, there was never man so notoriously
  abused. I am as well in my wits, fool, as thou art.

FESTE But as well? Then you are mad indeed, if you be
  no better in your wits than a fool.   90

MALVOLIO They have here propertied me, keep me in
  darkness, send ministers to me, asses, and do all they
  can to face me out of my wits.

FESTE Advise you what you say, the minister is here. (*As
  Sir Topaz*) Malvolio, Malvolio, thy wits the heavens re-   95
  store. Endeavour thyself to sleep, and leave thy vain
  bibble-babble.

79–80 'She loves . . . calls, ha?] OXFORD; *one line in* F   84 Master] F (M.)

| My lady is unkind, pardie. | Alack why
is she so? | She loveth another better
than me . . .' Perhaps Feste chooses
this particular song to torment Malvolio, since *his* lady (Olivia) is *unkind* and
loves another (Cesario). The music is by
Wyatt's contemporary at Henry VIII's
court, William Cornish (see Appendix).

74–119 Malvolio's numerous repetitions
of *fool* in this exchange echo ironically
back upon himself.

75 **pardie** by God (a corruption of French
par dieu)

84 **Master** At 2.3.125 Maria speaks of
'Monsieur Malvolio'; *Monsieur* is an
alternative modernization of F's 'M.'
here.

86 **besides** out of. Compare Sonnet 23.1–

2: 'As an unperfect actor on the stage
| Who with his fear is put besides his
part'.
five wits (usually regarded as common
sense, fantasy, memory, judgement,
and imagination)

87 **notoriously** scandalously. Perhaps this
is another Malvolio mannerism, like
element and *obstruction*: he uses *notorious* twice in the final scene to express
his sense of outrage (5.1.320, 334),
and Olivia picks up his phrase there
(5.1.369).

91 **propertied me** packed away, treated me
like a piece of furniture (or, if 'property'
has its theatrical sense—which was cur-
rent at the time—like an unused 'prop')

93 **face** bully

94 **Advise you** be careful

MALVOLIO Sir Topaz.

FESTE (*as Sir Topaz*) Maintain no words with him, good
fellow. (*As himself*) Who I, sir? Not I, sir. God b'wi' you, 100
good Sir Topaz. (*As Sir Topaz*) Marry, amen. (*As himself*)
I will, sir, I will.

MALVOLIO Fool, fool, fool, I say.

FESTE Alas sir, be patient. What say you sir? I am shent
for speaking to you. 105

MALVOLIO Good fool, help me to some light and some
paper. I tell thee I am as well in my wits as any man in
Illyria.

FESTE Well-a-day that you were, sir.

MALVOLIO By this hand, I am. Good fool, some ink, paper, 110
and light, and convey what I will set down to my lady.
It shall advantage thee more than ever the bearing of
letter did.

FESTE I will help you to't. But tell me true, are you not
mad indeed, or do you but counterfeit? 115

MALVOLIO Believe me, I am not, I tell thee true.

FESTE Nay, I'll ne'er believe a madman till I see his brains.
I will fetch you light, and paper, and ink.

MALVOLIO Fool, I'll requite it in the highest degree. I prithee be gone. 120

FESTE (*sings*) I am gone, sir,
                    And anon, sir,
                      I'll be with you again,
                    In a trice,
                    Like to the old Vice, 125
                      Your need to sustain,

---

121 *sings*] ROWE (*subs.*); *not in* F   121–32 I am gone . . . devil.'] *as in* CAPELL; *as eight
lines in* F, *divided after* 'anon, sir', 'again', 'Vice', 'sustain', 'wrath', 'devil', 'dad'

---

100 **God b'wi' you** A corruption of 'God
be with you'.
101 **amen** so be it (Latin): the standard
response to a prayer
104 **shent** rebuked
109 **Well-a-day** alas
121–32 Another song whose words may
or may not be by Shakespeare. Apart
from the first three lines, no contemporary music survives; but see the Ap-

pendix.
122 **anon, sir** straightaway, sir (a catch-
phrase also used by the harassed
drawer Francis at *1 Henry IV* 2.5.36
ff.)
124 **In a trice** immediately (literally 'at a
single pluck or pull' (*OED sb.*² 1a))
125 **old Vice** the type-character of the
Vice in the old morality plays. 'The
"old Vice" (buffoon) of the earlier Tudor

Who with dagger of lath
In his rage and his wrath
  Cries 'Aha' to the devil,
Like a mad lad,   130
'Pare thy nails, dad,
  Adieu, goodman devil.'   *Exit*

4.3   *Enter Sebastian*

SEBASTIAN

This is the air, that is the glorious sun,
This pearl she gave me, I do feel't and see't,
And though 'tis wonder that enwraps me thus,
Yet 'tis not madness. Where's Antonio then?
I could not find him at the Elephant,   5
Yet there he was, and there I found this credit,
That he did range the town to seek me out.
His counsel now might do me golden service,
For though my soul disputes well with my sense
That this may be some error but no madness,   10
Yet doth this accident and flood of fortune

---

stage was the predecessor of the Elizabethan fool, and the Vice twitting the devil was a thinly veiled form of the Elizabethan jester mocking the Puritan' (F. W. Sternfeld, *Music in Shakespearean Tragedy* (1963), p. 113).

127 **lath** wood

129 **Aha** a cry of defiance

131 **Pare thy nails** Compare *Henry V* 4.4.67–8, where Pistol is called 'this roaring devil i'th' old play, that everyone may pare his nails with a wooden dagger'. Presumably in some morality plays the devil had long nails with which to seize his victims, so paring them would reduce his threat and his power.
dad In some sixteenth-century morality plays, the Vice is the devil's son, inheriting and displaying his vices in comic form.

132 **goodman devil** 'master devil'. *Goodman* is a respectful form of address (*OED* 1). But *goodman devil* is an oxymoron and, although the phrase is technically addressed by the Vice to the devil, most Festes reasonably ad-

dress it as a parting shot to Malvolio— where *goodman* may take on the additional sense 'puritan', a puritan who is also from Feste's point of view a *devil*—the enemy.

4.3.4, 15, 16 **'tis not madness ... I am mad ... the lady's mad** Sebastian's soliloquy wavers between feeling that he is not mad and that he is, a sensation shared by several characters in the final scene.

6 **was** had been
credit report (*OED*'s only example of *credit* in this sense (*sb.* 3))

7 **range** roam through

8 **golden** valuable. See note to 5.1.372.

9 **disputes well with** maintains, reaches the conclusion, along with. This expression derives from the technique of *disputing* among medieval and Renaissance philosophers, especially in universities; but the meaning of *disputes ... with* as, essentially, 'agrees with', rather than 'argues against', is unique in Shakespeare (or, according to *OED*, anywhere else).

11 **accident** unexpected event
flood of fortune good fortune that has

So far exceed all instance, all discourse,
That I am ready to distrust mine eyes
And wrangle with my reason that persuades me
To any other trust but that I am mad,   15
Or else the lady's mad. Yet if 'twere so
She could not sway her house, command her followers,
Take and give back affairs and their dispatch
With such a smooth, discreet, and stable bearing
As I perceive she does. There's something in't   20
That is deceivable. But here the lady comes.
      Enter Olivia and a Priest
OLIVIA
Blame not this haste of mine. If you mean well
Now go with me, and with this holy man,
Into the chantry by. There before him,
And underneath that consecrated roof,   25
Plight me the full assurance of your faith,
That my most jealous and too doubtful soul
May live at peace. He shall conceal it
Whiles you are willing it shall come to note,

4.3.21.1 *a*] OXFORD; *not in* F

so abundantly overwhelmed me

12 **instance** example, precedent
  discourse reasoning; compare *Hamlet*
  Additional Passages J. 27–8 (4.4.9 ff.):
  'he that made us with such large dis-
  course, | Looking before and after'.
14 **wrangle** argue. Like *disputes* (l. 9) and
  discourse (l. 12), this term derives from
  philosophical debates in universities
  (*OED v.*²).
15 **trust** belief
17 **sway** manage, rule
18 **Take ... dispatch** undertake business
  (*take affairs*) and ensure that it is carried out (*give back their dispatch*)
19 **stable** poised, balanced (the only
  example of this usage in Shakespeare)
21 **deceivable** deceptive (according to *OED*
  a. 1, obsolete since *c.* 1688 in this sense)
23 **holy man** The association of this *holy*
  man with the *chantry* (see next line)

implies that he is the chaplain at-
tached to Olivia's house.
24 **chantry by** nearby chapel. A *chantry*
  was a chapel in which a priest sang
  daily mass for the souls of its founder
  or his relatives. It is a nice irony that
  Olivia should make her vows to Sebastian in the *chantry* where, presumably,
  the priest prays for the soul of her
  brother—the brother for whose sake
  she had initially vowed to shut herself
  away *like a cloistress* (1.1.27).
26 **Plight ... faith** i.e. enter into a solemn
  contract of betrothal, as binding as a
  marriage; the ceremony would follow
  later.
27 **jealous** anxious (now obsolete (*OED a.*
  5b), but with something of the modern
  meaning as well)
28 A short line, perhaps with an emphatic pause after *peace.*
29 **Whiles** until

What time we will our celebration keep   30
According to my birth. What do you say?
SEBASTIAN
I'll follow this good man, and go with you,
And having sworn truth, ever will be true.
OLIVIA
Then lead the way, good father, and heavens so shine
That they may fairly note this act of mine.   *Exeunt*   35

5.1   *Enter Feste the clown and Fabian*
FABIAN Now as thou lov'st me, let me see his letter.
FESTE Good Master Fabian, grant me another request.
FABIAN Anything.
FESTE Do not desire to see this letter.
FABIAN This is to give a dog, and in recompense desire my   5
dog again.
Enter Duke Orsino, Viola as Cesario, Curio, and lords
ORSINO
Belong you to the Lady Olivia, friends?
FESTE Ay sir, we are some of her trappings.

---

35 Exeunt] *Exeunt* |. *Finis Actus Quartus.* F
    5.1.0.1 *Feste the*] *not in* F   2 Master] F (M.)   6.1 *Orsino*] *not in* F   *as Cesario*] *not in* F

---

30 **What time** at which time (Abbott 202)
    celebration i.e. the wedding
31 **birth** rank
34 **heavens so shine** Perhaps this alludes
    to the proverb 'happy is the bride the
    sun shines on' (Tilley B663), or is
    simply a heartfelt wish that heaven
    should *fairly note* (look favourably on)
    her marriage.
5.1.1 **his** i.e. Malvolio's
5–6 **to give a dog ... dog again** On 26
    March 1603, John Manningham re-
    corded in his diary (see Introduction,
    p. 1) an anecdote about Queen Eliza-
    beth I and her kinsman Dr Boleyn,
    who 'had a dog which he doted on, so
    much that the Queen, understanding
    of it, requested he would grant her one
    desire, and he should have whatsoever
    he would ask. She demanded his dog;
    he gave it, and "Now, Madam," quoth
    he, "you promised to give me my
    desire." "I will," quoth she. "Then I

pray you give me my dog again." '
Perhaps this anecdote was well-
known; it certainly seems to lie behind
Fabian's phrase.
6.1 **Curio** He has no lines in this scene,
    but Orsino must be attended by some-
    one, so Curio, and presumably Valen-
    tine too, are the obvious choices.
    Otherwise one might suspect that the
    two actors doubled as the Officers.
7–43 For a discussion of this episode, see
    Introduction, p. 60.
7–8 **friends ... trappings** Orsino's conde-
    scending *friends* instantly provokes
    Feste's edged *her trappings*—i.e. her or-
    naments, her 'bits and pieces'. The
    two of them pick up their sparring
    from 2.4.66–77, and this tone affects
    the rest of their long exchange. It leads
    into Feste's *the worse for my friends* (ll.
    10–11), with the implication of 'fair-
    weather friends', which he goes on to
    'prove' (ll. 15–20), and then, when

ORSINO

I know thee well. How dost thou, my good fellow?

FESTE Truly sir, the better for my foes and the worse for   10
my friends.

ORSINO

Just the contrary—the better for thy friends.

FESTE No sir, the worse.

ORSINO How can that be?

FESTE Marry, sir, they praise me, and make an ass of me.   15
Now my foes tell me plainly I am an ass, so that by my
foes, sir, I profit in the knowledge of myself, and by my
friends I am abused; so that, conclusions to be as kisses,
if your four negatives make your two affirmatives, why
then the worse for my friends and the better for my foes.   20

ORSINO Why, this is excellent.

FESTE By my troth, sir, no, though it please you to be one
of my friends.

ORSINO *(giving money)*

Thou shalt not be the worse for me, there's gold.

FESTE But that it would be double-dealing, sir, I would   25
you could make it another.

ORSINO O, you give me ill counsel.

FESTE Put your grace in your pocket, sir, for this once,
and let your flesh and blood obey it.

---

24 *giving money*] COLLIER 1858; *not in* F

Orsino agrees with him, Feste swiftly
takes him at his word and asks for the
money that will prove Orsino a *friend*
of this kind, i.e. a flatterer.

18–19 **conclusions . . . affirmatives** i.e. as
in grammar four negatives make two
affirmatives, so, when a girl is asked
for a kiss, her 'no, no, no, no' may be
construed as 'yes, yes'. The point of
the comparison is to show how things
turn out to be the opposite of what you
expect: negatives prove affirmatives,
friends foes, and vice versa.

19 **your . . . your** This is not the possessive, 'belonging to you', but vague-
ly implies 'that you know of' (*OED a.*

5b), and is therefore thrown off (almost 'yer') when spoken.

24 **the worse** Orsino picks up Feste's *the
worse for my friends* and disproves it by
paying him.

25 **But** except for the fact
double-dealing (a) duplicity (b) giving
two coins

28 **Put your grace in your pocket** (a) put
your virtue where you cannot see it
(b) put your hand in your pocket, for
the money (punning on 'your grace'
as the customary form of address to a
duke)

29 **flesh and blood obey it** normal human
instincts follow the *ill counsel* (l. 27),
rather than *grace*

ORSINO Well, I will be so much a sinner to be a double- 30
dealer. (*Giving money*) There's another.

FESTE *Primo, secundo, tertio* is a good play, and the old
saying is 'The third pays for all'. The triplex, sir, is a
good tripping measure, or the bells of Saint Bennet, sir,
may put you in mind—'one, two, three'. 35

ORSINO You can fool no more money out of me at this
throw. If you will let your lady know I am here to speak
with her, and bring her along with you, it may awake
my bounty further.

FESTE Marry, sir, lullaby to your bounty till I come again. 40
I go, sir, but I would not have you to think that my
desire of having is the sin of covetousness. But as you
say, sir, let your bounty take a nap, I will awake it anon.

Exit

Enter Antonio and Officers

VIOLA

Here comes the man, sir, that did rescue me.

ORSINO

That face of his I do remember well, 45
Yet when I saw it last it was besmeared
As black as Vulcan in the smoke of war.
A baubling vessel was he captain of,
For shallow draught and bulk unprizable,

---

31 *Giving money*] COLLIER 1858 (*subs.*); *not in* F

---

30 **to** as to

32 ***Primo, secundo, tertio*** first, second,
third (Latin). Perhaps there is an allusion to a children's game 'Primus secundus' mentioned in Scot's *Discovery
of Witchcraft* (11. 10).
play game

33 **'The third pays for all'** Proverbial (Tilley T319); compare modern 'third time
lucky'.
triplex triple time in music (literally
'threefold')

34 **Bennet** Colloquial abbreviation of
'Benedict'. A London church, across
the Thames from the Globe Theatre,
was called St Bennet Hithe.

37 **throw** throw of the dice, gamble

47 **Vulcan** blacksmith of the Roman gods

48 **baubling** paltry, like a child's 'bauble'
or toy. 'Baubles' are also associated
with ships at *Troilus* 1.3.34, 'shallow
bauble-boats', and *Cymbeline* 3.1.26–
7: 'his shipping, | Poor ignorant bau-
bles'.

49 **For shallow … unprizable** of no value
because of its shallow draught and
small size. Would Shakespeare's audience have recognized this as the description of a *pirate* ship? According to
The Naval Tracts of Sir William Monson,
drawn up between 1585 and 1603,
pirates 'first cut down their half decks,
and all other weighty things overhead
[so that] no ship is able to equal them
in going' (cited by A. F. Falconer,
Shakespeare and the Sea (1964), p. 52).

With which such scatheful grapple did he make   50
With the most noble bottom of our fleet
That very envy and the tongue of loss
Cried fame and honour on him. What's the matter?

FIRST OFFICER

Orsino, this is that Antonio
That took the *Phoenix* and her freight from Candy,   55
And this is he that did the *Tiger* board
When your young nephew Titus lost his leg.
Here in the streets, desperate of shame and state,
In private brabble did we apprehend him.

VIOLA

He did me kindness, sir, drew on my side,   60
But in conclusion put strange speech upon me.
I know not what 'twas but distraction.

ORSINO (*to Antonio*)

Notable pirate, thou salt-water thief,

---

55 freight] F (fraught)

For the ambiguity of the presentation of Antonio, see Introduction, p. 41.
draught the depth of water which a ship needs to float her

50 **scatheful** injurious (Shakespeare's only use of the word)
51 **bottom** ship (literally, the ship's keel or hull)
52–3 **very envy . . . Cried** even enmity itself, and the voices of those who had experienced loss (of their ships) invoked
54–9 The Officer's speech is very curious. First, he bluntly addresses Orsino with no courtesy title. Then, although it seems as if he is being asked to provide evidence, rather like a police officer reporting to a modern law court, he introduces information about Orsino's nephew that is not strictly relevant to the *matter* (l. 53) and seems intended to discredit Antonio. When he does get to the evidence, he uses the contemptous *brabble* (brawl), implying that Antonio has now become a disreputable street-brawler. He seems to be spurring Orsino to revenge; no wonder

Viola intervenes.
55–6 **Phoenix . . . Tiger** Ships of the Illyrian navy. *Tiger* recurs as the name of a ship at *Macbeth* 1.3.6.
55 **freight from Candy** the cargo it had brought from Candia. *Freight* is identical in meaning to F's *fraught* (*OED sb. Obs.*), from parallel roots.
Candy Candia, the name of a town in Crete which came to stand for the whole island
57 **Titus lost his leg** *Titus* is an interesting choice of name in a context of mutilation, considering the events of Shakespeare's *Titus Andronicus*.
58 **desperate of shame and state** oblivious of the danger to his honour and his position (as a free man)
60 **drew on my side** drew his sword in my defence
61 **put strange speech upon me** spoke strangely to me
62 **but distraction** if not madness
63 **Notable** notorious
salt-water thief pirate (compare *Merchant* 1.3.22–3: 'water rats, water thieves . . . I mean pirates')

What foolish boldness brought thee to their mercies
Whom thou in terms so bloody and so dear   65
Hast made thine enemies?
ANTONIO   Orsino, noble sir,
Be pleased that I shake off these names you give me.
Antonio never yet was thief or pirate,
Though I confess, on base and ground enough
Orsino's enemy. A witchcraft drew me hither: 70
That most ingrateful boy there by your side
From the rude sea's enraged and foamy mouth
Did I redeem. A wreck past hope he was.
His life I gave him, and did thereto add
My love without retention or restraint,   75
All his in dedication. For his sake
Did I expose myself, pure for his love,
Into the danger of this adverse town,
Drew to defend him when he was beset,
Where being apprehended, his false cunning—   80
Not meaning to partake with me in danger—
Taught him to face me out of his acquaintance,
And grew a twenty years' removèd thing
While one would wink, denied me mine own purse,
Which I had recommended to his use   85

73 wreck] F (wracke)

64 **brought ... mercies** made you put yourself at the mercy of those
65 **dear** grievous (*OED a.*² 2). Though the meaning is close to 'dire', the words are distinct.
66 **noble sir** Antonio uses a courtesy title as the First Officer fails to do (l. 54). The contrast is the more noticeable since Antonio is not the kind of man to be mealy-mouthed even when his life is in danger.
67 **Be pleased that I** please allow me to
69 **base** foundation (synonymous with *ground*)
72 **rude** rough
73 **wreck** Several editors retain F's *wrack* to differentiate the figurative expression from an actual wreck, but *wreck* conveys the required sense; compare *COD* 2, 'greatly damaged or disabled . . . person'.
75 **retention** reservation. This appears to be an unusual use of the word—*OED* 4c gives only two examples, from 1603 and 1633—and it differs from that at 2.4.95.
76 **All his in dedication** i.e. dedicated my love entirely to him. This has something of the fervent religious tone of Antonio's earlier account of his love for Sebastian (3.4.352–6).
77 **pure** purely, solely
81 **meaning to partake** intending to share
82 **face ... acquaintance** brazenly deny knowledge of me
83 **a twenty years' removèd thing** as if we had not met for twenty years
85 **recommended** committed

Not half an hour before.

VIOLA How can this be?

ORSINO When came he to this town?

ANTONIO

Today, my lord, and for three months before,

No int'rim, not a minute's vacancy,   90

Both day and night did we keep company.

Enter Olivia and attendants

ORSINO

Here comes the Countess, now heaven walks on earth.

But for thee, fellow—fellow, thy words are madness.

Three months this youth hath tended upon me.

But more of that anon. Take him aside.   95

OLIVIA

What would my lord, but that he may not have,

Wherein Olivia may seem serviceable?

Cesario, you do not keep promise with me.

VIOLA Madam—

ORSINO Gracious Olivia—   100

OLIVIA

What do you say, Cesario? Good my lord.

VIOLA

My lord would speak, my duty hushes me.

OLIVIA

If it be aught to the old tune, my lord,

It is as fat and fulsome to mine ear

---

88 **When came he to this town** If the previous two half-lines, spoken by Antonio and Viola, are taken to make up a single line, this half-line may indicate a pause before Orsino takes control and attempts to test Antonio's story with a factual question.

89, 94 **three months** For the double time scheme in the play, see note to 1.4.3, and Introduction, pp. 41–2.

90 **vacancy** interval

92 **now heaven walks on earth** This phrase makes a sharp contrast with the ferocity of Orsino's speeches to Antonio (and indeed his subsequent ones to Olivia and Viola, ll. 113–27), as he momentarily resumes the hyperbolical language of conventional love poetry.

96 **but that he may not have** except that which I refuse him (i.e. her love). Beneath the graceful courtesy, there is something feline about Olivia's asking what Orsino wants when the one thing he wants is something she will not give him.

99–100 These lines are probably to be spoken simultaneously.

101 **Good my lord** This may be addressed to Viola (*lord* meaning 'husband'), in which case Viola may interrupt her; or to Orsino as a request to be allowed to speak to 'Cesario'; or even as a sharp rebuke to Orsino: 'Please be quiet!'

104 **fat and fulsome** gross and nauseating

As howling after music.   105
ORSINO   Still so cruel?
OLIVIA   Still so constant, lord.
ORSINO
What, to perverseness? You uncivil lady,
To whose ingrate and unauspicious altars
My soul the faithfull'st off'rings hath breathed out   110
That e'er devotion tendered—what shall I do?
OLIVIA
Even what it please my lord that shall become him.
ORSINO
Why should I not, had I the heart to do it,
Like to th' Egyptian thief at point of death,
Kill what I love—a savage jealousy   115
That sometime savours nobly. But hear me this:
Since you to non-regardance cast my faith,
And that I partly know the instrument
That screws me from my true place in your favour,
Live you the marble-breasted tyrant still.   120
But this your minion, whom I know you love,
And whom, by heaven I swear, I tender dearly,
Him will I tear out of that cruel eye

110 hath] CAPELL; haue F

108 **uncivil** barbarous
109 **ingrate and unauspicious** ungrateful and unpropitious
114 **Egyptian thief** In Heliodorus' *Ethiopica*, a Greek prose romance translated into English by Thomas Underdowne in 1569 and popular in Shakespeare's day, an Egyptian robber-chief tries to kill a captive whom he loves, when his life is in danger from a rival band. The point of the comparison is that it provides an example of a declaration of love wrung from a character *in extremis*; by using this story, and by threatening to kill Cesario (ll. 123–7), Orsino unconsciously reveals that it is Viola, not Olivia, whom he loves, thus preparing for their subsequent union.
116 **savours nobly** either 'tastes of, smacks of' or 'gives off a whiff of' nobility (*OED v.* 1, 2)

117 **non-regardance cast my faith** consign my fidelity to contemptuous oblivion. *Non-regardance* occurs nowhere else.
118–19 **the instrument | That screws** In the increasingly violent mood of the speech, the *instrument* is presumably one of torture, that *screws* (wrenches) the limbs.
120 **marble-breasted tyrant** the archetypal cold, hard mistress of much Elizabethan love poetry
121 **minion** sexual favourite, paramour (always used disparagingly in this sense by Shakespeare)
122 **tender dearly** regard highly (*OED, tender, v.²* 3), value. The expression is basically a financial one, 'value at a high rate', as at *Hamlet* 1.3.107: 'Tender yourself more dearly'.

Where he sits crownèd in his master's spite.

(To Viola) Come, boy, with me, my thoughts are ripe in   125
    mischief.

I'll sacrifice the lamb that I do love

To spite a raven's heart within a dove.

VIOLA

And I most jocund, apt, and willingly

To do you rest a thousand deaths would die.

OLIVIA

Where goes Cesario?

VIOLA   After him I love   130

More than I love these eyes, more than my life,

More by all mores than e'er I shall love wife.

If I do feign, you witnesses above,

Punish my life for tainting of my love.

OLIVIA

Ay me detested, how am I beguiled!   135

VIOLA

Who does beguile you? Who does do you wrong?

OLIVIA

Hast thou forgot thyself? Is it so long?

Call forth the holy father.   *Exit an attendant*

ORSINO *(to Viola)*   Come, away.

OLIVIA

Whither, my lord? Cesario, husband, stay.

ORSINO

Husband?

OLIVIA   Ay, husband. Can he that deny?   140

---

138 *Exit an attendant*] CAPELL; *not in* F

---

124 **in his master's spite** to the mortifica-
tion of his master
125 **ripe in mischief** fully prepared to do
harm
127 **a raven's heart within a dove** a pre-
datory bird's heart within a beautiful
and gentle one; compare *Romeo*
3.2.76: 'Dove-feathered raven'
128 **jocund** cheerful
    apt ready
129 **do you rest** put your mind at rest

131 **mores** such comparisons
133 **above** i.e. in heaven
135 **Ay** alas for
    beguiled cheated, robbed
136 **does do** In the original Arden edition
(1906), Morton Luce pointed out that
this 'was a less awkward construction
in the days when "do" had not completely differentiated its auxiliary func-
tions' (pp. 157–8). See Abbott 303.

ORSINO *(to Viola)*

  Her husband, sirrah?

VIOLA   No, my lord, not I.

OLIVIA

  Alas, it is the baseness of thy fear

  That makes thee strangle thy propriety.

  Fear not, Cesario, take thy fortunes up,

  Be that thou know'st thou art, and then thou art   145

  As great as that thou fear'st.

      Enter ⌈attendant, with the⌉ Priest

                        O welcome, father.

  Father, I charge thee by thy reverence

  Here to unfold—though lately we intended

  To keep in darkness what occasion now

  Reveals before 'tis ripe—what thou dost know   150

  Hath newly passed between this youth and me.

PRIEST

  A contract of eternal bond of love,

  Confirmed by mutual joinder of your hands,

  Attested by the holy close of lips,

  Strengthened by interchangement of your rings,   155

  And all the ceremony of this compact

  Sealed in my function, by my testimony;

  Since when, my watch hath told me, toward my grave

  I have travelled but two hours.

ORSINO *(to Viola)*

  O thou dissembling cub, what wilt thou be   160

  When time hath sowed a grizzle on thy case?

---

146 *attendant, with the*] CAPELL *(subs.); not in* F

143 **strangle thy propriety** deny your identity (as my husband)
146 **that thou fear'st** him whom you fear (Orsino)
149 **occasion** the course of events
152 **contract** See note to 4.3.26.
153 **joinder** joining (perhaps from French *joindre*)
154 **close** union
155 **interchangement** exchange (*OED* gives only one other example of this word, from 1796)

156 **compact** agreement (stressed on the second syllable)
157 **Sealed in my function** confirmed by my priestly authority
158 **watch** (a recent invention; see note to 2.5.57)
160 **dissembling cub** This alludes to the proverbial 'as wily (crafty) as a fox' (Tilley F629).
161 **grizzle** grey hair
    case literally 'fox-skin' (sustaining the metaphor *cub* in the previous line). In

Or will not else thy craft so quickly grow
That thine own trip shall be thine overthrow?
Farewell, and take her, but direct thy feet
Where thou and I henceforth may never meet.   165

VIOLA
My lord, I do protest—

OLIVIA   O do not swear!
Hold little faith, though thou hast too much fear.
    Enter Sir Andrew

SIR ANDREW For the love of God, a surgeon—send one
presently to Sir Toby.

OLIVIA What's the matter?   170

SIR ANDREW 'Has broke my head across, and has given Sir
Toby a bloody coxcomb, too. For the love of God, your
help! I had rather than forty pound I were at home.

OLIVIA Who has done this, Sir Andrew?

SIR ANDREW The Count's gentleman, one Cesario. We took   175
him for a coward, but he's the very devil incardinate.

ORSINO My gentleman, Cesario?

SIR ANDREW 'Od's lifelings, here he is. (*To Viola*) You
broke my head for nothing, and that that I did I was set
on to do't by Sir Toby.   180

171 'Has] F (H'as)

the original Arden edition, Morton Luce cites Turberville's *The Noble Art of Venery* (1576), p. 198: 'His [Raynard the fox's] case will serve to fur the cape | Of master huntsman's gown'.

162 **craft** craftiness (further sustaining the *cub* metaphor)
163 **trip** attempt to trip (or *overthrow*) someone else (a wrestling term: *OED sb.*¹ 5)
167 **Hold little faith** keep at least a little faith
169 **presently** at once
171–2 **'Has broke . . . coxcomb too** There has obviously been a second encounter offstage between Sebastian and the two knights, since none of the violence de-

scribed occurred during the one dramatized in 4.1.
171, 190 **'Has** See note to 1.5.141.
172 **coxcomb** A comic synonym for 'head', suggested both by the fool's cap and (in this bloody version) by the cockerel's red comb. Compare *Henry V* 5.1.41, 'your ploody [for 'bloody'] coxcomb', of Pistol's broken head.
175 **gentleman** i.e. attendant
176 **incardinate** This means 'appoint as a cardinal or to another priestly office', and is a blunder for 'incarnate', in human form.
178 **'Ods lifelings** by God's little lives (a mild oath)
179 **nothing** for no reason

VIOLA

Why do you speak to me? I never hurt you.
You drew your sword upon me without cause,
But I bespake you fair, and hurt you not.
   Enter Sir Toby and Feste the clown

SIR ANDREW If a bloody coxcomb be a hurt you have hurt
me. I think you set nothing by a bloody coxcomb. Here   185
comes Sir Toby, halting. You shall hear more; but if he
had not been in drink he would have tickled you othergates than he did.

ORSINO (*to Sir Toby*)

How now, gentleman? How is't with you?

SIR TOBY That's all one, 'has hurt me, and there's th'end   190
on't. (*To Feste*) Sot, didst see Dick Surgeon, sot?

FESTE O he's drunk, Sir Toby, an hour agone. His eyes
were set at eight i'th' morning.

SIR TOBY Then he's a rogue, and a passy-measures pavan.
I hate a drunken rogue.   195

183.1 *Sir*] ROWE; *not in* F   *Feste the*] *not in* F   190 'has] F (has)   194 passy-measures]
F (passy measures)   pavan] F2; panyn F1

---

183 **bespake you fair** addressed you pol-
itely (a common phrase of the period,
either with the *be-*, as at Marlowe,
Edward II 1.4.336, 'My gentle lord,
bespeak these nobles fair', or without,
as at *2 Henry IV* 5.2.33: 'you must
now speak Sir John Falstaff fair')
185 **set nothing by** think nothing of
186 **halting** limping (from the wound, or
reeling from drink, or both). In performance, he is often accompanied (and
supported) by Maria, who does not
otherwise appear in the final act.
187 **tickled** euphemism for 'beat'
187–8 **othergates** in a different (more
violent) way. *Gate* here means 'way,
manner, method' (*OED*, *gate*, *sb.*² 9).
According to Onions, it survived into
the twentieth century as a northern
and Warwickshire dialect expression.
190 **all one** all there is to it, no matter
191 **Sot** fool (or 'drunkard')
   Dick Surgeon The profession is used as
a surname (in the way now associated
particularly with Wales).

192 **agone** ago (past participle form of
Middle English verb *agon*, to pass by)
193 **set** This probably implies 'fixed', with
the eyes squinting at odd angles; compare *Tempest* 3.2.9, where the drunken
Caliban's 'eyes are almost set in [his]
head.'
194 **passy-measures pavan** This is probably Sir Toby's slurred attempt at Italian *passemezzo pavana*, a variety of the
slow dance called 'pavan' or 'pavane';
Sir Toby may think its slowly swaying
movements suggest drunkenness, and
pavan may well be a term of abuse with
him, since at 1.3.120–1 he seems to
prefer livelier dances: galliard, coranto,
jig. But although F1's *panyn* was cor-
rected to *pavyn* as early as F2, it is just
possible that the error is in the second
'n' rather than the first, and that Sir
Toby is trying to say 'passing-measure
paynim', that is, 'a pagan to a surpas-
sing degree'. Shakespeare frequently
uses 'passing' as an adjective, though
he never uses 'paynim'.

OLIVIA

Away with him! Who hath made this havoc with
　　them?

SIR ANDREW I'll help you, Sir Toby, because we'll be
dressed together.

SIR TOBY Will *you* help—an ass-head, and a coxcomb, and
a knave; a thin-faced knave, a gull?　　　200

OLIVIA

Get him to bed, and let his hurt be looked to.

　　　　Exeunt Sir Toby, Sir Andrew, Feste, and Fabian
　　　Enter Sebastian

SEBASTIAN (*to Olivia*)

I am sorry, madam, I have hurt your kinsman,
But had it been the brother of my blood
I must have done no less with wit and safety.
You throw a strange regard upon me, and by that　　　205
I do perceive it hath offended you.
Pardon me, sweet one, even for the vows
We made each other but so late ago.

ORSINO

One face, one voice, one habit, and two persons,
A natural perspective, that is and is not.　　　210

---

199 *you*] F (you)　　help—] MALONE (*subs.*); ~∧ F　　201.1 *Exeunt Sir Toby . . . Fabian*] DYCE
(*subs.*); *not in* F

197–8 **be dressed** have our wounds
　　dressed
199–200 **Will . . . gull** See Introduction,
　　pp. 62–3, for a discussion of this
　　moment.
199 **coxcomb** Used at l. 172 to mean
　　'head', with the overtone of 'fool's
　　cap', it now means 'fool'.
200 **thin-faced** See note to 1.3.16.
　　gull dupe, fool
203 **the brother of my blood** my own
　　brother
204 **with wit and safety** with a sensible
　　concern for my well-being, in reason-
　　able self-protection
205 **strange regard** distant look (he thinks
　　she is angry; she is of course amazed)
209 **habit** costume
210 **A natural perspective** i.e. an optical
　　illusion produced by nature, not by a

'perspective', or distorting, glass, a Renaissance invention described at
Richard II 2.2.18–20: 'perspectives,
which, rightly gazed upon, | Show
nothing but confusion; eyed awry, |
Distinguish form.' Sebastian, preoccu-
pied with Olivia and Antonio, apparently does not see Viola until l. 220;
but when does she see him? In most
performances, the moment is delayed
as late as possible, to intensify the
tension and its joyful release; but at
Stratford-upon-Avon in 1987, Harriet
Walter saw Sebastian at once but flat-
tened herself against a side wall, hardly daring to believe it, an image of
fearful joy, and one that gave plaus-
ibility to Sebastian's failure to see Viola
for eighteen lines.

SEBASTIAN

   Antonio! O my dear Antonio,
   How have the hours racked and tortured me
   Since I have lost thee!

ANTONIO Sebastian are you?

SEBASTIAN Fear'st thou that, Antonio?   215

ANTONIO

   How have you made division of yourself?
   An apple cleft in two is not more twin
   Than these two creatures. Which is Sebastian?

OLIVIA Most wonderful!

SEBASTIAN (*seeing Viola*)

   Do I stand there? I never had a brother,   220
   Nor can there be that deity in my nature
   Of here and everywhere. I had a sister,
   Whom the blind waves and surges have devoured.
   Of charity, what kin are you to me?
   What countryman? What name? What parentage?   225

VIOLA

   Of Messaline. Sebastian was my father.
   Such a Sebastian was my brother too.
   So went he suited to his watery tomb.
   If spirits can assume both form and suit

---

220 *seeing Viola*] OXFORD; *not in* F

---

215 **Fear'st thou** that do you doubt that
219 **Most wonderful** For a discussion of
   this climactic moment in performance,
   see Introduction, pp. 63–4.
221–2 **deity . . . everywhere**   godlike
   power of being everywhere at once,
   omnipresence. Hamlet uses the Latin
   version of *here and everywhere*, *Hic et
   ubique*, when the ghost that purports
   to be his father's spirit is heard crying
   from different places under the stage—
   the area known in the Elizabethan
   theatre as 'the hell' (*Hamlet* 1.5.158):
   both the phrase and the location raise
   the possibility that the ghost might be
   an evil spirit. Perhaps there is also a
   fleeting hint of witchcraft here, a reminder that popular belief associated
   twins with magic powers, even with

black magic.
223 **blind** a vivid way of expressing the
   unfeeling indifference of the waves to
   Viola's attractions
   surges large waves
224 **Of charity** (tell me) out of your kindness
226 **Of Messaline** See note to 2.1.15; and,
   for an account of the dramatic power
   of the reunion, see Introduction,
   pp. 64–6.
228 **So went he suited** he was dressed in
   that way. Viola has told us at 3.4.374
   that she imitates his clothing.
229–30 **If spirits . . . fright us** *Spirit* could
   mean 'devil' in Elizabethan English,
   and *come to fright us* sustains the hint
   of witchcraft from l. 222: Cherie Lun-
   ghi's Viola at Stratford-upon-Avon in

You come to fright us.
SEBASTIAN   A spirit I am indeed,   230
But am in that dimension grossly clad
Which from the womb I did participate.
Were you a woman, as the rest goes even,
I should my tears let fall upon your cheek
And say 'Thrice welcome, drownèd Viola.'   235
VIOLA
My father had a mole upon his brow.
SEBASTIAN And so had mine.
VIOLA
And died that day when Viola from her birth
Had numbered thirteen years.
SEBASTIAN
O, that record is lively in my soul.   240
He finishèd indeed his mortal act
That day that made my sister thirteen years.
VIOLA
If nothing lets to make us happy both
But this my masculine usurped attire,
Do not embrace me till each circumstance   245
Of place, time, fortune do cohere and jump

1979 nervously stretched out her hand and touched Sebastian tentatively, to make sure that he was not a *spirit.*

229 **form and suit** body and clothing

231 **dimension** bodily form
grossly naturally, corporeally. The idea of the pure spirit, or soul, clad or encumbered (hence perhaps *grossly*) in human flesh, goes back at least to Plato's *Phaedo* and was subsequently Christianized.

232 **participate** have in common with others (i.e. he had a body like everyone else—a final assertion of Sebastian's humanity, dispelling the various hints of black magic in the scene)

233 **the rest goes even** everything else goes to suggest (*goes even* literally means 'agree')

235 **Viola** This is the first time that her name is spoken on stage: Shakespeare has reserved it for this climax.

236–9 **My father ... thirteen years** For a discussion of the different ways in which this passage has been played, see Introduction, p. 65.

240 **that record is lively** the memory of that is vivid (*record* is stressed on the second syllable)

243 **lets** hinders (as frequently in Shakespeare; from Anglo-Saxon *lettan*)

245 **Do not embrace me** Viola is still prolonging the reunion, deferring the embrace until she resumes her identity as a woman, so that, as Barbara Everett says, 'as long as the play lasts she remains unembraced, the action never absolutely confirmed' (*EC* 35 (1985), 311), one of the ways in which this scene qualifies our sense of a harmonious resolution (see Introduction, pp. 69–73).

246 **cohere and jump** accord together and agree (*OED, jump, v.* 5). Compare *Shrew* I.I.188: 'Both our inventions meet and jump in one.'

That I am Viola, which to confirm
I'll bring you to a captain in this town
Where lie my maiden weeds, by whose gentle help
I was preserved to serve this noble count.   250
All the occurrence of my fortune since
Hath been between this lady and this lord.

SEBASTIAN (to Olivia)

So comes it, lady, you have been mistook.
But nature to her bias drew in that.
You would have been contracted to a maid,   255
Nor are you therein, by my life, deceived.
You are betrothed both to a maid and man.

ORSINO (to Olivia)

Be not amazed, right noble is his blood.
If this be so, as yet the glass seems true,
I shall have share in this most happy wreck.   260
(To Viola) Boy, thou hast said to me a thousand times
Thou never shouldst love woman like to me.

VIOLA

And all those sayings will I overswear,
And all those swearings keep as true in soul
As doth that orbèd continent the fire   265

---

249 **Where** at whose house
  weeds clothes (as frequently in Shakespeare; from Anglo-Saxon *waed*, garment)
253 **mistook** mistaken. 'Owing to the tendency to drop the inflection *en*, the Elizabethan authors frequently used the curtailed forms of past participles which are common in Early English' (Abbott 343).
254 **to her bias drew** inclined in the right direction. The metaphor is from bowls, and is frequent in Shakespeare: the *bias* refers both to the curve made by the bowl as it rolls along the pitch, and to the weight embedded in it which causes it to swerve.
255 **contracted** betrothed
257 **maid and man** This literally means 'a man who is still a virgin', but the phrase may imply that since Sebastian and Viola are alike in temperament as in appearance, Olivia has not simply been deceived; she may consider herself, in a sense, *betrothed* to them both.

259 **glass seems true** The *natural perspective* of l. 210 is still reflecting truth, not distorting it.
260 **happy** fortunate
261 **Boy** Actors often deliver the word lightly, to mark a shift from the emotional tension of the twins' reunion to something less fraught, though not less emotionally truthful: as so often in Shakespeare, humour is used to express feeling.
263 **overswear** swear over and over again. Here and in the next lines Viola revels in being able to express her love openly at last.
265 **orbèd continent** round container. For *orbèd*, compare *Hamlet* 3.2.149, 'Tellus' orbèd ground' (i.e. the earth), and *A Lover's Complaint* 25, 'th'orbèd earth'; *OED* gives no earlier examples. For *continent*, compare *Hamlet* Additional Passages J. 55 (4.4.9 ff.): 'tomb enough and continent' (*OED sb.* 1;

That severs day from night.
ORSINO   Give me thy hand,
  And let me see thee in thy woman's weeds.
VIOLA
  The captain that did bring me first on shore
  Hath my maid's garments. He upon some action
  Is now in durance at Malvolio's suit,   270
  A gentleman and follower of my lady's.
OLIVIA
  He shall enlarge him. Fetch Malvolio hither—
  And yet alas, now I remember me,
  They say, poor gentleman, he's much distract.
        Enter Feste the clown with a letter, and Fabian
  A most extracting frenzy of mine own   275
  From my remembrance clearly banished his.
  How does he, sirrah?
FESTE Truly madam, he holds Beelzebub at the stave's end
  as well as a man in his case may do. 'Has here writ a
  letter to you. I should have given't you today morning.   280

274.1 *Feste the*] *not in* F   279 'Has] F (has)

'container' is the usual sense of the
word in Shakespeare).

265–6 **orbèd ... night** i.e. the sun. The
  phrase echoes Genesis 1: 14: 'let there
  be lights in the firmament of the
  heaven, that they may divide the day
  and the night'.
269 **action** legal charge
270 **durance** imprisonment
272 **enlarge** free
273 **remember me** remember. The *me* is
  simply an intensifier (Abbott 220). See
  note to 3.2.30.
274 **distract** deranged, distraught—to
  which Wells, in Oxford, modernizes it.
  He argues that, in modern English,
  'distract' and 'distraction' imply merely a shift of attention, whereas 'distraught' indicates mental turbulence;
  and the anonymous *History of Hamblet*
  (1608) has 'running through the
  streets like a man distraught, not
  speaking one word but such as seemed
  to proceed of madness' (reprinted in

Bullough, 7, p. 90). But Warren argues that to read 'distraught' destroys
  both the quibble on *extracting* in the
  next line (and so weakens Olivia's equ-
  ation of her madness with Malvolio's),
  and the verbal echo of Viola's *distraction* in l. 62, which initiates the references to madness in the scene.
275–6 **A most extracting ... his** a distracting madness of mine drove his
  from my memory. For Olivia's comparison of her madness to Malvolio's,
  compare 3.4.14–15.
275 **extracting** distracting, banishing all
  else from my thoughts. Malone cites
  The History of Hamblet: 'to try if men
  of great account be extract out of their
  wits' (Bullough, 7, p. 92).
276 **remembrance** memory
278 **Beelzebub at the stave's end** the devil
  (who threatens to possess him) at a
  distance (proverbial: Tilley S807; the
  image is from quarterstaff fighting)
279 **'Has** See note to 1.5.141.
280 **today morning** this morning

But as a madman's epistles are no gospels, so it skills
not much when they are delivered.

OLIVIA Open't and read it.

FESTE Look then to be well edified when the fool delivers
the madman. (*Reads*) 'By the Lord, madam'—   285

OLIVIA How now, art thou mad?

FESTE No madam, I do but read madness. An your ladyship will have it as it ought to be you must allow *vox*.

OLIVIA Prithee read i'thy right wits.

FESTE So I do, madonna, but to read his right wits is to   290
read thus. Therefore perpend, my princess, and give ear.

OLIVIA (*to Fabian*) Read it you, sirrah.

    Feste gives the letter to Fabian

FABIAN (*reads*) 'By the Lord, madam, you wrong me, and
the world shall know it. Though you have put me into
darkness and given your drunken cousin rule over me,   295
yet have I the benefit of my senses as well as your ladyship. I have your own letter that induced me to the sem-
blance I put on, with the which I doubt not but to do
myself much right or you much shame. Think of me as
you please. I leave my duty a little unthought of, and   300
speak out of my injury.

                         The madly used Malvolio.'

OLIVIA Did he write this?

FESTE Ay madam.

ORSINO

This savours not much of distraction.   305

---

285 *Reads*] ROWE; *not in* F, *which however prints* 'By . . . madam' *in italic*   292.1 *Feste gives . . . to Fabian*] OXFORD; *not in* F

---

281 **epistles are no gospels** letters are (or
    contain) no truths (playing on the
    sense of *epistles* as 'New Testament
    letters' and *gospels* as 'New Testament
    accounts of Christ')
    skills matters (*OED v.*[1] 2b)
282, 284, 306 **delivered . . . delivers . . .**
    delivered The word goes through three
    different meanings in this episode. In
    l. 282 it means 'handed over', in l.
    284 'speaks the words of', in l. 306
    'freed'.

284 **edified** instructed
285 **'By the Lord, madam'** Feste obvious-
    ly rants the line as if he were raving
    mad.
288 ***vox*** (the appropriate) voice (Latin)
291 **perpend** pay attention. Used else-
    where by Pistol (*Henry V* 4.4.8; *Merry
    Wives* 2.1.110), Touchstone (*As You
    Like It* 3.2.65), and Polonius (*Hamlet*
    2.2.106), it is clearly intended to
    sound affected, as perhaps is Feste's *my
    princess* that follows.

OLIVIA

See him delivered, Fabian, bring him hither.

Exit Fabian

My lord, so please you—these things further thought
  on—
To think me as well a sister as a wife,
One day shall crown th'alliance on't, so please you,
Here at my house and at my proper cost.   310

ORSINO

Madam, I am most apt t'embrace your offer.
(*To Viola*) Your master quits you, and for your service
  done him
So much against the mettle of your sex,
So far beneath your soft and tender breeding,
And since you called me master for so long,   315
Here is my hand, you shall from this time be
Your master's mistress.

OLIVIA (*to Viola*)   A sister, you are she.

Enter Malvolio and Fabian

ORSINO

Is this the madman?

OLIVIA   Ay, my lord, this same.

How now, Malvolio?

MALVOLIO   Madam, you have done me wrong,

Notorious wrong.

OLIVIA   Have I, Malvolio? No.   320

MALVOLIO (*showing a letter*)

Lady, you have, pray you peruse that letter.
You must not now deny it is your hand.
Write from it if you can, in hand or phrase,

306.1 *Exit Fabian*] CAPELL; *not in* F   317.1 *and Fabian*] CAPELL (*subs.*); *not in* F   318–19
Ay, my lord . . . Malvolio?] *as* CAPELL; *one line in* F   321 *showing a letter*] OXFORD; *not in* F

307–8 **so please you** . . . **To** if you
  please . . . to
308 **think me** . . . **wife** think as well of me
  as a sister-in-law as you would have
  thought of me as a wife
309 **alliance on't** i.e. the relationship created by the double wedding
310 **proper** own

311 **apt** ready, willing
312 **quits** acquits, releases from service
313 **mettle** nature, disposition
320 **Notorious** See note to 4.2.87.
323 **from it** differently
  hand or phrase handwriting or phrase-
  ology

Or say 'tis not your seal, not your invention.
You can say none of this. Well, grant it then,   325
And tell me in the modesty of honour
Why you have given me such clear lights of favour,
Bade me come smiling and cross-gartered to you,
To put on yellow stockings, and to frown
Upon Sir Toby and the lighter people,   330
And acting this in an obedient hope,
Why have you suffered me to be imprisoned,
Kept in a dark house, visited by the priest,
And made the most notorious geck and gull
That e'er invention played on? Tell me why?   335

OLIVIA

Alas Malvolio, this is not my writing,
Though I confess much like the character,
But out of question 'tis Maria's hand.
And now I do bethink me, it was she
First told me thou wast mad; then cam'st in smiling,   340
And in such forms which here were presupposed
Upon thee in the letter. Prithee be content;
This practice hath most shrewdly passed upon thee,
But when we know the grounds and authors of it
Thou shalt be both the plaintiff and the judge   345
Of thine own cause.

FABIAN   Good madam, hear me speak,
And let no quarrel nor no brawl to come
Taint the condition of this present hour,
Which I have wondered at. In hope it shall not,

---

324 **invention** composition
326 **in the modesty of honour** with the
    restraint that becomes a noblewoman
327 **lights** signs, indications
330 **lighter** lesser
331 **acting** when I did
334 **geck** fool. Compare *Cymbeline*
    5.5.161–2: 'to become the geck and
    scorn | O'th' other's villainy'. Accord-
    ing to Onions, *geck* survived in Mid-
    lands dialect into the twentieth century.
335 **invention** trickery
337 **character** style of handwriting
340 **cam'st** (you) came (Abbott 401)

341–2 **presupposed | Upon** previously
    suggested to
343 **practice** trick. Compare John Man-
    ningham's description of the plot
    against Malvolio as a 'good practice'
    (see Introduction, p. 1).
    shrewdly sharply, maliciously
    passed imposed
345–6 **judge ... cause** Olivia reverses the
    proverbial saying that 'No man ought
    to be judge in his own cause' (Tilley
    M341) to express her outrage at the
    injustice that has been done to Malvolio.

Most freely I confess myself and Toby   350
Set this device against Malvolio here
Upon some stubborn and uncourteous parts
We had conceived against him. Maria writ
The letter, at Sir Toby's great importance,
In recompense whereof he hath married her.   355
How with a sportful malice it was followed
May rather pluck on laughter than revenge
If that the injuries be justly weighed
That have on both sides passed.

OLIVIA *(to Malvolio)*
Alas poor fool, how have they baffled thee!   360

FESTE Why, 'Some are born great, some achieve greatness, and some have greatness thrown upon them.' I
was one, sir, in this interlude, one Sir Topaz, sir; but
that's all one. 'By the Lord, fool, I am not mad'—but do
you remember, 'Madam, why laugh you at such a bar-   365
ren rascal, an you smile not, he's gagged'—and thus
the whirligig of time brings in his revenges.

MALVOLIO I'll be revenged on the whole pack of you.

                                    Exit

OLIVIA
He hath been most notoriously abused.

ORSINO
Pursue him, and entreat him to a peace.   370
He hath not told us of the captain yet.   ⌈*Exit Fabian*⌉

368.1 *Exit*] ROWE; *not in* F   371 *Exit Fabian*] ARDEN; *not in* F

352 **Upon** because of
352–3 **uncourteous . . . against him** uncivil qualities we discerned and
  resented in him
354 **importance** importunity
356 **followed** followed up, carried through
357 **pluck on** induce
360 **baffled** hoodwinked (or perhaps
  stronger, 'disgraced', since *baffle* was a
  technical term for the public disgracing
  of an unworthy knight (*OED v.* 1))
361–7 **Why . . . revenges** For ways of
  handling this speech in performance,
  see Introduction, pp. 67–8.
363 **interlude** comedy, playlet

367 **whirligig** roundabout (or spinning-top)
368 **I'll be revenged . . . pack of you** For
  the variety of interpretations inspired
  by this line, see Introduction, p. 68.
370 **Pursue him . . . peace** The Folio does
  not provide for anyone to obey Orsino's instruction, but it should presumably be a member of Olivia's
  household, and Fabian is the obvious
  candidate. As one of the conspirators
  against Malvolio, he might be thought
  unlikely to *entreat him to a peace*, but
  as a would-be peacemaker (see ll. 346–
  59) he stands as much (or as little)
  chance as anyone else.

When that is known, and golden time convents,
A solemn combination shall be made
Of our dear souls. Meantime, sweet sister,
We will not part from hence. Cesario, come—   375
For so you shall be while you are a man;
But when in other habits you are seen,
Orsino's mistress, and his fancy's queen.

Exeunt all but Feste

FESTE (*sings*)
          When that I was and a little tiny boy,
                    With hey, ho, the wind and the rain,   380
          A foolish thing was but a toy,
                    For the rain it raineth every day.

          But when I came to man's estate,
                    With hey, ho, the wind and the rain,
          'Gainst knaves and thieves men shut their gate,   385
                    For the rain it raineth every day.

378.1 *all but Feste*] DYCE (*subs.*); *not in* F   379 FESTE (*sings*)] F (*Clowne sings.*)

---

372 **golden time** *Golden* is a favourite adjective of approbation with Shakespeare: compare 'Golden lads' and
'golden chance' at *Cymbeline* 4.2.263
and 5.5.226; and Orsino's phrase also
occurs in Sonnet 3: if the friend has a
child, 'thou through windows of thine
age shalt see, | Despite of wrinkles,
this thy golden time' (11–12). Here,
golden has something of the nostalgic
overtone, of looking back to an ideal
world, that is present in references to
the classical 'Golden Age' (as at *As You
Like It* 1.1.113 and *Tempest* 2.1.174).
Shakespeare may intend something of
this in giving the phrase to Orsino,
ever the idealist, set against the harsh
reality of the wind and the rain in
Feste's closing song (and Orsino looks
forward to the *combination* of souls, not
bodies (ll. 373–4)).
convents comes about (literally 'is sur-
rounded, comes together' (*OED v.* 1,
3, 5))
374 **dear** loving
375 **hence** i.e. from Olivia's house

378.1 *Exeunt all but Feste* For possible
stagings of the end of the play, see
Introduction, pp. 69–70.
379–98 The words of Feste's song may
not be by Shakespeare. For a discussion of them, see Introduction, pp. 70–
3, and for the music, see Appendix.
379 **and a** An emphatic phrase, implying
'very' (Abbott 95, 96), frequently
found in popular songs and ballads:
compare 'King Stephen was and a
worthy peer' (*Othello* 2.3.82).
little tiny A common catchphrase; *little*
precedes *tiny* in all Shakespearian
examples.
381 **A foolish . . . toy** If *thing* has the likely
overtone of 'penis', then the line
roughly means: 'a little penis was
only a toy'—i.e. was useless—when I
was a child. Compare *little thing* at
3.4.290.
382 **rain . . . every day** Perhaps with
proverbial force, as in 'It never rains
but it pours' (though *ODEP*'s earliest
citation is from 1726 (p. 663)).
385 **shut** (past tense)

But when I came, alas, to wive,
  With hey, ho, the wind and the rain,
By swaggering could I never thrive,
  For the rain it raineth every day.   390

But when I came unto my beds,
  With hey, ho, the wind and the rain,
With tosspots still had drunken heads,
  For the rain it raineth every day.

A great while ago the world begun,   395
  With hey, ho, the wind and the rain,
But that's all one, our play is done,
  And we'll strive to please you every day.   *Exit*

393 had] F; 'had ARDEN   396 With] F2; *not in* F1   398 *Exit*] ROWE; *not in* F

389 **swaggering** blustering, bullying. Compare Doll Tearsheet on Pistol at *2 Henry IV* 2.4.68: 'Hang him, swaggering rascal'.
391 **beds** 'the various spots where he happened to fall' (Hotson, p. 171)—like the drunken tinker Christopher Sly, thrown out of the alehouse at the start of *The Taming of the Shrew*: 'This were a bed but cold to sleep so soundly' (Induction 1.31)
393 **tosspots** drunkards
398 **strive to please you** It is characteristic of epilogues to hope that the play has pleased: compare the King's 'strife to please you' in his epilogue to *All's Well* (l. 4), and Rosalind's hope in hers to *As You Like It* that 'the play may please' (l. 16).

THE MUSIC

Edited by James Walker[1]

Twelfth Night has often been called Shakespeare's most musical play, and this impression stems not so much from the amount of music (there is also a great deal in *Much Ado About Nothing, As You Like It,* and *The Tempest*) as from the dramatic use to which it is put.[2] The music is not distributed evenly throughout the play; most of it occurs in the first two acts, and is of two main kinds: the formal pieces played by the musicians, or musician, at Orsino's court (1.1, 2.4), and popular tunes sung in the drinking scene (2.3). Feste's songs (2.3, 2.4, 4.2, 5.1) straddle the two categories: he varies his style to suit his hearers. The words of these songs may or may not be by Shakespeare: he may be using or adapting existing songs, or fitting new words to existing tunes; in the drinking scene, he certainly adapts part of a song by Robert Jones to suit a new dramatic situation.

Some, but by no means all, of the original music has survived. Shakespeare's use of songs well known at the time has undoubtedly assisted the survival of, for instance, most of the material in 2.3. But the earliest surviving setting of Feste's concluding song dates from the eighteenth century (though it may make use of a tune dating from much earlier). For 'Come away death' (2.4) and 'I am gone, sir' (4.2), no early music survives; I have therefore composed settings which are compatible in style with the surviving originals, so that this edition provides material for all the songs required in a performance.

For the instrumental music which opens both the play and 2.4, a wealth of suitable material is available in the various keyboard collections of the sixteenth and seventeenth centuries, notably *The Fitzwilliam Virginal Book* (*c.* 1619). An excellent example of the kind of piece that Orsino describes in his first speech is provided by the keyboard pavan 'Lord Salisbury' by Orlando Gibbons (1583–1625).[3] This contains a double 'dying fall' (1.1.4) in its lengthy final sequence, whose suspensions, avoiding resolution in bar 5, turn upwards

---

[1] The music for 'Come away death', 'I am gone, sir', 'O mistress mine', and 'When that I was' is © Oxford University Press 1994. See title-page verso for information and performing and other rights.

[2] For a full discussion, see Peter J. Seng, *The Vocal Songs in the Plays of Shakespeare* (Cambridge, Mass., 1967), pp. 94–130.

[3] *The Fitzwilliam Virginal Book*, ed. J. A. Fuller Maitland and W. Barclay Squire, 2 vols. (1899), reprinted by Dover Publications (New York, 1963), 2. 479–80.

in order to fall at last through a scale enhanced by the false relation of the harmony's g natural and g sharp:

Ex. 1

O. Gibbons

It has been necessary to transpose most of the songs down in order to allow for the rise in pitch since Shakespeare's time. This brings pitches back to the range of the average voice, from which point individual adjustments can more easily be made.

THE SONGS

(i) **O mistress mine** (2.3.37–50)

The Elizabethan tune which has been traditionally associated with Feste's song may not have been the one used in the original performances. An expanded version of the title found in a seventeenth-century inventory, 'O mistress mine I must', implies that it was used with a different lyric;[1] but new words were often fitted to popular tunes, as in the Gamble version discussed below. In any case, this is the only contemporary tune remotely connected with the words, and its contours and rhythm are close enough to Shakespeare's lyric to make it worth attempting a satisfactory arrangement. The essential difficulty is that the tune is fashioned for a five-line stanza, whereas Shakespeare's stanzas are of six lines.

[1] See *A Shakespeare Music Catalogue*, ed. Bryan N. S. Gooch and David Thatcher, 5 vols. (Oxford, 1991), 3. 1834.

The basic, shortest version of the tune (see Ex. 2) was discovered in 1954 by Vincent Duckles in a commonplace book belonging to John Gamble (d. 1687),[1] who fits to the tune words from Philip Rosseter's *A Book of Airs* (1601), where they are set to quite different music. Gamble may have associated this tune and these words because the fifth verse of this poem begins 'Then mistress mine'; but while the tune fits the five-line stanza from Rosseter's book, it is one phrase too short for Shakespeare's.

Ex. 2

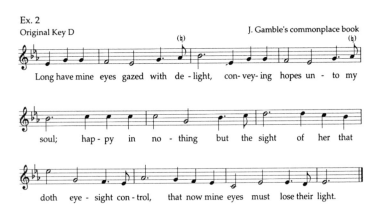

The keyboard variations on 'O mistress mine' by William Byrd (1543–1623)[2] present the tune as in the previous example (melodic details differ) and then add a refrain by repeating the last two phrases, giving seven phrases in all, one too many (see Ex. 3).

Ex. 3

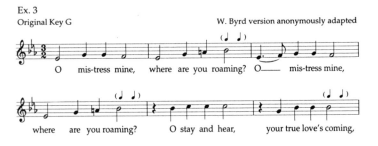

[1] 'New Light on "O Mistresse mine" ', *Renaissance News*, 7 (1954), 98–100.
[2] *The Fitzwilliam Virginal Book*, I. 258–62.

That— can sing both high and low. Trip—— no further,

pret-ty swee-ting. Jour - neys end in ———— lo-vers mee -

ting, ———— Ev - ery wise man's son——— doth know.

An even longer version is found in *The First Book of Consort Lessons* (1599) by Thomas Morley (1557–1602) in which the tune is arranged for a mixed ensemble. Again there are melodic differences and the repeat starts one line earlier, giving a total of eight phrases, two too many (see Ex. 4).

Ex. 4
Original Key G   T. Morley version adapted S. Beck

O mis-tress mine, where are you roa-ming? O mis-tress mine, where are you

roa-ming? O stay and hear, your true love's co-ming, O stay and hear, your true love's

co-ming, That can sing both high and low. Trip— no fur-ther, pret-ty

swee-ting, Jour-neys end in lo-vers mee-ting, Ev-ery wise man's son doth know.

Theatrical tradition has passed on a setting which, by repeating the first line of the stanza, is sung to Byrd's tune; unfortunately, this brings about a misalignment of the structures of stanza and tune, and the mid-point cadence comes a line late, implying a false rhyming of 'sweeting' with 'know'.

The defects of the traditional (Byrd) version have long been re-cognized, and many attempts have been made to find a better solution. In 1953 Sydney Beck published a paper on the problem in which he surveyed previous efforts and presented his own solution.[1] This, using Morley's tune, requires the first two lines of the stanza to be repeated, thereby avoiding the pitfalls of the Byrd version but still compromising the verse. The flaw lies in the double repetition at the beginning of the song, a device not found in Shakespeare's lyrics or in Elizabethan song (though end-lines are often repeated to form re-frains). These repetitions inflate the song and impede its natural flow.

For my solution, I have approached the problem from the other direction, and have adapted the tune to the stanzas by adding a phrase to the basic form of the tune (see Ex. 5). Because the third line of each stanza needs a firm cadence, this is where the phrase has to go. The following example offers a realization in which the added phrase is made out of the tune's own final cadence with only four up-beat notes added, shown by the dotted lines.

Ex. 5

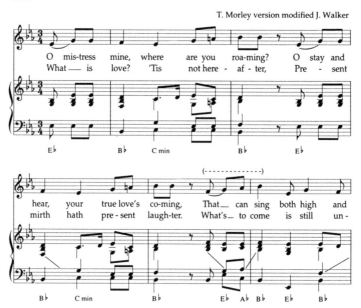

T. Morley version modified J. Walker

---

[1] 'The Case of "O Mistresse mine" ', *Renaissance News*, 6 (1953), 19–23.

low.   Trip___ no fur - ther, pret - ty swee-ting. Jour___ neys
sure.   In___ de - lay there lies no plen - ty, Then___ come

Eb   Bb min Ab   Ab Eb   Bb   Bb min Ab Eb

end in lov - ers mee - ting, Ev - ery wise man's son doth know.
kiss me, sweet and twen - ty. Youth's a stuff will not en - dure.

Eb   Bb Eb Ab Eb F min Eb Ab Eb Bb Eb

(ii) **Hold thy peace** (2.3.62)

Two versions exist: Ex. 6a is from Thomas Ravenscroft's collection
Deuteromelia (1609), Ex. 6b from a collection of Elizabethan rounds
made by Thomas Lant (1580). Either round would be effective, but
Ex. 6a has the more exciting rhythm owing to its added words 'and
I prithee'. A high pitch helps the 'caterwauling' effect.

Ex. 6a
Original Key C

T. Ravenscroft

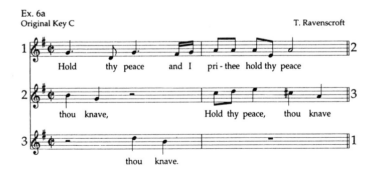

1   Hold   thy peace   and I pri - thee hold thy peace   2

2   thou knave,   Hold thy peace, thou knave   3

3   thou knave.   1

Ex. 6b
Original Key C (7th lower)   collected T. Lant

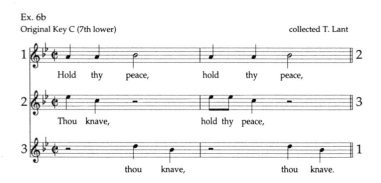

(iii) **Three merry men** (2.3.72)

Two versions exist: Ex. 7a is from a commonplace book in the hand
of John Playford (1623–86), printed in W. Chappell's *Popular Music
of the Olden Time* (1855–9), 1. 216; Ex. 7b is by William Lawes
(1602–45), published in John Hilton's *Catch that Catch Can* (1652).
Ex. 7a is the more directly effective and likely to be the original,
since it corresponds to the earliest known occurrence of the words,
in Peele's *Old Wives Tale* (1595), 21–4.

Ex. 7a

Ex. 7b
Original key C   W. Lawes

(iv) **There dwelt a man in Babylon** (2.3.74)

There are two possible sources: the tune of Ex. 8a is found in *The Mulliner Book*, a manuscript collection dating from the reign of Henry VIII. It is quoted and fully discussed in C. M. Simpson, *The British Broadside Ballad and its Music* (1966), pp. 410–12. Only the refrain would be required. Ex. 8b was entered in the Stationers' Register on 3 September 1580 as 'a new northern ditty of the Lady Greensleeves'. Edward W. Naylor (*Shakespeare and Music* (1931), pp. 182–3) claims that 'There dwelt a man' had long been sung to the tune of 'Greensleeves', and though he does not provide any evidence, its presence in John Caulfield's *A Collection of the Vocal Music in Shakespeare's Plays* (1864), p. 147, lends credence to the claim.

Ex. 8a

Mulliner Book

Ex. 8b

'Greensleeves'

(v) **O' the twelfth day of December** (2.3.79)

Since no original survives, a setting is offered here.

Ex. 9

J. Walker

(vi) **Farewell dear heart** (2.3.95–105)

A song by Robert Jones (flourished 1597–1615) from his *First Book of Songs or Airs* (published 1600). It was printed as a song in four vocal parts with lute tabulature, but here Shakespeare parodies it as a comic duet. The final four 'no's are in Jones and the Folio text, but E. H. Fellowes's edition (1925) suggests five, perhaps because a syllable on each note gives the end added vehemence.

Ex. 10
Original key G minor   R. Jones

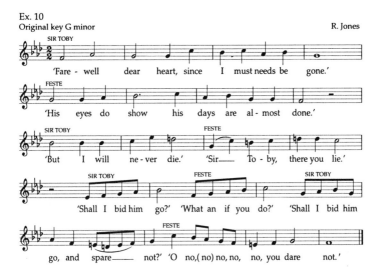

(vii) **Come away, come away death** (2.4.50–65)

It is disappointing that no setting has survived earlier than Thomas Arne's of 1741. If the tune given here is played through twice under the dialogue at 2.4.14–40, it should be approximately the right length, allowing the actors to begin speaking after it starts and to make the necessary pauses as they listen to it.

Ex. 11

J. Walker

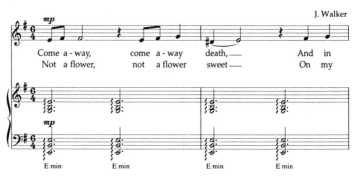

Come a - way, come a - way death, ____ And in
Not a flower, not a flower sweet ____ On my

E min   E min   E min   E min

sad ____ cypress ____ let me be laid. Fie a-way, fie a-way
black ____ coffin ____ let there be strewn. Not a friend, not a friend

A min+6   B maj   E min   C maj   A min   A min

Poco agitato . . . .

breath, I am slain by a fair cru - el maid. ____
greet My poor corpse, where my bones shall be thrown. ____

B maj   B maj   B maj   G maj   B maj

calmato

p

My shroud of white, stuck all with yew,
A thou - sand thou - sand sighs to save,

D maj   D   A maj   D maj   A maj   D maj

O—— pre - pare it. My part of death no
Lay me O where Sad true lo - ver ne - ver

D maj   B maj   E min   B min   B min

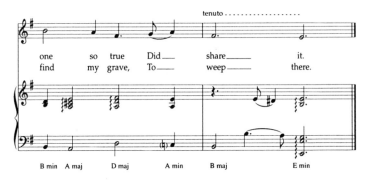

tenuto . . . .

one so true Did—— share———— it.
find my grave, To—— weep———— there.

B min A maj   D maj   A min   B maj   E min

(viii) **Hey Robin** (4.2.72–9)

Probably a collaboration between Sir Thomas Wyatt (1503–42) and William Cornish (*c.* 1465–1523), contemporaries at the court of Henry VIII. Feste sings the leading voice part of what is quite an elaborate three-part round, quoting the second verse, and slightly varying the words (given in the Commentary).

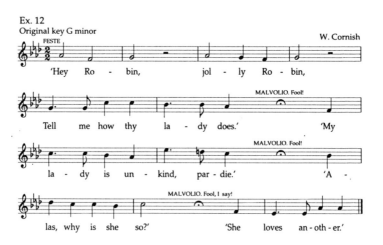

(ix) **I am gone, sir** (4.2.121–32)

The apparently tricky rhythm of this setting reflects Shakespeare's own implicit demand for a change of time signature at 'dagger of lath' and again at 'mad lad'.

you a-gain, In a | trice, Like to the | old Vice, Your need to sus-

tain, Who with | dag-ger of lath In his | rage and his wrath

Cries 'A-ha' to the | de-vil, Like a | mad lad, 'Pare thy

nails, dad, A- | dieu, good man | de-vil.'

(x) **When that I was and a little tiny boy** (5.1.379–98)

The earliest known version of the tune is in a volume of songs from the repertory of Vauxhall Gardens, including *The Celebrated Epilogue in . . . Twelfth Night . . . Sung by Mr Vernon . . . composed by J. Vernon* (Joseph Vernon, 1738–82), (1772). It appeared next in *Shakespeare's Dramatic Songs* compiled in 1816 by William Linley, I. 34 ff., who claimed that the composer was called Fielding. Chappell (I. 225) says that the tune was sung in the play in his day, and he printed a simpler version than Vernon and Linley (see Ex. 14). The tune was probably common property and could have been connected with the words from the beginning; its humdrum repetitions aptly fit the character of the song.

Ex. 14

Anonymous, arranged J. Walker

When that I was and a lit-tle ti-ny boy, With __ hey, ho, the wind and the rain, A foo-lish thing was but __ a __ toy, For the rain it rai-neth ev - ery day, With hey, ho, the wind and the rain, For the rain it rai-neth ev - ery day.

(Refrain)

INDEX

This is a selective guide to the annotations and the Introduction, although it does not duplicate the section headings of the latter. Citations from other texts are not listed. The Appendix to the Music is not included, nor are the songs in the play, as these are itemized in the Appendix. Characters in the play are only listed if their names are discussed. Asterisks identify entries which supplement the information given in *OED*.

a foolish thing was but a toy,
  5.1.381
*a foul way out, 2.3.172–3
a twenty years' removèd thing,
  5.1.83
abatement, 1.1.13
above heat, 1.5.126
access, 1.4.16
accident, 4.3.11
accost, 1.3.45
acquit you, 3.4.208
Actaeon, p. 35, 1.1.20
action of battery, 4.1.33
address thy gait, 1.4.15
adheres together, 3.4.75
Adrian, Max, as Feste, pp. 56, 60
advanced (= displayed), 2.5.29
advanced (= promoted), 1.4.2
affect, 2.5.22
affectioned, 2.3.137
after my degree, 3.4.74
agone, 5.1.192
Aguecheek, 1.3.16
a-hungry, 2.3.119
airs, 2.4.5
Alexander, Bill, director of *Twelfth Night*, pp. 6, 8, 10, 59–60
all his in dedication, 5.1.76
all one, 1.5.123; 5.1.190
allow, 1.2.56
All's Well That Ends Well, p. 70
amazed, 3.4.328
ample, 1.1.26
an, 1.3.11
anatomy, 3.2.59
and a, 5.1.379
a-nights, 1.3.4
antic, 2.4.3
any's, 1.3.18

appetite, 2.4.96
aqua-vitae, 2.5.186
Arion, 1.2.14
Armin, Robert, p. 56
as I am man . . . my master's love,
  2.2.36–7
as Maria goes . . . yellow stockings,
  3.4.14
as much to say, 1.5.51
as the sea, 1.1.11; 2.4.99
as to, 3.4.245
As You Like It, p. 70
Ashcroft, Peggy, as Viola, p. 64
aspect, 1.4.28
at my fingers' ends, 1.3.74
at one door . . . at another door,
  1.5.297, 301
authority, 1.2.18
Aveling, Edward, p. 59
ay, 1.2.20

babbling gossip, 1.5.262
back-trick, 1.3.115
baffle, 2.5.153; 5.1.360
balked, 3.2.22
Barentz, William, p. 54
barful strife, 1.4.41
barren, 1.3.75
barricadoes, 4.2.37–8
Barton, Anne, p. 63
Barton, John, director of *Twelfth Night*, pp. 6, 7, 12–13, 35, 38, 45, 55, 63; 2.3.15–16; 4.2.71
baubling, 5.1.48
bawcock, 3.4.108
beagle, 2.3.167
bear it out, 1.5.19
beauty's a flower, 1.5.47
become, 1.2.51

237

Index

bed of Ware, 3.2.44
beds, 5.1.391
Beelzebub, 5.1.278
before me, 2.3.166
begging but a beggar, 3.1.54–5
behaviour (= courtly gestures),
  2.5.15
behaviour (= outward appearance),
  1.2.44
belike, 3.3.29; 3.4.236
Bensley, Robert, as Malvolio,
  pp. 43–4
beshrew me, 2.3.75
bespake you fair, 5.1.183
bespeak our diet, 3.3.40
best persuaded of himself,
  2.3.138–9
betimes, 2.3.2
betters, 1.3.110
biddy, 3.4.111
bide, 1.5.59
Billington, Michael, pp. 6, 7, 36,
  57
birdbolts, 1.5.87–8
black in my mind, 3.4.24
black … yellow, 3.4.24
blanks, 3.1.102
blazon, 1.5.283
blind, 5.1.223
blood and spirit, 2.5.138
bloody argument, 3.3.32
bloody as the hunter, 3.4.215
bloody coxcomb, 5.1.172
bonds, 3.1.20
bonos dies, 4.2.13
botcher, 1.5.42
bottle-ale houses, 2.3.27
bound to, 3.1.75
bow to, 2.5.132
box-tree, 2.5.13
boy, 5.1.261
brain, 1.1.34–8
*branched velvet, 2.5.44
breach, 2.1.20
breast, 2.3.18
brock, 2.5.99
brother's dead love, 1.1.30
Brown, J. R., p. 33; 3.4.3,17
Brownist, 3.2.29
Bullough, Geoffrey, pp. 15–16
bum-baily, 3.4.171
but, 1.2.28; 2.4.2
buttery, 1.3.66

buttery-bar, 1.3.66
by my troth, 1.3.3
by'r Lady, 2.3.60
by the method, 1.5.217
by the nose, 2.3.54
by the very fangs of malice,
  1.5.175–6
by your favour, 2.4.24

Caird, John, director of *Twelfth
  Night*, pp. 54, 70
cakes and ale, 2.3.108
canary, 1.3.76
cantons, 1.5.259
caper, 1.3.113
Capilet, 3.4.276
carpet consideration, 3.4.228
carry it thus, 3.4.132
cars, 2.5.60
case, 5.1.161
cast away, 1.5.164
Castiliano vulgo, 1.3.39
catch, 2.3.17
catch the plague, 1.5.285
catechize, 1.5.57
caterwauling, 2.3.68
Cathayan, 2.3.71
Cesario, 1.4.0.1
challenge him the field, 2.3.119
chambermaid, 1.3.47
champaign, 2.5.151
*changeable taffeta, p. 36; 2.4.73
chantry, 4.3.24
character, 1.2.48
*check at, 2.5.109; 3.1.63
cherry-pit, 3.4.112
chev'rel, 3.1.12
Christian, 1.3.80
chuck, 3.4.108–9
cinquepace, 1.3.120–2
civil bounds, 1.4.21
clerestories, 4.2.38
clock strikes, 3.1.127.1
cloistress, 1.1.27
cloyment, 2.4.98
cockatrices, 3.4.189
cockney, 4.1.13–14
codling, 1.5.152
cohere and jump, 5.1.246
*coistrel, 1.3.37
cold scent, 2.5.116
come away, 2.4.50
come near me, 3.4.62

238